Data Mining, Data Warehousing & Client/Server Databases

Springer

Springer

Singapore
Berlin
Heidelberg
New York
Barcelona
Budapest
Hong Kong
London
Milan
Paris
Santa Clara
Tokyo

Data Mining, Data Warehousing & Client/Server Databases

**Proceedings of the
8th International Database Workshop
(Industrial Volume)
Hong Kong, 29–31 July 1997**

**Editors
Brian Siu, Paul KM Kwan
Benedict Lam, Peter de Vries**

Sponsored by

 HEWLETT®
PACKARD

 IBM.

 INFORMIX®

 ORACLE®

 NCR

 SAS®

 SYBASE®

Borland (HK) Limited
City University of Hong Kong
Hong Kong Polytechnic University
WinClient Technologies (HK) Ltd

 HONG KONG
COMPUTER
SOCIETY

 Springer

Brian Siu
Division of Technology, City University of Hong Kong, Tat Chee Avenue
Kowloon, Hong Kong

Paul KM Kwan
Information Technology Department, New World Telephone Ltd.
Rm. 801-6, East Wing, New World Office Building, 24 Salisbury Road
Tsimshatsui, Kowloon, Hong Kong

Benedict Lam
Information Services Department, Hong Kong Air Cargo Terminals Ltd.
6/F, Cargo Terminal 2, Hong Kong International Airport
Kowloon, Hong Kong

Peter de Vries
Information Technology Consultant, Pier 1 Ltd., 35A Tai Mong Tsai Road
Sai Kung, New Territories, Hong Kong

ISBN 981-3083-53-0

© Springer-Verlag Singapore Pte. Ltd. 1997
Printed in Singapore

Typesetting: Camera-ready by editors
5 4 3 2 1 0

Preface

The first International Hong Kong Computer Society Database Workshop was held in Hong Kong in 1989. This book covers the eighth annual database workshop in the series.

The main theme of this workshop concerns with data mining, data warehousing and client/server databases. Advances in data gathering, storage, and distribution technologies have outperformed the techniques for analyzing and understanding data. There is an urgent need for automated data mining and knowledge discovery in databases.

Data mining is used to discover patterns, clusters and models from data, which are then rendered in operational forms that are easy for people to visualize and understand. It is a general rule that the bigger the database, the more difficult it is to sustain high levels of performance. The key objective of data warehousing is to provide business executives with flexible access to vast quantities of information through loosely structured queries.

Data warehousing is a continual process which enables a corporation to assemble operational and other data from a variety of internal and external sources. It transforms that data into consistent, high-quality, business information, distributes that information to the points of maximum value within the organizations and provide easy, flexible and fast access for busy non-technical users.

In client/server systems, users are capable of interconnecting various platforms efficiently and transparently to distribute data and application programs across heterogeneous systems in a computer network. Application processing is developed between client and server workstations. The processing is initiated by the client and performed by the server, and both client and server cooperate to run an application. A client/server system increases processing power by separating the database management system from the application -- the client as the front-end system handling the user interface and the server as a back-end system accessing the database.

The objective of this workshop is to bring together database practitioners, researchers and vendors to share and explore topics in data mining, data warehousing and client/server database. We would like to take this opportunity to express our thanks to those who contributed to this function, and trust you will find this a useful and practical database technology reference book.

Organizing Committee
8th International Database Workshop
June 1997, Hong Kong.

Acknowledgments

There are, of course, many people and organizations to whom we are indebted for their help, contribution and sponsorship in the development of the tutorial, workshop and proceedings. Without their efforts and contribution the workshop would not be possible. They deserve a special acknowledgment.

We would like to thank all contributing authors, from various companies and institutions, for their papers. We would like to thank our sponsors for their financial assistance, and the City University of Hong Kong for providing the venue for the tutorial sessions. We are grateful for careful reading and evaluating by the program committee members.

Our sincere thanks to all.

The Editors

Sponsors
(in alphabetical sequence)

Borland (HK) Ltd.

City University of Hong Kong
(Department of Computer Science)

Hewlett-Packard Hong Kong Ltd.

Hong Kong Polytechnic University
(Department of Computing)

Hong Kong Computer Society
(Database Special Interest Group)

IBM China/Hong Kong Corporation

Informix Software (HK) Ltd.

NCR (HK) Ltd.

Oracle Systems (HK) Ltd.

SAS Institute Ltd.

Sybase Hong Kong Ltd.

WinClient Technologies (HK) Ltd.

Organizing Committee

Chairman - General	Brian Siu, City University of Hong Kong
Chairman - Academic Stream	Irene Kwan, Hong Kong Polytechnic University
Chairman - Industrial Stream	Paul Kwan, New World Telephone Ltd.
Vice Chairman	Kevin Ho, Ewig Industries Company Ltd.
Secretary	Benedict Lam, Hong Kong Air Cargo Terminals Ltd.
Treasurer	Kai-Hing Lau, K.H. Lau & Company
Publications	Brian Siu, City University of Hong Kong Philip Tsang, Open University of Hong Kong
Publicity	Vivian Wong, Oracle Systems (HK) Ltd. Peter de Vries, Pier 1 Ltd.
Registration	Michael Tsui, Borland (HK) Ltd.
Hotel/Venue Liaison	Tommy Ho, Kintetsu World Express (HK) Ltd. Raymond Lo, VISA International Ltd.
Local Arrangement	Peter de Vries, Pier 1 Ltd.
Hon Advisors	Joseph Fong, City University of Hong Kong Irene Kwan, Hong Kong Polytechnic University Danny Ha, Databank Training & Consulting Services
Council Advisors	Raymond Cheng, Hong Kong Computer Society Peter Kwan, Hong Kong Computer Society George Leung, Hong Kong Computer Society

Message from DBSIG Workshop Chairman

On behalf of all the members of the workshop organizing committee, I extend to all of you a warm welcome to the 8th International Database Workshop.

The first International Hong Kong Computer Society Database Workshop was held in Hong Kong in December 1989. Its main objective was to promote database technologies. Its scope has a broad coverage of advanced database technologies, methodologies and software tools. This event has been held for the past 7 years. The themes of the past workshops were:

1st, in 1989: "Conversion to Database Systems"
2nd, in 1990: "Data Modelling Techniques"
3rd, in 1991: "Distributed Database Systems"
4th, in 1992: "Database Management Horizon"
5th, in 1994: "Next Generation Database Systems"
6th, in 1995: "Database Reengineering and Interoperability"
7th, in 1996: "Multimedia, Knowledge-based & Object-Oriented Databases"

This year, once again, the workshop has an objective to bring together practitioners, researchers and vendors to share their experiences and research findings. Its aim is to benefit the researchers, IS/IT practitioners and executives in the application and management of database technology. The theme of this year is on data warehousing, data mining and client/server database.

The data warehousing and data mining are the emerging technologies which deliver decision support capabilities and knowledge discovery. The highly competitive nature of business in the 1990s has led to the constant quest for ways to sustain and gain competitive advantage. Under the constant changing business environments, the need for information to support the business is not being met. "Organizations are literally data-rich with disparate data and information-poor for integrated data" [p.xi, BRA96] "It was the data warehouse that provided the foundation for the fulfillment of the promises of earlier technologies such as DSS and EIS." [p.v, INM96] This "new style of processing proved to be very valuable to the competitive world in which organizations were attempting to gain and protect market share and to maximize both short-term and long-term profits." The technologies "attracted and kept a large portion of the attention of serious system developers and the business community." [Ibid]

The workshop this year is well supported by academic researchers and vendors of the IT community. We have received more than 58 papers. A total of 30 papers were submitted from academic institutions and more than 26 papers were submitted from vendors and consultants. All the papers came from 14 counties: Australia, New Zealand, Korea, Singapore, Japan, Taiwan, China, France, Germany, Norway, United Kingdom, Ireland, Canada, and USA.

On behalf of Database Special Interest Group (DBSIG) of the Hong Kong Computer Society, I would like to take this opportunity to express my thanks to those who have contributed to this event. We thank the members of the program committee for their efforts to make the workshop a success, and express our gratitude to the sponsoring companies and institutions.

I am grateful to the hard-working committee members for the sacrifice and the long hours they have spent to organize this workshop. Without their full support, this workshop could not have been a success. I would like to thank the advisors of the organizing committee, the HKCS Council and the HKCS office for their support to the event.

It is our mission to promote information technology and serve the community. I believe you will find this workshop useful and practical, and beneficial to you and your institutions.

Paul K. M. Kwan
DBSIG Workshop Chairman
Hong Kong Computer Society
pkwan@newworldtel.com

[BRA96] Brackett, Michael, "The Data Warehouse Challenge - Taming Data Chaos", John Wiley & Sons, 1996
[INM96] Inmon, W.H., Claudia Imhoff, Greg Battas, "Building the Operational Data Store", John Wiley & Sons, 1996

Table of Contents

Keynote Paper

Data Warehouse Performance Management Techniques
Andrew Holdsworth, Oracle..*1*

Papers

Developing Applications using ORDBMS Technology
Stephen Yao, Informix...*30*

Emerging Technologies for Business Intelligence
Ian Parkes, COL Limited...*36*

Data Warehouse Approach
Dave Gleason, Platinum..*50*

Data Warehouses and Metadata: The Importance of Metadata Management
Stephen Gardner, NCR..*61*

A Case for Real-time Client-Server OLAP for Multidimensional Financial
and Business Analysis
Perry Yu, Hyperion Software..*72*

Advanced Technology for Data Warehouse Solutions
Ray Ruff, Sybase...*86*

What is Data Mining and how to apply data mining techniques to exploit
information from your data warehouse or data mart
Paul Chik, SAS Institute..*94*

Data Mining: The software that finds patterns never seen before
Samson Tai, IBM...*103*

A Data Warehouse is for Life, Not just for Christmas - Owning a Data
Warehouse: Your responsibilities
Peter Hall, Hewlett-Packard..*113*

Data Warehouse Key Components and Process: Using a Rational Approach
to build Your Data Warehouse
Dale Mietla, NewTHINK, Marvin Miller, DEC, George Kong, DEC.....................*128*

Successful Data Warehousing: Driving Value from your Meta Data Initiative
Cass Squire, Prism Solutions..*148*

Building a Data Warehouse: Its Methodology and Returns on Investment
Danny Lau, SAS Institute...*160*

Semantic Layer for Data Warehousing
Yuen Wai Sing, Business Objects...*168*

Moving Data Warehouses to the Net
Vincent Boudville, Infosis Software...*183*

Born to be Parallel
Albert Leung, NCR..*196*

Data Mining in the age of Object/Relational Database Management Systems
Tony Banham, Informix...*217*

Aligning IT with a Consumer-Oriented Business Model
James Alderton, NCR..*226*

12 Steps of Creating a Successful Data Warehouse
Ringo Chan, Oracle..*227*

Using the Web to Transform Data into Knowledge
C. S. Lo, SAS Institute..*249*

An intelligent business workbench for the insurance industry: using data
mining to improve decision making and performance
Grant Keats and S.Loo, University of Auckland, New Zealand..............................*256*

Discover missing semantic from existing relational databases
S.Huang, S.Li and H.Chen, Tatung Institute of Technology, Taiwan.......................*275*

Client/Server Web database design and implementation: a CGI-SGML
approach
P.Tsang, C.Diu and S.Tse, Open University of Hong Kong, Hong Kong................*287*

Data Warehouse Performance Management Techniques

Andrew Holdsworth, Oracle Services, Advanced Technologies,
Data Warehousing Practice

Abstract

This document describes the management and technical issues involved in a Data Warehouse project. Eventually these techniques will be refined through time and experience to become part of Oracle's overall Data Warehousing strategy.

Introduction to Data Warehouse Performance

The process of Data Warehouse performance management is similar to that of the design of a Data Warehouse. It is similar in that like the design and analysis phases, the techniques utilized are very different from the processes adopted in a conventional OLTP type system life cycle.

In a conventional system life cycle there exists usually numerous levels of analysis and planning. In the Data Warehouse environment the system builders are seldom given this luxury and are required to assemble a Data Warehouse in a rapid manner with little time for performance analysis and capacity planning.

This makes the Data Warehouse performance management process extremely difficult as the work loads very often cannot be predicted until finally the system is built for the first time and the data is in a production status. As a system goes production for the first time only then may a system administrator discover there are performance problems.

If there are to many performance problems in the running of the Data Warehouse the viability of the project becomes marginal or questionable. It is important to remember the success of a Data Warehouse can only be measured once the data is loaded and users are able to make business level decisions by extracting data from the Data Warehouse.

This background information describes the atmoshere on any Data Warehouse project at any phase. There are so many unknowns through out the process be it loading, query work load and future work load the database administrators life is one of continual uncertainty.

This process of continual uncertainty is not necessarily a bad thing either. The reason for this can be determined from the need for a Data Warehouse. If the users knew everything about the contents of their data they would not need a Data Warehouse. As the users do not know what they do not know how can the Data Warehouse team accurately assess their computing requirements. *In essence the process of performance management and planning in the Data Warehouse is a mixture of intuition and well-educated guess work.*

This document will not rehash existing capacity planning techniques as these are all largely based upon knowing the system requirements prior to deployment of the system.

The performance of a Data Warehouse is largely a function of the quantity and type of data stored within a database and the query/data loading work load placed upon the system. When designing and managing such a database there are numerous decisions that need to be made that can have a huge impact on the final performance of the system.

Unfortunately many of the decisions made in the construction of a Data Warehouse are made in ignorance of the performance characteristics of the Data Warehouse hardware and software environments. This has resulted in massive differences in expectations between system users and system designers and administrators. It is essential that system/database administrators work closely with the Data Warehouse designers to understand and best characterize the database performance requirements. This will enable the system/database administrators to make a better best guess for the system configuration that will yield good performance.

Business Requirements for Data Warehouse

The business requirements for a Data Warehouse usually involve some of the following criteria:-

- Ensure Consistency of Data from Disparate Data Sources.
- Load and Maintain a List of Various Business Tables.
- Provide Structured Query Access to the Data Warehouse.
- Provide Ad Hoc Query Access to the Data Warehouse.
- Provide Reporting Access to the Data Warehouse.
- Provide Exports and Summary Data to other Analytical Query Systems.
- Periodic Update and Purging of the Data Warehouse Data.

For each system each of these requirements will have a varying degree of importance based upon the Data Warehouse's target deployment strategy. These should determine the initial capacity planning requirements for the Data Warehouse and a when making these estimates all efforts should be made to satisfy the most critical business requirements.

It should be also noted that having successfully built and implemented your Data Warehouse the Warehouse, *you must guard against the warehouse becoming a victim of it own success.* A well implemented Data Warehouse will by definition be regularly used. If the project is a success the users of the system will increase beyond the point anticipated when the system was first built. For this reason all estimates should include some margins or factors of safety for system growth and estimation errors. It is important to remember that the sizing of Data Warehouse systems is not a precise science.

Performance Definition of Acceptable Performance

The simplest definition of acceptable performance is that the Data Warehouse is able to meet all of the business requirements in the required time scales.

With all these types of issues the definition of acceptable becomes blurred because some of the business requirements are simply unacceptable or impossible. The impossible or "would like to have" issues need to be identified early in the life of the Data Warehouse.

Many of these problems are often caused by ignorance of the data or naivity with regards to the chosen technology for the Data Warehouse.

Example: A Data Warehouse is required to run queries on a large table that involves full table scans. The response times for these queries are very critical. To reduce the query response times parallel query is utilized. Running one of these queries utilizes 75% of all system resources on the machine for a minute. The business requirements determine that over two hundred users need to perform this query each once about every 2 minutes. Clearly here we have problem in that this sort of problem probably cannot be solved by any machine. In this example it is possible to see where a well informed set of system designers can ensure they do not commit to deliver a business requirement that is clearly impossible to deliver.

In this example a proactive database administrator may notice that all these queries could be satisfied by a simple summary table. In this case the business requirements could be satisfied with ease. In essence it takes more than just raw machine horsepower to solve Data Warehouse problems and in fact a proactive entrepeneurial approch is what is really required.

This example is given to show when embarking on a Data Warehouse project it is important to be very careful when developing service agreements and similar agreements all parties understand what they imply. This is particularly important bearing in mind the unknown quantity of some of the Data Warehouse workloads. The following business functions are particularly difficult to assess for capacity planning purposes:-

Data Loading and Scrubbing: Very often the amount of data processing is unknown until the process actually begins or after the data is in production and users find data errors and anomalies. The data processing and conversion processes can be very resource and time intensive. In many cases the full database meta model is not complete until the data has been cleaned up. The process will yield more exceptions than envisaged and meta models may be subject to considerable amounts of change after this process is complete.

Ad Hoc Queries. This work load will strike fear into a system or database administrator. Ad Hoc Queries by definition mean a highly variable workload that can be put on the system at any time for a unspecified length of time. Numerous Ad Hoc queries that involve parallel table scans may bring the system to a complete halt. With Ad Hoc Queries a mechanism for governing their execution is required to ensure the predictable workload users can function with minimal impact.

It may be determined having built the Data Warehouse some of the requirements cannot be satisfied on the machine or indeed on any machine. However by re-engineering parts of the application and the creation of summary tables it may mean that the business requirements can be fully or partially satisfied. This should be regarded as normal evolution of the Data Warehouse. The process of continual re-engineering as user workload increases should be an every day occurrence on an active Data Warehouse.

Performance within Budget Requirements

It is fully understood that on many Data Warehouse projects the hardware capital budgets will impact the size of the machine that may be used. The rest of the document describes how to build a balanced system. Should hardware budgets limit the size of the Data Warehouse machine all parties should be aware and modify their expectations accordingly. It should be noted however that well sized machine initially will allow more freedom and give the project a higher chance of success and subsequent growth.

It is important to have the Data Warehouse in production as soon as possible. *Economies in hardware specification that cause time delays are only false economies in the sense that you cannot generate revenue from a Data Warehouse that is not in production.*

Capacity Planning for the Data Warehouse

Producing a Balanced Design or Configuration

When configuring a Data Warehouse system it is important to insure that all components are balanced. What this means is that all active components (CPU, Memory and I/O) are all effectively used and when one component reaches its maximum operating range all the other components approach their maximum at the same time.

This practice has been perfected by engineers for centuries. A Civil engineer building a bridge will design each component to fail at the same time. After all, the strength of a structure is determined by the weakest link in the structure. In addition an engineer will optimize the structure to use the most cost effective materials and construction methods to build the structure.

This principal can be applied to configuration of the Data Warehouse. We know that the CPU is the most expensive non renewable resource on the system. With this fact appreciated the memory and I/O subsystem should be constructed to ensure that the CPU can be kept busy and the design held in balance. Failure to do this makes the memory or I/O subsystem the weak link in the structure.

CPU Requirements and Scaleabilty

CPU sizing and requirements for a Data Warehouse are a function of the database size and the user workload. Both of these factors should be considered when determining the size and the number of CPUs.

The database size will impact the number of CPUs simply because a database needs to be administered. A database requires periodic reorganization which requires extracts of data, data reloads and data re-indexing. A database requires backing up and restoring in the case of a media component or operational failure. All of these processes requires CPU resources. As the data volume increases it becomes more important to run these operations in parallel to make the database batch windows and availability requirements. For this reason the database size will have a large impact on the number and size of the CPUs required. As a rule of thumb if the database size drives the CPU requirements a recommended would be to assume about 5 Gig of Data per CPU assuming fairly conventional availability requirements. This rule is not a true linear rule because when the database size increases some economies of scale can be exploited. Also as systems increase in size their I/O subsystems tend be upgraded and more efficient.

When adding additional CPUs to a system the scaleability with regards to additional CPUs should be considered and fully understood. It is naive to assume in a multiple CPU environment (SMP or MPP) that you will achieve linear scalability on all operations for all the CPUs. It is important to understand which operations scale well and under what conditions which operations are inherently single threaded and do not scale at all.

In summary characteristics of CPUs are simple and predictable. Faster CPUs process single threaded jobs faster than slow ones. If your Data Warehouse workload has a number of single threaded jobs or processes look to get the machine with the most powerful CPUs. Multiple CPUs allow multiple jobs to run concurrently hence increasing system throughput. The increase in throughput is a function of the scaleability of the system. Multiple CPUs also allow the Data Warehouse to take advantage of the parallel features or the Oracle RDBMS (7.1 Onwards). Again the speedup that can be gained from these features is a function of the scaleability of the system.

From these simple facts it is possible that a machine with few very powerful CPUs may provide a better solution than a machine with multiple low powered CPUs and vice versa. Historically machines with more CPUs have been able to support more users and provide more consistent response times then machines with fewer CPUs because they are less sensitive to a large process dominating the whole machine. Again making an initial assessment of the Data Warehouse workload will help guide the selection of the correct CPU configuration.

Table 1 describes the types of CPU configurations and comments on their Scaleabilty and single threaded performance.

Table 1.

CPU Environment	Single Threaded Performance	Scalability	Comments
Single CPU	equivalent to CPU rating	None	Big CPU machines give the best performance e.g. HP and DEC Alpha
Low End SMP (Small Intel, Sun 1000)	Poor	Good	Good scaling can be anticipated in 1 4 CPU range
High End SMP (DEC Alpha Turbo Laser, HP, Pyramid, Sun 2000, Large Intel)	Excellent	Good	Good scaling can be anticipated in 1 12 CPU range
MPP (IBM SP/2 Pyramid RM1000)	equivalent to CPU rating	Varied	Excellent scaling on processes that are designed to scale

Scalability is a function of many items of which a great number of them are out the control of the system administrator and are built into the hardware, operating system and RDBMS. There are however a number of items which are under the control of the capacity planner and system administrator which will effect the scalability of the system.

One of the core issues is to ensure that the system is balanced such that the CPUs can be fully utilized. The CPUs are the most critical resources on the machine so they should be the most fully utilized when ever possible. A fully utilized CPU means that the most work is being done and the Data warehouse is effectively working at its optimum rate. If performance is not satisfactory the number or type of CPUs requires increasing or upgrading.

In modern SMP and parallel processing machines it is often difficult to get the CPUs fully utilized because there is bottleneck in the system and the system is out of balance. The balance can be re-established by the increasing other system resources such as memory or I/O bandwidth.

When conceptually modeling the Data warehouse machine it is useful to imagine the I/O subsystem as a pump to supply data to the CPUs. With an increase in Memory the pump may have to work less hard as the data is in memory and less pumps are required to keep the CPUs busy. With an increase in I/O bandwidth (Disks and Controllers) we are effectively creating a bigger pump. As we increase the number of CPUs on a system the requirement for a bigger I/O subsystem becomes more apparent.

Sizing of the I/O subsystem is crucial to the scaleabilty of any parallel operations in Data Warehouse. Failure to recognize this and address it early in any Warehouses evolution will result in time consuming rebuilds and user frustration.

Memory Requirements

Memory on any RDBMS application is used for a number of distinct tasks. For each of these should insufficient memory resources be available a bottleneck will occur in the system causing the CPUs to work at a lower efficiency and the system performance to drop.

The main memory on the machine is used for the following distinct tasks:-

- Process and Operating System Virtual Memory.
- Buffer Caches.
- Sort Space.

Process and Operating System Virtual memory

This memory is used to allow execution of the actual processes on the machine. This memory embraces all the elements of memory described in this section, however when considering just the process space and operating system overhead the requirements in the Data Warehouse environment are relatively modest. This is because relatively few active processes exist.

The other elements of memory may contribute to the situation where the sum of all the active virtual memory exceeds the actual amount of memory. In this scenario the operating system has to manage the virtual memory by prioritizing the least busy pages of memory and storing them on disk. This process is often called paging and in more pathological cases an entire process state may be stored on disk and this is causes swapping. In any case should this happen performance will be heavily degraded and for this reason a system should not be allowed to page or swap. Should paging or swapping occur it may be necessary to scale back memory allocation to the database to ensure process can run in memory. If this is unacceptable for performance reasons further memory should be purchased.

There is however usually limits to the amount of memory that can be physically assembled or addressed on most modern machines. In many cases the amount of memory is constrained by the number slots in the computer backplane. If the backplane to the machine can accommodate a great deal of memory the operating system may not be able to address the memory effectively. This is due to the fact that most operating system are 32 Bit systems and will hit addressable limits at 2 Gig and 4 Gig respectively depending if signed or unsigned machine integers are utilized. With the development of 64 Bit operating systems many of these type of issues and problems will be eliminated.

Buffer Caches

The majority of main memory in RDBMS applications has usually been applied to the construction of very large buffer caches. This cache block is often sizable by tuning parameter. Large caches are very advantageous to database applications if you consider the performance issues. To read a data page from memory takes about 20--30 micro-seconds and to read a page from disk takes about 20-30 milli-seconds. Knowing these numbers, if the most often used data pages are kept in memory considerable performance advantages can be gained. Our RDBMS uses sophisticated Least Recently Used algorithms to determine which pages shall remain in memory or will get flushed to disk. Many tuning documents will refer to cache hit ratios. This ratio is very simply the fraction of times when a data page is accessed relative to the times it is located in memory. This number should be conventionally in the high 90s on normal systems.

There are additional caches within the database that also require correct sizing. These are usually associated with building caches of information to support data dictionary activity. These can be sized in shared pool parameter.

The other data cache that usually gets neglected is the operating system file system cache. Very often this can grow to be very large especially if the database is built using file system files as opposed to raw disks. It is important to understand the implications of the size of this cache as very often incorrect decisions are made about performance without fully understanding the size and impact of the file system cache.

Sort Space

Any database will spend considerable time and resources sorting large sets of data. This process will run faster if the sort process can run entirely in memory without the need to use intermediate disk storage in the process of sorting. The amount of memory and process uses for sorting is controlled by sort area parameter. However when using the parallel query option the total amount of memory used for a sort may be the degree of parallelism multiplied by the sort area parameter. If multiple concurrent queries execute simultaneously this can add up to a considerable amount of memory. Care should be taken to assess and control the amount of sorting memory that gets used to avoid the possibility of paging and swapping occurring.

Memory in the Data Warehouse

In Data Warehouses the allocation of memory should be a function of the type of workload on the system. If the Data Warehouse is performing parallel table scans, sort and joins of large tables with very little indexed access there is very little point in building a large buffer cache as the chances of get a good cache hit ratio are minimal. It this situation the memory should be allocated to the sorting process. If however the Data warehouse is working off keyed access to data like in a star query it will be important to get good cache hit rations and the system memory should be configured into buffers. Naturally all systems are a cross between the two extremes, however, knowledge of type operation and how best to configure for each type will yield huge performance gains.

64 Bit Computing

Earlier reference to machines with a 64 Bit operating system was made to supporting very large memory configurations. These are now a commercial reality with machines from DEC and future machines from SGI, HP and Sun. To take advantage of the large memory configurations requires no additional work other than to increase the size of the init.ora parameters. It has been noticed that significant speed ups have been achieved using buffer caches in the order of 4-8 Gigabytes and total sort size in Gigabytes.

Disk and I/O Subsystem Requirements

It is described earlier in this document that the I/O subsystem can be compared to a pump that pumps bytes of information at the CPUs to enable them to perform a workload. This is largely true. In addition the I/O subsystem provides a permanent data store for the information. This second factor is unfortunately what usually drives capacity planners in their sizing of a Data Warehouse I/O subsystem. What usually happens is that a database I/O subsystem size is determined from storage requirements rather than performance requirements.

The following notes describe the problems involved when configuring an I/O subsystem and provided hints as to how best match hardware configurations to potential user workloads.

I/O Subsystem Components

The main components in the construction of an I/O subsystem will be an array of disk drive devices which are controlled by a number of disk controllers. The controllers are usually then linked to the main system bus via various components with various names such as I/O adapters, Channels etc. The precise names and the architecture for each vendor will be different as they adopt different design philosophies. When working with the hardware vendors it is important to ensure you explain your design objectives in disk I/O terms so that they can build a balanced I/O subsystem.

As stated earlier the disk drive(s) will be the core component of any I/O subsystem. Disk drive technology whilst it has improved over the last few years has not improved at the speed of CPU development. On average CPU speeds double every 18 months however disk performance may at best only increase a few percent over the same period of time. For this reason as CPUs become more powerful there will be a need for more powerful I/O subsystems and hence more disk drives. Disk drive manufacturers whilst not increasing disk performance greatly (mainly due to laws of physics) have greatly increased the storage capacity of a disk, reduced the cost of manufacture and have increased the reliability of their components.

The increased size of disk drives has provided cheaper mass storage (it cost as much to make a 4 Gig disk as a 2 Gig disk) but has confused the industry because the disk throughput has not increased proportionately. In a database application to increase the I/O bandwidth the number of disk drives needs increasing. However if the number of drives is halved due to having bigger disks a performance problem is only inevitable.

In summary the performance of the disk drive is very static at about 30 I/Os per second as good working average and will remain at this level for a considerable period of time. It is important to not be side tracked by disk storage capacity when dealing with performance issues. In large modern SMP machines there is usually significant over capacity in terms of disk storage space if the I/O subsystem is configured to keep the CPUs busy. This statement assumes the database size is less than about 100 Gigabytes in size. For larger databases the number of spindles may mean the I/O subsystem is indeed more powerful than the CPUs and a capacity planning model by volume is required rather than capacity planning by throughput.

Capacity Planning Estimation Techniques

The previous section described that most I/O subsystem capacity planning should be done by anticipating system performance and ensuring that the I/O subsystem can keep the CPUs busy. A great deal of this will be alien to administrators who are used allocating disk space by volume.

It is important to remember that in a Data Warehouse most of the work loads are indeed unknown. With this fact understood it would seem sensible to design an I/O subsystem that will keep the CPUs busy. This means that the one query that utilizes all system resources will work as fast as possible and that is after all the objectives of the Data Warehouse to get the query results to the users as fast as possible.

With this in mind and the fact that there are so many unknowns it is best to use a very simple method of estimating the disk requirements. On embarking the process of estimating the number of disks, controllers etc. the capacity planner usually has only a few inputs namely:-

- The size of the database

- The number of CPUs

- An initial estimation of activity on the Data Warehouse e.g. Table Scans, Star Queries, Conventional Queries etc.

From these it is possible to work up a possible configuration bearing in mind additional operation factors such as the following:-

- Is the database to be mirrored.
- How space is required to stage the database prior to data load.
- How much space to allow for Indexing and Temporary Sort Space.

The best way to show how to work up hardware estimate is by performing a worked example. These calculations follow a back of an envelope style, and the quality of the results will be a function of the quality of the assumptions made whilst working with the client in the analysis and early requirement phases.

Worked Example

A customer wishes to build a Data Warehouse to support their customer information system. The database consists of about 10 core tables that comprise about 60

Gigabytes of data. They are going to perform a great deal of table scan activities as they mine the data for purchasing trends. They know the data is coming from a number of legacy systems and anticipate many problems consolidating the data. They anticipate regularly sweeping or scrubbing entire tables and creating updated copies. For this reason they know the processing requirements are going to be extremely high and for this reason have ordered a 20 CPU Sparc Server 2000E. They have configured 2 Gigabytes of memory into the system and now they need estimates as to the size of the I/O subsystem. They have requested that the database is fully mirrored in case of media failure.

Assessment of Database Size and Volume based Estimate

(base data+indexes+temp) * Factor for Admin.

(60 + 15 + 30) * 1.7 = 179 Giga Bytes

The factors are arbitrary and are based upon experience they can be altered when applicable.

The disks available are 4 Gig Volumes so the number of disks prior to mirroring will be 179 / 4 = 45 Disk Drives

Assessment of Disk Drives from CPU performance

#CPUS * Disks/CPU estimate

20 * 8 = 160 Disk Drives

In this case the number of disk drives to keep the CPUs busy exceeds the storage requirement. Using a volume based estimate could mean that there could be an I/O bottle neck on the database.

Mirroring the database would double the number of disk drives to 90. Mirroring will also assist query processing as reads can be satisfied by multiple spindles. However the scale up is not perfect so we can assume an I/O scale up of about 50%.

This means that the effective number of drives using a volume based estimate would approach about (1.5 * 45) 68 drives again well short of the 160 drives calculated to keep the CPUs busy.

At this point these estimates need to be communicated to the project team and cost benefit assessment needs to be made. To get all CPUs busy will require doubling the number of disk drives. An assessment needs to be made to see if budget limitations allow the project buy almost twice the number of disks. At this point it usually becomes a judgment issue and compromises are required. Other factors that should be considered when making this estimate.

- Is the number of CPUs going to increase in the future
- Are the CPUs going to upgraded to faster ones in the future
- What are the chances of the database further increasing after phase one of the project.

All these issues encourage early investment in disks however budgets will usually override the technical arguments. It is stated that this process is a very imprecise science and I/O subsystem capacity planning is one of the hardest to get correct. However if the database administrators cannot negotiate enough I/O resources there will be I/O bottlenecks later. If obtaining hardware resources are not an issue 160 Disks should be obtained as part of creating a balanced system.

Configuration for Performance

Having secured considerable amounts of disks on which to build the Data Warehouse thought has to be given as to how to best layout the database so the full potential of the I/O subsystem can be realized.

The process of spreading parts of the database out over multiple disk drives is commonly known as striping. When striping a database the database administrator has a number of options on how to perform the striping operations. It has been stated earlier that the work loads on the database will be fairly unpredictable and for this reason it is important to come up with a disk configuration that does not penalize any type of workload.

The types of I/O that is likely to take place on the database files will be either random single block reads and writes or sequential reads and writes. The majority of I/O activities will be read I/O s upon the database however an understanding of what writes take place is required.

The core database I/O activities are described in Table 2.

Table 2.

I/O Type	Database Activity
Sequential Read	Table Scans, Read from Temp segment, Recovery of Database from Redo Log
Sequential Write	Direct path Load, Log Writer Write, Write using Sort Direct Write (7.2), Write using unrecoverable option (7.2).
Random Read	Any Indexed or key access operation
Random Write	Dirty buffer write

Avoiding Contention

When organizing and building the database it is essential to avoid contention. Contention can be defined as disk I/O operations that negatively impact another process performing a disk I/O operation. An example of this is two processes simultaneously wishing to read two different parts of a disk. One process will have to wait until the first disk I/O is performed before the second I/O request is performed. This introduces the issue of queuing for a device. Contention can be made worse if each process then wishes to read the next block after the block they just read. In this case to perform the I/O operation the disks would have to seek to the position to perform the I/O. This takes time and if there was no contention at all the disk I/O would take very little time at all. In order to minimize contention we are effectively attempting to reduce disk queue lengths and minimize seek operations on the disk.

In the previous table it shows the type of I/O operations performed within the database. There are certain process that continually perform sequential I/O and this process is critical to the performance of the database. In particular the log writer performs sequential writes when logging database transactions and sequential reads when recovering the database. The log writer I/O operations are designed to be and need to be very fast. For this reason the database redo log files should always be located on a dedicated disk without interference from other processes.

Similarly when locating the database files the database designer needs to follow the same logic. It is important to separate those database objects that are subject to sequential I/O such as tables when they are being scanned and those subject to single block random I/Os such as index blocks and tables being accesses by key access.

To resolve the contention it is recommended that a truth table of anticipated access paths to each data object be built as it gets defined within the database. Using the table it will be possible to see if an object can coexist on the same disks as other object or if it should be given a dedicated set of disks.

Techniques for Striping

There are two methods of striping a data object. The first method is manual striping in which the database administrator physically locates an object over multiple devices by creating multiple data files. The other method is to use machine or hardware striping. Hardware striping allows the database administrator to define a single logical file that spans multiple physical devices. The administrator is also able to define the size of the stripe taken from each device.

The advantages and disadvantages of the various striping techniques are described in Table 3.

From this table it is easy to see when striping the database the administrator needs to decide whether to invest time on manual striping or to use machine striping with a small performance penalty. In Data Warehouse where the workload profile is unknown it is recommended that machine striping is used to stripe all objects. To eliminate contention for disks it is recommended that tables that are subject to multiple concurrent parallel scans be given a dedicated set of disks striped to give satisfactory I/O bandwidth and load balancing abilities.

Table 3.

Striping Method	Advantages	Disadvantages
Manual Striping	Best performance for single query parallel scan. Good for benchmarks. Conceptually Simple.	Difficult to setup and administer in future use. No ability to load balance if multiple parallel scans on the same object.
Machine Striping	Easy to setup and administer. Load balances if multiple parallel scans occur on the same object	Performance penalty of about 5-10% when performing single parallel query.

The final issue with machine striping is that of stripe size. This issue is a hotly debated issue. The stripe size will drastically impact table scan performance as well as database operational issue such as backups and restores. When setting the strip size the administrator should attempt to insure that each I/O can be satisfied within one stripe. This means if table scanning the stripe size should be at minimum blocks size times the value of database block read count parameter. It is unlikely however that the table scan will align itself with the stripe boundaries so a larger number is actually required. *Do not allow the system administrator to set the stripe size to the DBMS blocks size.* This has been shown on many occasions to be very degrading to all database operations. *A recommended size for the stripe size is about 1 Meg and on very large systems 5 Meg.*

Tape and Media Management Requirements

When building the Data warehouse at some point in time the database will need to be backed up and restored. As many of these databases are very large sophisticated tape and media management system will be required.

When evaluating the media system the following issues should be addressed:-

- Cost of Loss of Data.
- Speed of Backup and Restore.
- Amount of Operator Intervention Required.

- Compactness and size of media storage.
- Cost of overall Media management subsystem as a percentage of whole system cost.

Data Placement Techniques within a Data Warehouse

Compromising Administration against Spaced Used

Having determined the size and made best guesses on the access patterns on each object within the Data Warehouse, the database designer or administrator needs to formulate a strategy as to how best store the object within an Oracle database. This process usually involves determining which object should reside in each Oracle database tablespace. The database designers and administrators will then ensure that each tablespace is created with the correct I/O characteristics such as striping to ensure satisfactory I/O performance.

The object to tablespace mapping involves a number of variables but the most important thing is to remember the design objectives of this phase. When determining an object to tablespace mapping there two core objectives that must be addressed. These are as follows.

- Give sufficient I/O subsystem bandwidth to each database object (Table, Index or Cluster)
- Layout the database objects in a manner that will minimize future database administration and system downtime.

Whilst these objectives should be obvious they very often conflict and this places great responsibilities on the database designer and administrator to resolve these issues and understand the impact of any compromises.

There are some very simple rules of thumb to creating an object to tablespace mapping. These are as follows.

- Give Large objects their own tablespace.
- Group objects of similar access patterns together into a single tablespace. For Example Tables, indexes.
- Separate objects with high degrees of space management activity into their own tablespace. For example temporary or sort segments, rollback segments and derived or summary tables.

Working to reduce fragmentation and row chaining

Fragmentation and row chaining will have serious performance and operational impact on your data warehouse. This degree this affects each Data Warehouse will largely be determined by the nature of each workload. There are however some things a database designer and administrator can do on creation of the database and its objects to attempt to minimize these problems.

Fragmentation within a tablespace will be caused by the dynamic allocation of extents for database objects and their subsequent de-allocation. This process over time will leave gaps and holes within the database that cannot be used and will eventually waste database space and make some database operations inoperable. Once this happened a database re-organization is usually inevitable.

To eliminate fragmentation is impossible however there are steps that can be taken to minimize or at least slow down the process. These are as follows:-

- When creating database objects ensure that the storage parameter increase allowance is set to zero. This parameter when left at the system default of 10% probably causes more fragmentation than any other single issue.
- When creating objects within a single tablespace it is best to adopt a uniform extent size for all objects within the tablespace. This prevents a great deal of fragmentation because any reallocated extents will be immediately reused. This technique is essential for temporary and rollback segment tablespaces.
- In tablespaces where large objects are being stored make the extent size approximately one tenth the size of the data files for that tablespace. In this way monitoring space utilization will be simple and require minimal effort.

Impact of Direct Loader and Parallel Features on Fragmentation

Use of the Direct Loader and the parallel features is essential on any Data Warehouse database of any significant size. These facilities however work in a manner that can cause fragmentation and all database administrators should be aware of these features. These are as follows.

- When loading data using the direct path loader in parallel mode the loader will truncate the last extent to be populated in the data load from the length specified in the storage clause to the length of the populated extent. This means when using multiple direct loads into the same file gaps can be created that cannot be filled.
- When building Indexes in parallel or utilizing the unrecoverable create table as select each parallel slave process will allocate extents according to the storage

clauses and again will truncate the length of the last extent allocated. Again this can create gaps in the database of empty space.

Data Cleaning

The data cleaning or scrubbing process can itself make or break the entire Data Warehouse project. The data may require so much processing that in the life of the Data Warehouse it is never perfect.

It is recommended that if possible most data cleaning is done prior to insertion into the database. Much of this work can be done with tools designed specifically for the process. These tools also have the advantage in many cases that they provide historical mapping data to map the Data Warehouse data representation back through the cleaning process to the operational data. This issue may be crucial when building very complex corporate Data Warehouses. In smaller more bespoke systems the cleaning process simply filtering the data may be sufficient.
The data cleaning process prior to data loading should however allow for the following features or characteristics.

- Product data output suitable for loading by the Direct Loader. This allows rapid loading into the database with minimal overhead. A full explanation of the benefits of the direct path approach is covered in the application section of this document.

- The cleaning process should function in parallel. With larger and larger databases this process cannot afford to run as single threaded process. The process must be able to run in parallel to facilitate data cleaning within a reasonable operational time window.

- The cleaning process should be self documenting and should generate summary statistics and exceptions to the process.

- The project should determine "How Clean ?" the data needs to be before putting the data into production. A great deal information of useful work can be done on imperfect data. A cost/benefit approach needs to be applied on when to stop cleaning and the process of Data Warehousing begins. This is very analogous to cleaning the bottom of a boat. Once most of the nastiest weeds and barnacles have been removed there is nothing to stop the boat being used. There is however a law of diminishing returns once the boat bottom has reasonable level of finish.

- Small numbers of rows (100s) can be manually corrected or cleaned up later whilst in the database using SQL. However the bulk of data modification and transformation needs to be done prior to loading into the database.

Types of Data Cleaning and Transformation

There will be various types of operation that is required to clean a set of data. Some of this should be done external to the database. Some of the cleaning processes it is possible to use the database utilities to clean and validate the data. If the direct path loader is used to load the data the data loading process is very rapid. A table may get loaded into the database for analysis only to determine more data cleaning is required. The data may be cleaned in the external files and the table may get reloaded. multiple times. Another solution is to use the Unrecoverable option of the Create Table as Select (CTAS) in parallel and recreate the cleaned table within the database. The purpose of this discussion is to demonstrate that for each data cleaning problem there is multiple solutions and it will be the skill of the Data Warehousing project to determine the best process. The problems of data cleaning can be classified under the following classes of problems:-

Application Cleaning

This can be summarized as manipulation of the data to make the warehouse function. An example of this would include unification of customer identifiers from diverse data sources.

Data Inconsistency Cleaning

This can be summarized as the process of cleaning up the small inconsistencies that introduce themselves into the data. Examples include duplicate keys and unreferenced foreign keys.

Column Level Cleaning

This involved checking the contents of each column field and ensuring it conforms to a set of valid values. These may be enumerated data types or actual values. Free format and text fields should be stored in the correct collating sequence. For example convert EBCDIC to ASCII.

Table 4 is not complete but it does however attempt to describe some of the most common data cleaning problems.

Table 4.

Problem	Class of Problem	Potential Solution	Simplicity of Solution
Unification of data into common Entities from multiple systems.	Application.	Use of tools or well documented transformation mechanisms.	Largely depends on diversity of data. Should initially be regarded as complex.
Elimination of Duplicate values.	Data Inconsistency.	Use SQL joining table to its self or use RDBMS Constraint utilities.	Simple to perform. Can be very time consuming.
Elimination or resolution of orphaned records.	Data Inconsistency.	Use SQL with Anti-Join Query or use RDBMS Constraint utilities.	Simple to perform however time consuming. Will require business experience to resolve inconsistencies.
Invalid Dates	Column level Inconsistency.	Can be eliminated on data load. However application may need to further reduce applicable date ranges.	Many of these problems derive from storage mechanisms in legacy data. Use tools or filters to pre-process data into format suitable for database.
Invalid Column Values	Column level Inconsistency/ Application.	For large sets of rows pre-process prior to data load or if loaded recreate table using CTAS. For small data quantities use SQL UPDATEs.	This will be function of business rules complexity. Remember other fields may be suitable for other query work. Use Cost/ benefit to determine if this processing is required immediately.
Number Precision	Column level Inconsistency/ Application.	As for invalid column values.	Complex to determine optimum levels of number precision. However precision should not exceed accuracy of data.

Assessing Data Cleaning Requirements

When estimating or bidding for any Data Warehouse project the data cleaning component represents the least quantifiable and exposes any project to the most risk of cost and time overruns. In this section an attempt is made to identify the parameters that make the data cleaning process simple and those that increase complexity and hence risk. Readers of this document should be aware for data sourced from old legacy systems very often a customers staff will not be able to give you accurate schema information about their own data and the process of data cleaning could be better renamed as data discovery. Do not expect perfect data and supporting documentation from customers as much of the knowledge on these systems existed over 5-10 years ago when these systems were developed. The staff who held this knowledge base will have left the organizations a great deal of time ago.

Factors that Contribute to Simpler Data Cleaning

- Single source of data
- Source data stored in the database
- Source data stored in relational database

- Source data stored in same byte order as DW
- Source data uses same collating sequence
- Source data uses relational constraints
- Source data uses column level constraints

Factors that Contribute to Complex Data Cleaning

Multiple diverse sources of data

Data not initially stored in relational format

Data not stored in same byte order (Byte swapping required)

Data stored in different collating sequence

Data coming from application that enforces minimal validation and constraint definitions.

Application Performance Techniques

SQL Statement Design and Tuning Techniques

Tuning SQL statements is area where this is literally no substitute for experience and practice. A great deal of SQL statement tuning is subjective and usually exploits some knowledge about the data that the current optimizer is unable to fully model or represent. The optimizer improves with every release of Oracle as better statistics and plan generation algorithms are incorporated into the kernel. As users however everybody should be fully aware that the SQL optimizer has limitations and these will be recognized by experience. Fortunately for developers it is possible to "hint" SQL statements and manually override the optimizer to manually achieve optimum execution plans.

For more formal methods of tuning SQL statements please refer to the database documentation or the book "Oracle Performance Tuning" by Corrigan and Gurry. These documents describe the mechanics and well as the background to this process. In Data Warehouse applications the query execution plans in many cases if they are not correct may mean the results cannot be derived in reasonable time. For this reason identifying the good and bad plans becomes very important and should be part of any Data Warehouse process.

The usual mistakes and areas for investigation in SQL statements are as follows.

Table Scan or Indexed Access

When accessing each table in a query there is two fundamental methods (hash clusters excluded). These consist of scanning the entire table or using an index on the keyed fields within the "where" clause of the query. There is a very simple rule of thumb when an index is better than a full table scan. If you going to retrieve less than 20-25% of a table then index access is better solution otherwise use a full table scan. In many cases where consultants have forced queries to use indexes they slowed down queries because a table scan is faster. It is important to always consider the selectivity of indexes prior to their use. Use of an index does not imply an optimum execution plan.

Incorrect Join order and Type

This is particularly prevalent on SQL statements written to execute lower version of the Oracle RDBMS. This is because the optimizer will only optimize the SQL statement fully if there are 5 or less tables in the SQL statement. If a 7 table join is required it will probably generate a sub-optimum execution plan. Additionally with newer release of the database there is 3 methods to join each table namely, nested loops, sort merge, and hash joining. In a complex query the number of possible join mechanisms becomes a very large set of combinations. In order to determine the best execution plans the SQL statement tuner needs to use the guidance provided by the optimizer with his or her knowledge of the data to determine the best join order and join mechanism.

Lack of Index Definition or Poor Index Definition

Poor index design is responsible for great number of performance problems. The selectivity of an index can be greatly increased by the use of concatenated index to include many of the "where" clause predicates and hence reduce the size of an index range scan and the subsequent number of table lookups. Further refinements can be made to the design of a concatenated index by appending the remainder columns from the select list of the query such than not table lookup are performed in the query at all. In this case the query is entirely satisfied from within the index.
Another issue index designs is that very often little thought is given to key ordering when specifying a concatenated index. If possible is best to place the columns in order of selectivity with the most selective column first. This is particularly important to verify index definitions and designs generated by case tools as these tools tend to generate the index definition according to the dictionary ordering of columns and not by selectivity of the columns.

Unnecessary Sorting

A great deal of time in any query can be wasted by unnecessary sorting and filtering. Some of the most common of these may involve the use of a "union" statement where a "union all" would have been suitable. In this case the "union all" eliminates the need for a sort to eliminate duplicate rows in the set operation.

A more common example is when using an "order by" clause. If an index range scan is used and the index is built according to the ordering specified by the "order by" clause the query is able to retrieve the data presorted and then eliminate the sort operation to satisfy the "order by" clause.

Implicit Datatype Conversion

This problem is a very common problem in all types of system ands its discovery and subsequent correction has increased the performance of thousands of systems worldwide. It is particularly common on tables that have a key that consists entirely of digits however it is stored as character or varchar field. Examples of these would be check numbers, serial numbers, sku numbers or any key that whist containing only digits no arithmetic operations are performed upon it. The usual fault made by the SQL programmer is when assigning equality statements in the "where" clause predicate list. On specifying a the equality the equals sign is used but the variable is not surrounded by quotes. This forces the statement to be executed as numerical comparison rather than a lexical comparison. This will implicitly force a full table scan rather than using the desired index.

Example:

Table Custommer has a primary key cid. This is ten byte character field which comprises entirely of digits.

This SQL will perform an implicit data type conversion by performing an implicit to_number on the data. This will execute as full table scan.

> select * from customer
>
> where cid = 9999999999;

However this SQL will perform a lexical comparison and will use the primary key index.

> select * from customer
>
> where cid = '9999999999';

The Transactional Options within Oracle

There are two basic mechanisms to manipulate data within an the database. The conventional route is via SQL by use of Update, Delete and Insert statements. This mechanism uses the full transaction layer that has been optimized for high performance OLTP applications. This mechanism uses rollback segments for the storage of read consistent images and redo logs to ensure the changes are made permanent. Whilst the use of SQL is excellent for OLTP when manipulating the size of objects found in a Data Warehouse this approach reaches various practical limitations. The alternative approach is to make use of the direct interface to the database that bypasses the entire SQL and subsequent transactional layer.

Since the latest versions SQL*Loader has been shipped with a direct path option. This option provides a rapid mechanism for loading of data into the database. It does this by bypassing the SQL interface and writing database blocks directly to file. This process by passes the buffer cache, the transaction layer avoiding the overhead of logging and for this reason is very fast. The only disadvantage of this mechanism is that it does not provide full database recovery and the database should be backed up after the data load. Whilst this is not ideal for mission critical OLTP systems it is ideal for Data Warehouses where rapid loading and subsequent backup is what is required without the addition of numerous transaction logs. In the various new releases of Oracle this basic philosophy has been extended to other operations to allow parallel direct path loading into a single table and most what will be the most useful for Data Warehouse operations the "unrecoverable" clause on "create index" and "create table X as select .." operations. This functionality allows rapid creation and loading of tables that do not require any of the overheads of the transaction layer and they function in parallel. This allows rapid movement of data into and within the database and does not stress the read consistency models and also reduces the time for database reorganization operations.

Use of Parallelism in a Data Warehouse

Data Warehouse databases are by their very definition are in the class of a Very large database or VLDB. For this reason to practically load and administer these databases a single CPU will not be adequate to perform all operational functions. For this reason multi-CPU machines and software to enable jobs to execute in parallel are essential.

To exploit fully the parallel nature of these machines and software great care has to be taken to ensure that the process does not serialize upon common resource or as it more commonly referred to as single threading upon a resource. An example of this would be parallel table scan were multiple CPUs are attempting scan a table that was stored on one disk drive. Very rapidly it would become obvious that it was impossible to keep the CPUs busy because they single threading upon this disk drive.

From this very simple example it is very simple to understand that when performing operation in parallel everything has to be done to eliminate single threading. Unfortunately detecting single threading is by no means a trivial task and again requires a great deal of experience and internals knowledge. If single threading is suspected it is best to collect the statistics defined in later sections on this document and seek help from staff familiar with the hardware and software components.

Use of Partitioning in a Data Warehouse

A great deal has been written about partitioning within database in numerous books and publications. These notes will not rehash the same principals other than to give the some the key benefits of partitioning in a Data Warehouse.

The first issue is that database administration may make some sort of partitioning inevitable. If a table grows to large such that basic operations such as re-orgs and index builds take to long the table will require partitioning. The manner in which this partition occurs will have large impacts on the final applications.

The second issue is that partitioning can be used to speed query performance. If a table is partitioned horizontally by specified key boundaries such as date ranges queries can be made more selective by only querying those partitions which satisfy the query criteria.

Purging and Deleting of Data

Systematic purging of data from the Data Warehouse is one of the more difficult and resource intensive operations. This operation needs to be executed periodically in a minimum of elapsed time. Usually at this time it is also best to de-fragment and reload the data for optimum query performance.

To purge data from the database there are number of options that may be adopted. Each one has its benefits and disadvantages. Data Warehouse designers and administrators need to build a purging strategy into the long term Warehouse strategy. The options for purging of data are shown in Table 5.

Table 5.

Purging Mechanism	Advantages	Disadvantages	Example
SQL Delete Statement	Simple to program. Works well for small data quantities.	Very slow for large data volumes. Can cause excessive rollback segment and redo log I/O. Will leave holes in the database.	delete from sales where salesdate between '1-Mar-95' and '31-Mar-95'; commit;
Use of Horizontal Partitioning	Requires a ranged horizontal partitioned solution to allow purging process to simply drop partition of data to be purged.	Purge process very fast. However will impact query and data load programming.	drop table salesmar95;
SQL Delete Statement	Simple to program. Works well for small data quantities.	Very slow for large data volumes. Can cause excessive rollback segment and redo log I/O. Will leave holes in the database.	delete from sales where salesdate between '1-Mar-95' and '31-Mar-95'; commit;
Use of Horizontal Partitioning	Requires a ranged horizontal partitioned solution to allow purging process to simply drop partition of data to be purged.	Purge process very fast. However will impact query and data load programming.	drop table salesmar95;
Selection of Delete Compliment into new table.	Can select compliment of delete statement into a new table. e.g. query the rows you wish to keep and then remove the old table. This process can run in parallel and will de-fragment the database. For large deletes it will not be constrained by single threading and the overhead of the transaction layer. This is particularly useful when partitioning is not an option.	Requires significant D.B.A. attention during the process. however this process is very fast.	create table newsalesas select * from sales where salesdate>'31-Mar-95' or salesdate<'1-Mar-95'; drop table sales; rename newsales to sales;

Specialist Data Warehouse Query Techniques

One of the most important query types that will be exploited within a Data Warehouse practice is the star query. As great deal of Data Warehouses are constructed using a star schema. To fully exploit this model some latest DBMS kernels attempt to optimize star queries.

A star schema consists of a central intersection table or more commonly called "fact" table with a large number of satellites tables related to the central table. The satellite tables define the dimensions of the star query. An example of a star schema would be a central sales table that stores the value of each sale. On the fact table there would be a large number of foreign key references to the satellite tables. These could be product, product type, business period, geographical region, and sales organization. The star query is composed by referencing the outer satellite queries within the query 'where' clause predicates. The specification of all the join conditions insures all the tables are correctly linked. An example of the type of business question that a star query would consist of would may read as follows:

Give me the sum of sales of soft drinks sold in the states of California and Texas in the month of June from Vending machines.

This query may be written in SQL some thing like this:

```
select sum( sales ), state
from months m, sales_line s, products p, location l, sales_fact f
where f.mid = m.mid
and    f.sid = s.sid
and    f.pid = p.pid
and    f.lid = l.lid
and    m.month = 'June'
and    s.route = 'Vending Machine'
and    p.product_type = 'Soft Drinks'
and    l.state in ( 'CA', 'TX' )
group by state;
```

This query will executed as Cartesian join of the outer satellite tables to produce a combination product. The join to the central fact table is than completed by performing nested loop join. This is done by building an concatenated index on all the foreign keys in the fact table. The order this index is specified will require tuning according to the selectivity of the various keys.

To further speed this query if the sales column is appended to the index the whole query will be satisfied in the index without even having to look at the fact table. This query is very fast. In queries that use more than 5 tables insure that the tables are specified in join order with the fact table last and use an "ordered" hint within the query.

Monitoring the Data Warehouse

Bottleneck Detection

Bottleneck Detection is the process where by the database administrator will detect for what reason the database performance level has reached a plateau. To increase the performance from this plateau may require the addition of more hardware resources or reconfiguration of the system software(O/S, RDBMS or Application). The following notes provide an insight as to determine the various types of bottlenecks. For more complex bottlenecks seek specialist tuning and performance assistance.

Hardware bottlenecks

Table 6 describes what utilities use to determine hardware bottlenecks and the statistical information that should be interpreted from the statistics.

Table 6.

Hardware Resource	Monitoring Tools	Results Interpretation	Addition Comments
CPU	"sar -u", vmstat, iostat	When the CPU is fully utilized it should split 60-80% User Code 40-20% System Code	If there is no idle time and the CPU is utilized as described. The system is CPU constrained. Either buy more CPUs or rework application to use less CPU.
Memory	"sar -?", vmstat	There should be no paging or swapping activities	If paging or swapping occurs consider either reducing memory buffer sizes or it this is unacceptable buy more memory.
Disks	"sar -d", iostat	The key statistics are:-I/Os per second per device. (Should be less than 30) Device queues (should average between 1.0 and 1.5) Device response times (Should average at 0 milli sec wait time and 20-30 milli sec service time)	In addition high wait I/O value from "sar -u" will indicate I/O bottlenecks. If disk statistics look good and still high wait I/O investigate disk controller and channel bottlenecks.

RDBMS Bottlenecks

Unlike hardware bottlenecks where detection is very simple RDBMS bottlenecks are more subjective and require considerable knowledge and experience of the DBMS Kernel internals. With this fact in mind this document does not attempt to address every database internal bottleneck. This document describes a method that a system administrator can take effective statistics that when given to database performance specialist they can be interpreted easily.

The core database statistics to collect are those provided by us in memory performance tables. These are often referred to as the V$ and X$ tables. There are numerous of these tables which are all documented in various documents. The most important thing is to collect these results in a format that is useful for performance analysis as well as long term performance tracking.

These statistics are best captured using a snapshot tool like the utlbstat & utlestat scripts shipped with the database or some of the more sophisticated scripts shipped from the performance studies group with Oracle UK. These snapshot tools in essence measure the deltas in the database statistics over finite period of time. They then generate a report that can be used to determine bottlenecks.

The second set of statistics are the real time statistics and are useful to watch in real time as the database is showing its performance problems. The key statistical table to watch in real time is v$session_wait. This allows to get real time information about the state of each database process. Use of this table allows the database administrator very simply determine internal bottlenecks as any process in a wait state will be displayed with the wait event. This tool is particularly useful resolving scaleability problems.

Developing Applications using Object Relational DBMS (Industry Case Study)

Stephen Yao, Director, Business Development, Informix Greater China Region

Abstract

Relational Database Technology has been widely accepted and used by almost every organisation from small desktop to mainframe computer systems. However, this 20 years old RDBMS technology as well as the Structure Query Language (SQL) was originally designed to manipulate characters and numbers in the form of rows and columns. In the early 90's, Object Oriented DBMS caught a lot of attention because of the ability to model real life data. However, the major programming paradigm shift and the effort required to migrate applications from RDBMS to OODBMS has driven the development on Object Relational ORDBMS technology. ORDBMS incorporates the extensibility of OO DBMS on top of the commonly used SQL language. Using a programming example, this article describes the basic steps involved in building a next generation application using the ORDBMS technique including schema design, type hierarchy and actual SQL programming syntax.

The following article provides an in-depth look at what's really involved in building a next generation of business application using Object Relational Database Management Systems (ORDBMS) techniques. This will be done by using the overall example of an Insurance application, which combined both inherent ORDBMS capabilities as well as several extensible object modules to handle complex information such as maps, image, document etc.

My goals are to help you understand how the new ORDBMS and extensible functionality might be used in a real-world application as well as to show that creating this new class of applications is relatively easy.

Let me start off by describing the need of the Insurance industry and the application that I use as an example through out this paper. The insurance industry needs to succeed :

1. Accurate estimates: There's information in their database on past accidents and automobile damage, and by accessing similar historic information one should be able to truly compare a new insurance claim with similar ones in the past.

2. Faster turn-around: The competitive environment in any business means that companies like Horizon want to respond to customers as quickly as possible. The demonstration performs a rapid yet accurate assessment of appropriate information

and minimises the "hand" work that needs to be done, resulting in very quick turn-around for the customer.

3. "Front of shop" service: Taking advantage of tools like WWW makes is again a competitive advantage.

The application uses both native Informix Universal Server (IUS), an ORDBMS object oriented features such as new data types, prepackaged DataBlades, and a web interface built with the Informix Web DataBlade. DataBlade Modules are snap-in object extensions that expand the general purpose capabilities of the Informix Universal Server. Let's have a closer look at the application flows :

1. Customer enters claim over internet

2. Agent reviews in-basket

3. For each outstanding claim, agent:
   • Reviews customer's policy
   • Compares with similar past accidents (visual and text records) to determine cost exposure
   • Determines appropriate response based on cash reserves
   • Returns information to customer on claim disposition and appropriate repair options and locations

This application would not have been practical using traditional RDBMS technology because it needs to manipulate the following complex information :

1. Geographic locations: The information for repair shops, home, and office locations, although available, cannot be efficiently stored or queried in a traditional RDBMS. This type of activity has historically been done in a GIS system, but this is a very expensive approach, and the tools do not integrate well (hence the "duct tape" analogy).

2. Images: Again, these are at best stored as BLOBs within a traditional RDBMS. Technology to search for images "like" another have been available only as a client implementation, and searching an entire image base for "similar" dents was just not practical.

The design of this application is somewhat different due to the advanced capabilities of ORDBMS and the power that DataBlades provide. It includes :

1. Database design: SQL3 and ORDBMS provides you with custom data types. By taking advantage of these types, or adapting pre-defined types from DataBlade modules, you can greatly simplify the overall design project.

32

2. Integrating DataBlade modules: Many of the complex needs within the Horizon demo are easily met by the functions and data types provided as standard DataBlade components. When designing this type of project, it is useful to review the available DataBlade modules and identify which capabilities are available. Again, selecting appropriate DataBlade modules will dramatically simplify the project.

3. Add custom code: Finally, the option exists to create custom code that can run within the server, which will greatly improve the overall application performance.

Beginning with SQL3, there are several changes in how you design your DataBase that you can consider. Changes includes Inheritance and type hierarchies plus entities.

The relational model extends to an object model :
- Rows and Collections
- Smart Large Objects
- Abstract/User Defined Data Types
- Functions and Triggers

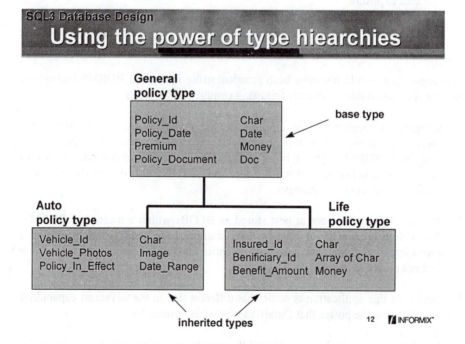

SQL3 Database Design
Using the power of type hiearchies

General policy type

Policy_Id	Char
Policy_Date	Date
Premium	Money
Policy_Document	Doc

base type

Auto policy type

Vehicle_Id	Char
Vehicle_Photos	Image
Policy_In_Effect	Date_Range

Life policy type

Insured_Id	Char
Benificiary_Id	Array of Char
Benefit_Amount	Money

inherited types

12   INFORMIX

SQL3 Design: Defining Row Type :

```
create row type policy
      (policy_id char(40), policy_date date,
      premium money, policy_document doc);

create row type date_range
      (begin_date datetime, enddate datetime);

create row type auto_policy
      (vehicle_id char, vehicle_photos image,
      policy_in_effect date_range)
      under policy;

create row type life_policy
      (insured_id char(9),
      benificiary_id set(benificiary_id char(9)),
      benefit_amount money)
      under policy;
```

SQL3 Design: Creating New Functions

```
create function value(policy auto_policy)
      returning money return premium/time_remaining(date_range);
      end function;

create function value (policy life_policy)
      returning money
      return benefit_calculation(benefit_amount,policy_date);
      end function;
```

and note .... select value(p) from policy p;
returns value specific for auto & life through ***overloading***

To integrate the varies complex datatypes to solve a complicated business problem including :

1.   Complex Databyte: Text Search :

   <u>Business Problem</u>: How many accidents involve the 'wrong side of the road'

```
      select count(*) from claims
            where contains (report, '( 'wrong' , 'side' , 'road') );
```

2.   Complex Databyte: Image Search :

Business Problem: What is the average claim paid for a given type of accident

```
select avg(assessed_at) from claims
      where image_like (acc_image,'my image') = 'T'
      and claim_paid is not null;
```

3.   Complex Databyte: Spatial Search :

Business Problem: How many customers live in a given area?

```
select count(*) from customers where contains(home_location,
box'(x1,y1,x2,y2)');
```

Business Problem: How many customers live in each county?

```
select Co.name, count(*) from customers Cu, counties Co
      where contains(Cu.home_location,Co.Boundary)
      group by Co.name order by 2;
```


Putting it all together :

Business Problem: What is the average amount paid on claims within a given area where the accident involved the wrong side of the road?

```
select avg(c.assesed_at)
      from claims c, policies p,customers cu
      where contains (c.report,('wrong','side','road')
      and contains (cu.home_location,box'(x1,y1,x2,y2)')
      and c.policy_id = p.policy_id
      and p.holder = cu.customer_id
      and c.claim_paid is not null;
```

The Custom Coding lets you add specialized, customized behaviors to applications which is truly the power of ORDBMS. Developers use DataBlades for commodity functions and extend via ADTs, User Defined Functions, and User Defined Routines. For sophisticated developers, they can program the extended functions in C, C++, Java and for the average user they can use Stored Procedural Language (SPL).

In summary, I hope this article gives you an overview of ORDBMS capabilities as well as the true extensibility of user defined databytes, standard 3rd party DataBlade object components and custom object modules. In today's competitive business world, the example I used illustrates how an insurance application benefits from incorporating complex information to achieve faster turn around on claim processing, more accurate estimation and better customer services. The ORDBMS technology can be applied to re-engineering business applications across many industries. Lastly, adopting ORDBMS techniques is a nature extension to the traditional RDBMS systems and creating this new class of applications is relatively easy.

About the Speaker :

Mr. Stephen Yao has 15 years experience in the IT industry in varies positions starting as a system developer to his current role as the director of business development responsible for emerging technology development related to the Internet, Multi-media and recruitment of Datablade developers in the region. Prior to joining Informix, Mr. Yao was the Regional Product Manager for Data General Corporation. He is a graduate of University of New Brunswick, Canada major in Computer Science.

Stephen Yao
Director, Business Development
Informix Greater China Region

www.informix.com

Emerging Technologies for Business Intelligence

Ian Parkes - Special Projects Director, COL Limited

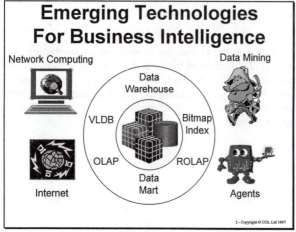

Although its hard to predict the future, even the near term, it is apparent that the technologies listed here all have a good chance of impacting the field of BI and DSS. The technologies in the core are already at the centre of debate.

Those on the edge are slowly capturing our attention. In this presentation, we will take a brief look at the status of these different initiatives.

Data Warehouse

The Data Warehousing Institute

u **"Top 10 Mistakes"**
  - u **The wrong sponsor**
  - u **Believing Performance/Capacity/Scalability Claims**
  - u **Data warehouse design = Transaction DB Design**
  - u **Data with Confusing Definitions**
  - u **Loading Information "because it was there"**
  - u **Technology Manager .v. User-Oriented**
  - u **Focus on Internal Record-Based Data**
  - u **Setting Unrealistic Expectations**
  - u **Politically Naïve Behaviour**
  - u **Once it's Up, it's Finished**

3 - Copyright © COL Ltd 1997

The foundation for much of the work on Business Intelligence has been the acceptance of the Data Warehouse concept. But, as always with the introduction of new approaches, there has been a learning curve and mistakes have been made.

One survey, which is interesting in its own right, and also helps to explain the importance of some of the more recent technologies, is the Data Warehousing Institute's "Top 10 Mistakes" in building a data warehouse.

Many of the issues listed are those traditionally found at the boundaries between IT and end-users, but the sheer scale of the data warehousing task can significantly magnify these problems into real "show-stoppers".

If, as the META group claims, it costs US$3million and takes 3 years to build, the expectations for the average data warehouse are understandably high.

To gauge these risks in the real-world, lets consider some practical examples...

Database Growth Rates

While most data warehouses and data marts start out small (under 25 gigabytes), few remain that way. The average warehouse is expected to *quintuple* in size over the next few years. (Aberdeen Group)

4 - Copyright © COL Ltd 1997

The scale of data warehousing is already achieving the ultimate accolade of the IT world - a new three letter acronym - VLD

Database have literally exploded in size.
In the past 5 gigs was large, then it was 50, now its multiple terabytes.

Very Large Databases

Company	Size (Terabytes)
Wal-Mart	24.0
MCI	3.0
Sears	1.7
Lucent	1.2
Equitable Life	1.0
Tel-Way	.7
Transquest	.7
Kmart	.7
Barclays Bank	.7
Health Source	.6
BEZEQ	.6

5 - Copyright © COL Ltd 1997

A case in point is Wal-Mart which recently announced that it was growing its 3 terabyte database to 24 terabytes in order to do "market basket" analysis -- in order to determine which products people buy together and to plan more efficient store layouts and product promotions.

The difficulty with these large stores are multifold. One difficulty is that it is impossible to analyse them in their terabyte form. Joins done on terabytes of data are measured in hours and days, not seconds and minutes.

38

Because of this many enterprises like MCI have divided their data warehouses into smaller data marts, although in this case the data marts are still around 100 gigabytes (large by most peoples standards).

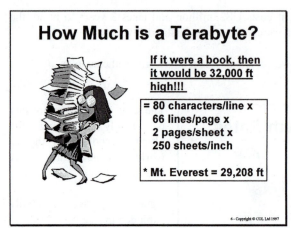

With a little arithmetic you can show that its a book about 32,000 feet high. Mt. Everest is only 29,000 ft!

Remember the Data Warehousing Institute's warning about "politically naïve behaviour - "This will help managers make better decisions"

And here is the problem - while the Data Warehouse has proved to be a great place to store and manage data, it is NOT the delivery system that end-users wanted.

What was, and is, wanted is a system that genuinely supports the decision making process.
Enter the DSS - Decision Support System.

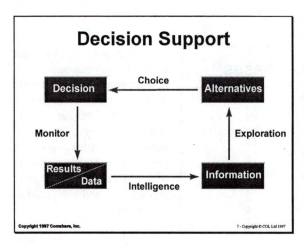

The old definition of a DSS application was simply to take data and turn it into information. While useful to get started; it is no longer good enough.

A complete decision support application requires a closed loop process that continues through exploration, choice, and monitoring.

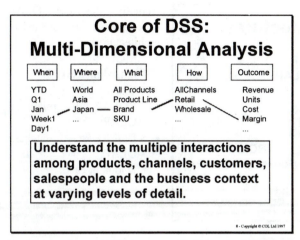

At the heart of today's DSS applications is the ability to view data and information from a multidimensional perspective.

To look at the interrelations and interplay of several variables all at once.

In the past it was sufficient to call the tools and systems supporting multi dimensional analysis simply DSS.

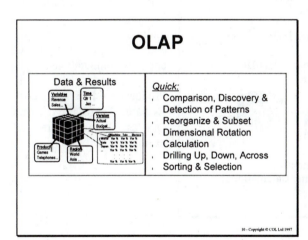

Today, the preferred term is OLAP -- online analytical processing as opposed to OLTP.

The software and applications falling under this rubric all attempt to provide the end user with the ability to quickly execute the tasks listed here.

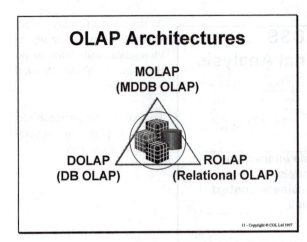

Actually, the term OLAP encompasses three major architectures.
- MOLAP - multidimensional OLAP;
- ROLAP - relational OLAP;
- DOLAP - database OLAP.

Let us look at each.

MOLAP or multidimensional OLAP is characterised by a specialised database that is multi-dimensional as opposed to relational

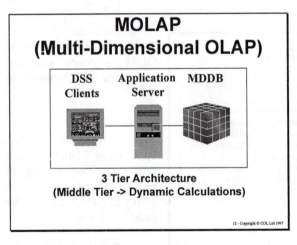

It is a database honed for fast indexing into multidimensional structures and fast calculation of complex computations.

Products like Arbor's Essbase, Applix's TM/1 and Oracles Express are all examples.

Characteristics include:
- Consistently fast response time
- Based on summarised information
- High levels of computational complexity
- Read/Write Access
- Suitable for Planning / Analysis tasks

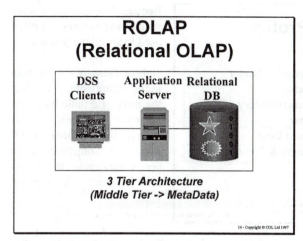

In contrast ROLAPs store the data in specialised relational formats.

The key to these architectures is often the middle tier which performs the task of translating the user's actions into backed SQL calls that satisfy the user "multidimensional" requests.

Microstrategy's DSS Agent is an instance of this type of technology.

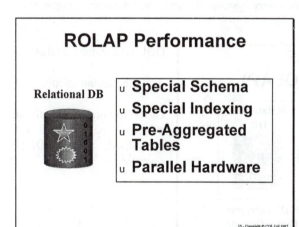

Because a relational database is not honed for fast multidimensional retrieval, they rely on a number of tricks to speed retrieval time.

One of the major things a ROLAP does is transform a normalised representation into a specialised non-normal scheme such as a star schema.

A star schema consists of a fact table with all the data -- sales, costs, etc. -- and a set of dimension tables that are keyed into the fact table.

Joins of the fact table with the dimension tables are used to produce a multidimensional view -- sales by product by location by time.

Star joins can get exceedingly complex and can required 100s of lines of SQL to produce even simple multidimensional displays.

42

ROLAP Profile

Response Time	Varies by Query
Content	Detail Actual/History
Compute Complexity	Low
Access	Read Only
Application Focus	Query & Comparison

16 - Copyright © COL Ltd 1997

Because Star joins are slow, specialised indexes are often used to speed the process.

One of these is the bit map index. Simply put, you select the rows of a table based on a select statement (select males), that produces a 1 if it is true and 0 otherwise. Then you concatenate these bits into a long bit mapped index.

Now, when you do joins you simply join the bitmaps which is much faster although it requires you to know which selects to do ahead of time.

ROLAPs are fine for large scale query systems but lack the necessary computations needed for many DSS applications.

DOLAP (Database OLAP)

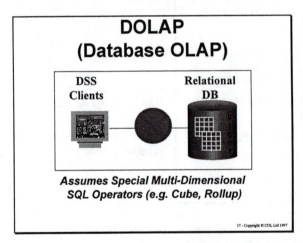

DSS Clients

Relational DB

Assumes Special Multi-Dimensional SQL Operators (e.g. Cube, Rollup)

17 - Copyright © COL Ltd 1997

DOLAP is database OLAP.

It is the ultimate utopia.

OLAP performed directly on a normalised database with specialised SQL OLAP operators.

Unfortunately, like all utopias its an idea not a reality. If you look at the major database vendors you will see that they've all conceded the idea that at a minimum a specialised calculation engine is needed for OLAP -- Oracle & Express; IBM and Arbour.

How do you navigate through a terabyte or even 100 gigabytes? You don not. As Nicholas Negroponte, head of MIT's Media Lab suggests, this is the point at which you delegate rather than navigate.

Delegate, Don't Navigate

Future human computer interface will be rooted in delegation, not the vernacular of direct manipulation -- pull down, pop-up, click -- and mouse interfaces. "Ease-of-use" has been such a compelling goal, that people forget that many people don't want to use the machine at all. They want to get something done.

Nicholas Negroponte, Head of MIT Media Lab "Being Digital", 1995

18 - Copyright © COL Ltd 1997

Data Mining

One place you can delegate is to you friendly data mining tool.

Some people call OLAP and ROLAP data mining, but its not.

Data mining is an automated process of discovery and extraction of things that you did not know about and that are useful things to know.

Data Mining Tasks

Associations/Affinity: Associations between Items	Rule Induction CART, CHAID
Sequence/Temporal Patterns: Time-based Affinity	Rule Induction CART, CHAID
Clustering: Grouping items according to statistical similarities	Decision Trees, K-Nearest Neighbor
Classification Assign new records to existing classes	Decision Trees, K-Nearest Neighbor
Forecasting/Prediction Predicts future value of a variable	Neural Nets Genetic Algorithms

21 - Copyright © COL Ltd 1997

Data mining technologies actually cover a range of tools and algorithms. Most experts divide them into the five categories listed here, although there are basically 3 categories:

- Association (including sequence and clustering) - that is discovering things that occur together in the data;
- Classification - determining whether something fits a predefined pattern;
- Forecasting.

Sample Applications of Data Mining

Retail	Market Basket Analysis
	Time-based Purchases
	Promotional Analysis
Banking	Fraud Detection
	Customer Segmentation
	Life Cycle Management
Telecom	Call Analysis
	Customer Loyalty/Churn
Insurance	Fraud Dection
	Product Design
	Risk Analysis

22 - Copyright © COL Ltd 1997

As this list of sample applications shows DM has enjoyed increasing use, especially with data sets that involve customer transactions.

E.g. association technologies applied to market basket analysis, and clustering applied to things like customer turnover (determine who is likely to stop or start being a customer).

On paper data mining has promising future. However, when employed with multi-dimensional data it suffers a number of limitations.

Drawbacks for Multi-Dimensional Analysis

- ⊔ **Techniques assume relational table format (limited ways to handle hierarchies)**
- ⊔ **Work well in a "batch" but not "ad hoc" environment**
- ⊔ **Best used by analysts who understand data requirements and algorithms**
- ⊔ **Standard statistical techniques often perform as well**

23 - Copyright © COL Ltd 1997

Most of these techniques only work with relational or flat files, not hierarchies and multidimensional data (in fact you have to throw away the hierarchy in most cases to analyse it).

Second, the techniques are so complex that they cannot run in real time (so they cant support ad hoc analysis) and they often require a rocket scientist to run and interpret the results.

Finally, as several research studies have shown it is not clear whether they perform better than standard statistical techniques with which more people are familiar.

A second way to delegate is to assign the task of looking through the data to software agent -- a process that can take a numerical pattern of interest (like high cost overruns where the costs is a substantial dollar figure) and rifle through the data in search of data that fit the pattern; and then when the process finds it, it notifies you.

OLAP Agents: Defined

> A triggered or scheduled background process that utilizes detection rules to automatically monitor, filter, or query a large or frequently changing data set, searching for patterns defined by the rules, and informing interested users when the patterns occur.

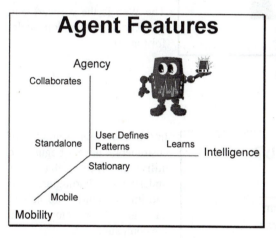

25 - Copyright © COL Ltd 1997

These processes are called software agents.

Researchers envision agents as travelling through cyberspace, interacting with other agents and learning from their masters interactions.

In fact most "commercial" agents run on a single machine, look for patterns the end user defines and work alone.

Agent Features

Agency

Collaborates

Standalone — User Defines Patterns — Learns — Intelligence

Stationary

Mobile

Mobility

Although they are still quite primitive, they are still enormously useful in real-world applications.

Exception Agent Example

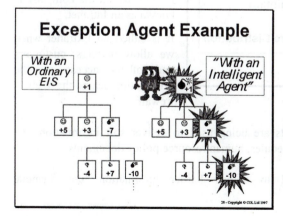

With an Ordinary EIS

"With an Intelligent Agent"

28 - Copyright © COL Ltd 1997

This example demonstrates how traditional reporting techniques mask the underlying problems.

The Agent is able to apply the search criteria at all levels of the hierarchy and "promote" these problems for immediate management attention.

46

No discussion of the future of DSS would be complete without a mention of the Web.

We are all familiar with the publicly accessible Web, which continues to grow at an astounding rate.

Web Growth

90 Million Web Pages, 170000 Pages Added Daily

29 - Copyright © COL Ltd 1997

The Web has garnered explosive support primarily because it is cheap, easy to administer and deploy, simple to use and because it provides global access on a 7 day x 24 hour basis.

The Web is the software and application distribution model for tomorrow.

Why the Web?

- u **Open, Cross-Platform**
- u **Global, "7x24" Access**
- u **Inexpensive**
- u **Easy to Install & Maintain**
- u **Simple to Use**
- u **Centralised Software Distribution**

30 - Copyright © COL Ltd 1997

In the same vein, a number of customers have begun to utilise the Web -- that is its underlying technologies, tools and infrastructure -- to deliver data and information within the company.

A Web within the company is known as an Intranet.

It is called an Extranet when we allow partners, customers and others access to the information behind the Web firewall.

For the most part, these Intranets are being used to deliver soft information like corporate news, status reports, schedules, human resource policy documents.

Occasionally, their being used to deliver harder information like financial management tables and charts.

In most of these cases the information is distributed in the form of static HTML documents (HTML) which are manually created or converted from their original format (e.g. a Word document or to the HTML format.

The simplicity of the Web arises because it is based on 5 key standards:

- A globally distributed TCP/IP network of Web servers and clients (called browsers);
- A hypertext markup language (HTML) for creating documents;
- An addressing scheme (URLs) for accessing documents on a particular Web server;
- A hypertext transport protocol (HTTP) requesting and delivering documents;
- A common gateway interface (CGI) that functions as an API enabling clients to interface to globally distributed external programs and data sources.

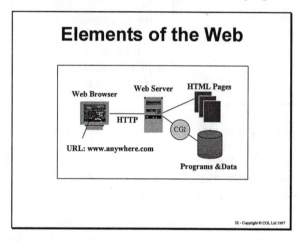

A number of OLAP, ROLAP and database vendors have utilised these key elements to provide thin client delivery of the data in a data warehouse or a data mart.

Basically, when an end user accesses a Web page requesting a particular view of the backend data, the Server hands the request to the CGI program.

The CGI program retrieves the necessary data from the backend database along with an HTML template specifying how the retrieved data are to be formatted as well as the next set of actions that the end user can perform once the data have been displayed.

The resulting data are typically displayed as HTML tables and HTML forms. The elements of the HTML forms are used to control the end user interactions.

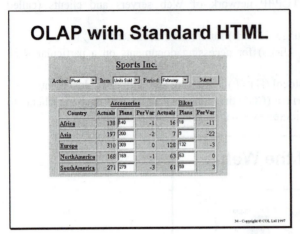

For the most part, the data and results returned by these CGI programs (standard or specialised) are displayed as HTML tables and forms.

Here, for example, the data from a multi-dimensional cube are displayed as a table. Various forms controls are used to define the actions and selections that the end user can make.

Tables and forms can be quickly rendered by virtually any browser supporting HTML 3.0.

There are drawbacks to using tables and forms to display DSS data and to guide the end users navigation through these data.

In summary we can suggest that reliance on pure Web standards to dynamically deliver DSS applications and data suffers from a number of weaknesses, especially when you compare the resulting system with a three-tier client/server system. Not only is the client thin, but the rest of the components are also thin.
Yet, the Web offers substantial benefits when used for particular kinds of custom and packaged DSS applications.

The trick is to combine the benefits of the Web with those of a three-tier system.

This enables end users to access DSS applications and data with any Java-enabled browser .

For example, There are three applets in Comshare's "DecisionWeb" -- a grid, a chart and a dimension controller. These Java applets enable the same kind of dynamic display and interaction as a standard client/server desktop.

So from a list of initial mistakes, we have moved on from Data Warehouses, through Very Large Databases to OLAP, Data Mining, Software Robots and the ubiquitous Web.

We might be forgiven for thinking these are all just waiting for us to use tomorrow...

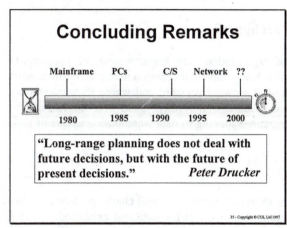

... Peter Drucker suggests we really make our future decisions today.

While it is hard to predict even the emerging or near term future, you are best protected if you keep the end user and the task in mind, and that you rely on "open components" so that near term mistakes are easily corrected.

... Perhaps we need to make these mistakes today.

Data Warehousing Approach

Dave Gleason, PLATINUM Information Management Consulting

Why Implement a Data Warehouse?

Today, an increasing number of organizations are implementing, or planning to implement, a data warehouse. This is being done in an environment where Information Systems budgets are under constant downward pressure and where IS managers are being asked to do more with less resources. Why then, amid ever increasing cost cuttings are more and more organizations looking to data warehousing as one of their business solutions?

Turning Data into Information

Most organizations today have no shortage of data. The real challenge, however, lies in transforming that data into information. Most of the data that exists today is in a form that, while optimal for feeding transaction-driven processes, is difficult for humans to interpret. the data warehouse, when properly designed and constructed, extracts the information value from this data and puts it into a form that can be easily understood and interpreted by the people who need to use it to make decisions. In the past, an organization could maintain its competitive advantage just by using information technology to automate repetitive tasks and control complex processes. Now, however, these traditional uses for data processing are no longer enough to keep a company competitive. It is essential to leverage the informational value of data, to provide true decision support capabilities. Data warehouses exist to do just that: to maximize the decision-making power that is hidden in every organization's data.

Bringing Solutions to Users

When computer systems were first installed in major companies, they were relegated to so-called "back office" tasks. These included tasks such as accounts receivable, billing, and order entry. Over time, their roles evolved into more mission-critical ones. Still, however, data was usually processed by a central IS department, which acted on user requests to provide data and data processing to end users.

Today, those end users are demanding quicker and quicker access to corporate data. They are changing the traditional relationship between IS and user departments, in which IS supplies reports and services to end users. This relationship is being replaced by a new one in which end users are active participants in the use and manipulation of data. In many organizations today, end users are creating their own databases, often on personal computers with spreadsheet software or end user database software. This is happening because these users need to get the data faster than ever before, and they need the ability to analyze that data. not just to read reports.

Data warehousing affords users the ability to perform sophisticated analysis of data, using customized views of that data. It puts the power of that data into the hands of end users, by giving them easy access to the right data and the right tools for analyzing that data.

Supporting Strategic Decision Making

Data warehouses are invaluable for the support of decision making at all levels of an organization' especially for major strategic decisions. Today, evaluating the course of action for strategic decisions often means suspending normal business while all available resources scramble to collect the information needed for evaluation. Data warehouses collect and maintain all of the required information and put it in a format that can be easily manipulated and analyzed. This saves valuable time and expense when strategic decisions need to be made.

Data Warehouse Implementation Decisions

Many factors must be considered when planning, designing, and implementing a data warehouse. Some of the common technical and implementation issues that need to be addressed for a successful data warehouse implementation are discussed below.

Technical Considerations

A data warehouse serves a very different function from a traditional operational, transaction-driven information system. Accordingly, it places many different demands on its technical architecture .

Technical Platform. It is important to choose the platforms that best serve the needs of the organization. Mainframe computers and client server architectures each have their own strengths and weaknesses, and one must carefully consider the choices. Often, the best choice is an environment with multiple, heterogeneous platforms. For instance, some of the data warehouse data may reside on the host in a mainframe database, while other data is stored on powerful UNIX servers in a client server environment. Subsets of the data warehouse data could be replicated to smaller regional or departmental servers. Of course, this kind of open environment requires a great deal of coordination and sophistication to manage effectively.

Mainframe

Strengths
- Existing investment in most organizations.
- Skill levels and support organizations currently exist.
- Proven technology, with high processing power and large data capacity.

Weaknesses
- Fewer flexible, easy-to-use end user tools available.
- No GUI available.
- Many corporate mainframes are near capacity and cannot support CPU-intensive ad hoc user querying.

Client Server

Strengths
- Provides the largest array of flexible, end user tools.
- Provides true interactive GUI for ease of use.
- Removes ad hoc query load from transaction-driven mainframe systems.

Weaknesses
- Less-proven technology than that of the mainframe.
- Skills may not already exist in the organization.
- Additional hardware requirements may drive total data warehouse implementation costs upward.

Database Management Systems (DBMS). There are many DBMSs that can be used to implement a successful data warehouse. The overriding consideration, however, is that the DBMS must be relational. The design of a database for a data warehouse is different from that of a traditional operational database, and as such it places unique demands on the DBMS. For these reasons, it is wise to use a database that has proved to be effective for data warehousing implementations.

In the mainframe environment, data warehouses are implemented almost exclusively in DB2 for MVS. On a client server platform, numerous databases are available, such as Oracle, Sybase, Informix, DB2/X, and others. The final choice depends on such factors as anticipated data volume and corporate standards.

Communications Infrastructure. When planning for a data warehouse, many organizations neglect to anticipate the cost and effort associated with bringing access to corporate data directly to the desktop. This cost and effort can be significant, since traditionally many organizations distribute data to users in printed reports, and not all users have direct electronic access to information. This may mean that communications networks have to be expanded, and new hardware and software may have to be purchased. It is important to identify and anticipate these needs when planning for a data warehouse.

Design Considerations

Several issues must be addressed concerning the design of the data warehouse. It is critical that a strategy be formulated for addressing these issues in a consistent manner, before actual construction of the warehouse begins.

Data Content. A common misconception about data warehouses it that they can not, or should not, contain as much detail as the original transaction-driven databases that feed them. In reality, while the data in a data warehouse is not formatted the same as the data in an operational system, it can be just as detailed. It is true, however, that some information is stripped out of transaction data before it is placed in the warehouse. But entire detailed transactions are not stripped, only those fields within transactions that are meaningless to human beings. That is, many fields in a typical operational database exist solely to trigger some other operational process, but are not meaningful to people trying to interpret the data. All fields that are not meaningful to a person in the context of analysis and decision making are removed from the data as it flows from its original database into the data warehouse.

Data Distribution. One of the biggest challenges when designing a data warehouse for a large organization is the data distribution strategy. Assuming the data volume is too large to be placed on a single database server, it then becomes necessary to address how the data will be divided and which users will have access to which types of data. There are several "axes" along which data can be divided, including:

- *Location.* Different servers can be established to hold different locations' information. For example, in an organization with four regions, there may be four regional data warehouse servers, each containing information for that specific region in a common format.

- *Temporal.* The data can be partitioned according to the time period to which it pertains. For example, you may choose to implement two servers devoted to the current and previous year's data and a third server dedicated to all historical information greater than one year old.

- *Subject area.* Different servers can be established with different subject areas on each server. For example, there may be a "manufacturing" server, which stores manufacturing, raw materials, and logistics information, and a separate "financials" server which stores all finance and accounting information.

Realistically, the best solution for a given organization is usually a hybrid of one of more of these approaches. Given the fact that individual servers are usually connected by a wide area network (WAN), the data on any server is theoretically accessible from any client workstation. However, the performance impact of accessing large volumes of data across a network can be enormous. The goal, then, is usually to try to place different types of data as close to their users as possible. By combining the three axes above with a thorough understanding of the information needs of different types of users, a coherent, effective data distribution strategy can be devised.

Data Manipulation Tools. A number of tools on the market are specifically designed to help in the implementation of a data warehouse . These tools provide a facility for defining the transformation rules that will be applied to operational data to transform and refine it into the format needed for the subject-oriented data warehouse. They provide an easy to use interface that allows developers to rapidly specify a large number of data transformation rules. Then, they generate program code to perform the transformations. Each product, of course, takes a slightly different approach to this process, but the underlying philosophies are similar. When evaluating these tools, the following points must be considered:

• The tool must be compatible with your environment. It must be able to extract data from all or most of the heterogeneous platforms and database systems that will feed your warehouse. It should also be able to produce output that can be easily loaded into your data warehouse database.

• There is a learning curve associated with these tools. A developer can often, after only a few hours of training, use the tool to produce a simple data transformation. However, complex transformations are the norm rather than the exception in data warehousing, and require further training.

• A robust user interface is essential, These tools have varying degrees of user friendliness and varying capabilities to handle complex transformations. Each allows the transformation rules defined with the tool to be augmented with custom-written exit routines, but this is inefficient and should be avoided whenever possible.

• Handling of meta data, which is data about data is also very important. This includes how one defines the layout of the source and target data structures to the tool. While all of these tools allow you to manually define these data structures, it is far easier to define them automatically. This can be done by scanning the data structures into the tool or by loading the meta data definitions of the data structures into the tool. The other important component of meta data is how the tool communicates the transformation rules that have been defined. The tool should produce output that clearly specifies exactly what transformations were indicated for every source and target data structure. Supplying this information on reports is helpful, but the ability to implement an electronic interface from the data manipulation tool to another source, such as a repository, is also important. As discussed below, the ready availability of meta data can be a key component of a successful data warehouse.

Data Movement Tools. Perhaps the most often neglected component of the data warehouse architecture is the data movement capability. Many organizations expend considerable resources in evaluating and selecting tools for data manipulation, end user querying data storage and retrieval (i.e. the database software), only to neglect to plan for actually moving the data from its source to the warehouse environment.

The data that needs to be transformed and loaded into the warehouse is very rarely all sitting on the same machine, in the same environment. Instead, it is usually spread out, through far-flung reaches of the organization. Data could reside on various mainframes, client server machines, and network file servers. It could be stored in a wide variety of technologies and data formats, ranging from old legacy databases to flat files to relational databases.

All of this data needs to be periodically gathered and made available to the data manipulation routines, and then presented to the data warehouse database for loading or updating. This must happen on a regular schedule, with a minimum of human intervention. In order for end users to consider the data warehouse as a reliable source of information, usable for strategic decision making, the process of data movement must be automated; there can be no doubts in the users' minds about whether a scheduled load or update of the data warehouse has taken place. There are several tools available on the market today which can automate the process of moving data from one environment to another; their use in a data warehouse environment should be considered mandatory.

Performance Considerations. It is relatively difficult to predict the performance of a typical data warehouse In part this is because the usage patterns against the data are hard to define. When designing a traditional operational system, it is usually possible to identity approximately how many occurrences of each transaction type will take place in a given time period A data warehouse, on the other hand, is not transaction driven; there are no key metrics that one can use to predict how often certain types of data will be accessed.

Also, when planning the physical design of a database that supports transaction processing, it is common to denormalize the data structures to improve the efficiency of specific high-volume transactions. Tuning the data warehouse introduces new challenges.

One way to solve this problem is to use summary tables which provide denormalized, presummarized views of the data in the warehouse. Many user queries can be executed directly against these summary tables, reducing the need for costly multi-table joins. The key to successful use of summary tables, however, is that they must be closely tied to the ways in which users access the data. This means that you must have a clear understanding of the user's information needs and tailor summary tables to meet those needs. Over time, as those needs change, there must be a mechanism to create new summary tables.

Implementation Considerations

Front-End Tools. In its purest definition, a data warehouse project includes designing and populating the data warehouse database, but not necessarily implementing a front-end tool to allow users to access the warehouse data. In practice, however, consideration must be given to how users will access this data.

At the minimum, you should define a suite of tools for use against the warehouse. These can often be tools that are already used by your organization. Of course, the warehouse is usually an open database, and any technically compatible tool could be used with it. However, defining a standard suite of tools for which your organization can provide support and assistance is beneficial.

Currently, no single tool on the market can handle all possible data warehouse access needs. Therefore, most implementations rely on a suite of tools. Choosing this suite requires defining different types of access to the data and selecting the best tool for that kind of access. Examples of access types can include the following:

• Simple, tabular column reporting
• Graphing and charting
• Information mapping, as is used with geographical information systems
• Predefined, repeatable queries
• Ad hoc, user-specified queries
• Complex textual searching
• Reporting of quantitative data, with interactive drill-down capability
• Very complex, robust queries, with multi-table joins and sophisticated search criteria

In addition, you may elect to build sophisticated mini-applications to retrieve and format warehouse data. Mini-applications often take the form of custom-developed screens or reports that retrieve frequently used information from the warehouse and format it in a standardized way. This approach can be very helpful for data warehouse users who are not yet comfortable with ad hoc querying, but it can never totally replace ad hoc, drilldown queries. There will always be situations where reports and screens show irregularities, and the user must drill down into the data to investigate.

User Sophistication Levels. In most organizations, users have different levels of technical sophistication. Some users may already use end user reporting tools to write custom reports and queries. Others may have little or no computer experience. Since the goal of the data warehouse is to put the data in the hands of users, their varying skill levels must be addressed.

It is, of course, not realistic to expect all users to eventually become technically adept at designing queries and using the front-end tools. There will instead be several different classes of users, with different needs for ease-of-use and flexibility. Many organizations divide the user communities into "crawlers," "walkers," and "runners" for the purposes of classifying front-end tools.

• *Crawlers.* These are the users who are most comfortable retrieving information from the warehouse in predefined formats. Often, this involves running an existing command or query to get results. There is very little need for these users to write their own complex queries.

- *Walkers.* These users typically use a combination of predefined queries and simple queries that they write themselves. They may also perform interactive drill-down querying to investigate results of simple queries.

- *Runners.* These are the users who tend to write their own, very complex queries. They need front-end tools that allow them maximum flexibility and adaptability.

Meta Data. One of the problems that many organizations face when they roll out a data warehouse is how to communicate to the end users what information is in the data warehouse and how it can be accessed. Without a clear understanding of what definitions apply to information in the warehouse and how that information should be combined, users may make invalid interpretations of the information from the data warehouse.

The key to providing users with a road map to the information in the data warehouse is meta data. Meta data can describe exactly what information is in the warehouse, as well as where it came from. It can describe the rules that govern data use and valid ways in which the data can be transformed.

Meta data needs to be collected as the warehouse is designed and built. Then it has to be made available to warehouse users to guide them as they use the warehouse. A number of tools have been announced to help warehouse users understand the contents of the data warehouse and how to use its information. These tools deserve careful consideration: a clear strategy for collecting, maintaining, and distributing meta data is very important.

Data Warehouse Experience

The issues discussed above represent only some of the issues and concerns that must be addressed for a successful data warehouse implementation. PLATINUM Information Management Consulting has worked with many clients to help them ensure the success of their warehouse efforts.

Many additional considerations must also be addressed when rolling a data warehouse out to the user community. Some of those are discussed below.

Cultural Considerations

To be successful, you must view a data warehouse implementation as much more than just an technology project. For a data warehouse represents a new way of using information to support daily activities, decision making, and corporate strategies. Implementing a data warehouse is truly a cultural change for most organizations, and as such, great care must be taken to prepare the organization for the change.

Because technical planning alone is not sufficient to ensure a successful warehouse implementation, it is critical to identify other factors that must be addressed when developing roll-out plans for your data warehouse.

Training and Exploration

Training is even more important in a data warehouse implementation than in the rollout of a new transaction processing system. This is because, in order for the data warehouse to be successful, its users must develop a high level of information proficiency. That is, they must become adept at using the information in the warehouse to help them perform their duties and make decisions. This often requires more intensive training than is given with new operational applications, where it is enough to train users in how to operate the screens and interpret the reports of the new system.

One of the key components to providing proper training for warehouse users is data warehouse exploration. In the exploration phase, representatives of the data warehouse implementation team should work closely with the end users, in order to understand how the users work and to tailor the warehouse to the way the users do business.

One of the challenges in implementing a data warehouse is that it often changes the way people work. This means that you can not design a solution that meets 100% of all user requirements based on current requirements. As soon as users begin to use the data warehouse, the requirements may shift as the way they perform their jobs shifts. To follow this moving target, the data warehouse team must explore the warehouse with the users and make small changes to the warehouse and its front-end tools as the user requirements change. Using this method can ensure that you do not spend an inordinate amount of time working to meet requirements that turn out to be short lived; it also eases the end users' transition to using a data warehouse.

Client Success Profiles

We have worked with many organizations over the past six years to implement successful data warehouses. Below are profiles of three of these clients, each of which had very different needs and a different environment for its data warehouse efforts.

Large US Health Insurer. This large health insurer became aware of the importance of corporate reporting architectures in the late 1980s when a strategic planning study questioned their ability to introduce new products by the year 2000 due to inability of business areas to consistently and correctly access data that was already being maintained in the environment. To get a full "snapshot" of the firm's experience with their customers, individual areas had to integrate data from varying systems, some more than 30 years old, built at varying times and with different technology.

We were hired to help this client developed a corporate reporting architecture that would consistently put critical business information at the fingertips of those business users that needed it. The client was interested in bring disparate data from more than 20 different transaction systems into one integrated set of homogeneous databases. We worked with the client management to set up a master project plan that incrementally brought the system up, with data being integrated one subject area at a time. Throughout the whole project the concept of "incremental benefit for incremental cost" was used. After all databases were available to the business users, a final phase was executed that migrated reporting from a variety of reporting structures to the warehouse, thereby providing a consistent source of corporate reporting information to the whole firm.

During the user rollout, more than 1000 users were put through training on how to use the ad hoc query tools, to understand what data is available through the warehouse, and how to use meta data to find warehouse data relevant to their business issues. Today, on an average month, more than 350 users use the warehouse to answer business questions, with approximately 75% of the users residing in business areas rather than the IM area.

Throughout the life of the project, our associates played roles in planning, defining architectures, designing databases, mapping source to target systems, providing capabilities to manage meta data, and actually coding systems. All our involvement was in conjunction with client teams and we complimented client personnel with varying level of involvement throughout the effort.

Large US Utility Company. This company turned to data warehousing as the answer to a difficult problem: they had to quickly migrate all data and reports off a VM machine, and replace all of that functionality as they did so. For several years, end user departments at this company had built a massive end user reporting environment on the VM rnachine, with data being pulled from the operational legacy systems on the MVS mainframe. As the data volumes on the VM machine exploded, and support costs spiraled out of control, the company decided to remove the VM machine, and migrate all of the end user reporting functionality to other platforms.

The data warehouse was identified as a key component for providing this end user reporting functionality. In the previous environment, users had grown accustomed to writing their own queries and reports to satisfy their individual reporting needs. The company quickly realized that there was no way the Information Systems department could meet all of these needs when the VM machine was removed. One of the reasons for the escalating costs of the VM machine was that different departments and users were building their own decision support and reporting environments, with no central coordination or cooperation. This led to a huge amount of redundant extract files, and no consistency with the way certain information was handled .

Faced with this massive undertaking, the company turned to us for help in evaluating architecture options and understanding the scope of the warehouse effort. We worked closely with the client to perform a thorough analysis of the current decision support reporting environment. Using this information, we built a meta data-driven scoping model which mapped current reports to the enterprise data model, and the data model to the source operational systems. We then fully populated this model with information about the data in those source systems, including its time consistency, volume, completeness, etc. We also met extensively with key users, to compile critical high level information needs. All of this information was fed into the scoping model, further analysis and algorithm were applied. The end result was a multi-year "road map" to the data warehouse, This road map identified specific warehouse projects, assigned a rough scope and level of effort to those project, identified which high-level information needs would be addressed in each project, and mapped the project's data onto the enterprise data model.

Large International Pharmaceuticals Company. We are working with this multi-national manufacturer of pharmaceuticals and health care products to design and implement a global data warehouse. As competition in the pharmaceutical industry grows more and more intense worldwide, the client is looking for opportunities to develop strategic decision support solutions which can be leveraged globally. One of the challenges inherent in this approach is that there are vastly differing levels of technological readiness and infrastructure from country to country within the company.

This client engaged us to assist them in gathering requirements for this worldwide warehouse. Our consultants participated in designing and conducting an 11-country requirements gathering initiative, which included site visits to each country. They then conducted extensive analysis of requirements and existing technical architectures in order to produce a strategic project plan for building a common data warehouse and implementing it in each market.

We continue to work with this client on the multi-year effort to design a global data warehouse to meet both local market needs and regional and executive management needs. We have been instrumental in gathering and analyzing detailed user requirements, establishing the data architecture framework for the data warehouse, building end user decision support tools to support specific information needs, and rolling out repository functionality to users. This project demonstrates our commitment to providing full data warehouse support on a global basis.

About the Speaker

Eldon Li is currently the Principal Consultant, Data Warehouse at PLATINUM technology Ltd and he has more than 20 years of IT experiences in the IT field. Prior to joining PLATINUM technology, Mr. Li has been worked for IBM China / Hong Kong Corporation as Advisory Systems Engineer for more than 10 years and responsible for database marketing and implementation. Apart from that, he also responsible for Data Warehouse marketing and implementation in the past 3 years.

Data Warehouses and Metadata:
The Importance of Metadata Management

Dr. Stephen R. Gardner, Director of NCR's Advanced Technology Research

Abstract

Metadata is popularly defined as data about data. In a relational database, metadata is the representation of the objects defined in the database. In otherwords, the definitions of the tables, columns, databases, views, and any other objects. When used in association with data warehousing, metadata refers to anything that defines a data warehouse object - a table, a column, a query, a report, a business rule, or a transformation algorithm.

Understanding these definitions is critical for all aspects of the data warehouse development process. Metadata management must be tightly controlled from developing extract programs which extract data from the source operational systems, to transformation of the data into the target data warehouse. The data warehouse is only useful to gain competitive advantage, if the data that is transformed to populate the information store is able to accurately answer the business questions, for which the warehouse was built.

1.   What is Metadata?

Metadata consists of the following types of objects:

- Location and description of data warehouse servers, databases, tables, names, and aggregations
- Rules for automatic drill-up/drill-down and across business dimension hierarchies such as products, markets, and charts of accounts
- End user defined custom names or aliases for the more technically named data headings and facts
- Rules for end user defined custom calculations
- Personal, workgroup, and enterprise security for viewing, changing, and distributing custom aggregations, calculations, and other end user analyses
- Descriptions of original sources and transformations
- Logical definitions of tables and attributes of the data warehouse
- Physical definitions of tables and columns, as well as their characteristics
- Mapping of data warehouse tables to each other
- Extract history
- Alias information
- Aggregation algorithms

- Subject area location
- Relationship history
- Ownership/stewardship
- Access patterns
- Reference tables and encoded data
- Aging and purging criteria
- Data quality indicator
- Security
- Units of measure
- Identification of operational sources
- Simple attribute to attribute mapping
- Attribute conversions
- Physical characteristic conversions
- Encoding and reference table conversions
- Naming changes
- Key changes
- Defaults used
- Default reason
- Logic to choose from multiple operational sources
- Algorithmic formulae used

2.   Why is Metadata Important?

Metadata is the roadmap or blueprint to data. Just as a library card catalog points to both the contents and location of books within the library, metadata points to the location and meaning of various informational objects within the warehouse.

In a similar way, the data warehouse also must maintain a catalog of items that it manages. End users are like library customers - they originate requests for information based on a selection that they made from a catalog. The process that fulfills their request must know where the information is located within the data warehouse.

The data warehouse must therefore contain a component that fulfills the catalog functions for the information that it manages. This catalog must be organized to supply the following capabilities:

- It must serve as a map to locations where information is stored in the warehouse.
- It must have two dimensional components for every item

     1.   The definition needed by the database technology (table name, table owner, etc.).

     2.   The definition needed by the business user.

- It must provide a blueprint for the way in which one kind of information is derived from another.
- It must provide a blueprint for extractors that extract data from operational systems and load them into the data warehouse.
- It must store the business rules that are built into the data warehouse.
- It must store the access control and security rules to enable administering security.
- Metadata must track changes over time.
- Metadata must be versioned to capture its change history.
- The structure and content of the data warehouse needs to be stored.
- The system of record for the data warehouse must be clearly and formally identified.
- The integration and transformation logic must be made available as a regular part of the data warehouse metadata.
- The history of refreshment needs to be stored.
- Metrics need to be stored so the end user can determine whether a request will be a large or small one before the request is submitted.

3.   Importance of Metadata During Development

The data warehouse development process is an engineering process. It must, therefore, be explicitly documented to provide reproducibility and for evolutionary quality improvements. Metadata that is created as a result of this process must, therefore, be versioned for change management purposes. For example, every operational schema of the data warehouse catalog must be versioned. The business rules and process rules that were used for conversions, scrubbing, transformation, and aggregation must be captured.

The design of metadata for a data warehouse is a dramatic shift in the paradigm for information analysts who have been analyzing and designing databases to support operational systems. The focus during the design of an operational database is to create normalized data models attributed with atomic data. Until now, the primary concern was to eliminate data redundancy by using normalization. The objective of eliminating data redundancy is to prevent problems of update and for maintaining data consistency.

The design of metadata for the data warehouse needs a complete change in mindset. The focus of the design of metadata for the data warehouse is to represent a rich range of relationships to the analyst, often with a large amount of redundancy. Because updates are not a primary issue within the data warehouse, no price is associated with the data redundancy other than the storage overheads.

Another shift in paradigm for the information analyst is the emphasis of operational systems on current metadata. Most operational systems operate only with the current organization of the database and data. Old data is hopefully archived, along with the older versions of the database organization. Within the data warehouse, the organization of previous versions of the operational database are important because the metadata must be used to extract historical data.

An important aspect of metadata is the need to maintain mappings all the way from the sources to the data warehouse through the process of extraction, refinement, and re-engineering. These mappings need to be maintained for the following purposes:

- Verification of data quality
- Synchronization and refresh
- Integration

4.   Data Source Extraction

Metadata is a key component in the task of integrating operational data from multiple sources into the data warehouse. Metadata is needed for the following data extraction activities:

- Identification of source fields
- Tracking changes in data organization over the history of the data
- Applying defaults intelligently for data fields that were purposely or inadvertently not entered
- Resolving inconsistencies in encoding schemes
- Attribute-to-attribute mapping
- Attribute conversions
- Full descriptions of source and target schemas
- Itemized source to target mappings
- Conversion variables defined during the transformations
- Data transformation rules
- Data retrieval options
- Exception handling options
- Conversion steps
- Conversion reports

5.   Data Refinement and Re-engineering

The data refinement and re-engineering phase of data transformation is responsible for cleaning up the data from the various source systems. Metadata must track the following activities:

- Integration and partitioning
- Aggregation
- Pre-calculation and derivations
- Transformations and remappings

6.   Storing and Managing the Metadata Persistently

After the warehouse is deployed, the metadata is the roadmap for the end user. Not all metadata generated during the development process of the data warehouse is usable or of interest to the user of the warehouse. Among the metadata that is of interest is the metadata that defines which information is available and accessible by the user. Also, definitions of reports and queries that are available to the user are of interest to the business user of the warehouse. Users also are interested in receiving estimates of query execution times. Metadata generated during the development phase of the data warehouse must be stored and organized properly. There are two approaches for the storing and management of this metadata:

1. **Use of a dedicated commercial or homegrown data warehouse information directory** - This information directory stores and manages the metadata and is dedicated to the data warehouse application.
2. **Use of a commercial or homegrown repository/data dictionary** - A repository or data dictionary is a general-purpose cataloging device, usually used to store, classify, and manage metadata. This repository or data dictionary is generally used for more than just the storage of metadata for the data warehouse.

As the importance of metadata management assumes a primary role in the development and deployment of data warehouses, vendors are offering integrated information directory services that tackle the various aspects of metadata management. These information directories are built on the following assumptions:

- Data warehouse administrators and designers have separate need to manage technological metadata in the form that it exists.
    - Metadata for data sources
    - Data cleanup rules
    - Rules for data transformation
    - Rules for mapping source data to target
    - Metadata for data targets

- Business end users, however, want to see and understand metadata at a business level.
  - Business terms used to describe data
  - Associations between technical names/aliases and the business terms that describes them to the business user
  - Description of data warehouse data sources in business terms
  - Description of predefined reports an queries that are available inside the data warehouse
  - Contact information for the owners of the data items
  - Authorization requirements for access to data items
- Business users need some form of a navigation facility that enables them to find their way through the data warehouse.
  - Query and access - this capability is used to inquire and to perform drill-down
  - Launch previously created queries and reports
  - Send requests for data distribution
  - Attach data warehouse access and query tools

The components described above are supported to various degrees of detail by an ever increasing number of vendors. Unfortunately, support for all aspects of these components is very limited. The primary focus of vendor support to date has been directed towards the technical component. The fact of the matter is that metadata is tool-specific, and cannot be shared across different tool sets.

There are several commercial implementations of data dictionaries and repositories that are in general use by organizations on a day-to-day basis. Most of these repositories use a relational database for storing and managing metadata. Some new repository solutions based on Object-Oriented Database Management Systems (OODBMS) technology are also emerging.

To date, the use of standards is limited. Most commercial repositories are built to vendor-defined standards. The information model also has seen very limited standardization. As a result, the classification of metadata has not followed broadly accepted standards which, therefore, makes the job o interchange difficult and complex.

7. Metadata Standards

With the increasing interest in the role of metadata in the data warehouse, the realization has come that metadata standards are truly needed to allow vendors of metadata management products to exchange metadata information. Unfortunately, metadata standardization has been evolving very slowly. The challenge in metadata standardization is in the following areas:

- **Metadata administration** - The primary objective of data administration has been to standardize the definition of metadata within an enterprise. Standardizing the definition of metadata involves setting up well understood and well communicated processes for naming metadata elements, standardizing datatypes and lengths, and maintaining expressive and descriptive glossaries.
- **Metadata representation and classification** - The primary objective of a representation and classification scheme is to categorize metadata into classes that are based on technology. Because of the number of storage technologies used by an enterprise, this classification can be quite diverse. Part of the classification scheme also needs to express and manage the relationships between the different classes of metadata.

Efforts are under way by a consortium of vendors, known as the Metadata Council, to standardize metadata interchange between diverse vendor products within the data warehouse arena. These efforts are directed toward specifying the format and structure of metadata so that vendor products can interchange metadata information. Though an admiral attempt at standardization, the obvious flaw in this approach is the lack of support by the majority of the vendors in the data warehouse arena.

The figure below is a representation of the Metadata Council's interchange standard logical model for shared metadata.

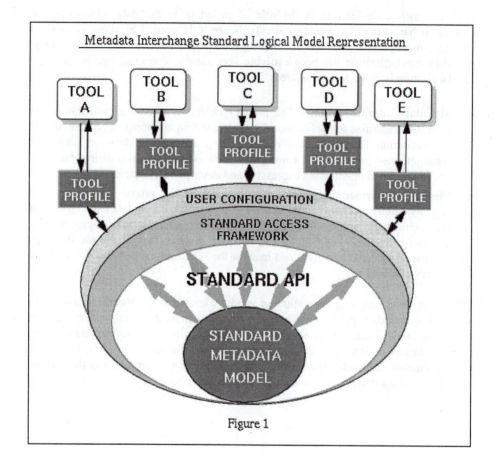

Figure 1

Additionally, the Metadata Council has proposed the following standard for tools, which is depicted by the drawing below, which was taken from Appendix D of the first draft of standards by the Metadata Council.

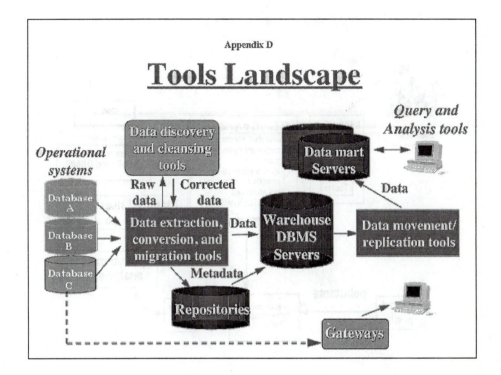

Figure 2

And finally, pictured below is an example of a coordinated view of metadata, from both the technical and business user point of view.

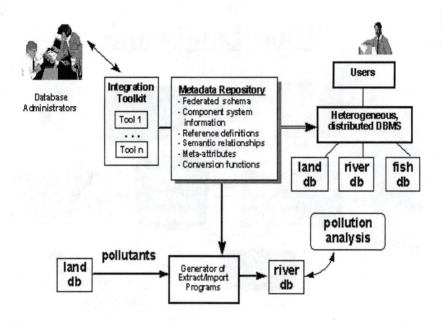

Figure 3

8.   Summary

- Metadata is an important component of a data warehouse.
- Metadata is the roadmap into the data warehouse.
- Understanding the metadata is important for the various components of the data warehouse to function correctly.
- The metadata must be understood by both the builders and end users of the data warehouse.
- The metadata must be centrally managed in an information directory or repository.
- The state of the practice is evolving. Currently, vendors have demonstrated the maximum support for the technical directory component of the information directory.
- Metadata standards are still evolving. A Metadata Council has been formed, but has limited support, by only a few vendors.
- The data warehouse represents a consumer challenge to supplying metadata information to the end users.

About the Author

Dr. Stephen R. Gardner has over 24 years of experience in the information systems industry. Since 1972, he has been providing solutions for both operational and data warehouse applications utilizing relational and hierarchical data base management systems. He has specialized in the migration of legacy systems to open client/server environments. His experience has been utilized by companies in the telephone, retail, financial, and manufacturing industries to provide mission critical solutions to meet their business demands. Dr. Gardner has conducted extensive advanced technology research analyses, resulting in numerous papers and industry presentations.

Dr. Gardner is the Director of NCR's Advanced Technology Research providing thought leadership to NCR associates involved in Scalable Data Warehousing. He was previously associated with Gardner Consulting, Inc. as a principal and senior consultant.

Dr. Gardner is a professor at LaSalle University where he also received his Ph.D. in Computer Science (Magna Cum Laude), his Master of Science degree in Computer Science (Cum Laude), and his Bachelor of Science degree in Computer Science.

A Case for Real-time Client-Server OLAP for Multidimensional Financial and Business Analysis

Perry P. Yu, Senior Manager, Hyperion Software Asia Pte. Ltd.
Email: perry_yu@hysoft.com

Abstract

OLAP (On Line Analytical Processing) has matured to become a major element in Data Warehousing (DW) as well as a core technology in the more traditional DSS (Decision Support System) and EIS (Executive Information System). Different claims made by OLAP vendors are making it difficult for IT to select the appropriate architectures. This paper introduces the most popular architectures available for implementing OLAP for multidimensional financial and business analysis. The latest technology updates, and the benefits and drawbacks of different approaches: ROLAP (Relational OLAP), MOLAP (Physical Multidimensional Database), and RAP (Real-time Analytical Processing) are discussed. Although one size does not fit all, this paper will present the key factors in deciding upon the optimal technology to support increasingly important real-time dynamic applications, what-if scenario analysis, user-friendly interfaces, and operations in a mobile and distributed environment.

1.   Background

1.1.   Data Warehousing and OLAP: Management for Change

Ever competitive and changing business environment creates a need for ever more complex analyses of increasing volumes of business data. In the 1990s, increasingly sophisticated business systems provide large amounts of raw data often in the terabyte and petabyte ranges to support such analyses. Technologies resulting from this need to turn vast volumes of business data into meaningful management information include Data Warehousing (DW) and On Line Analytical Processing (OLAP).

DW provides a means of storing data in a fashion optimized for decision support. This optimized data is often kept separately from the operational data from which it is derived. Data can be managed to support fast, multidimensional queries. Derived metrics can be effectively computed, wherever possible, and the integrity of the data can be preserved when the data is loaded into the warehouse.

One area which has become increasingly important is the process of getting data out of the DW (or out of the operational systems in the absence of a DW) to the actual business analysts and other users. OLAP provides this means and is now viewed as a key technology for providing knowledge workers with access to business data in a meaningful, intuitive fashion. A DW, if present, serves as an OLAP backend storing descriptive information about data (called *metadata*) as well as detailed or summary data for the analysis.

The term OLAP was first coined by Dr. E.F. Codd, the inventor of the relational model, to describe a genre of software that is used for analyzing business data in a top down hierarchical fashion. It is significant to note that in his white paper where he coined the term OLAP, Dr. Codd cautioned that "relational databases were never intended to provide the very powerful functions for data synthesis, analysis and consolidation that are being defined as multidimensional analysis." [COD94]

OLAP tools, however, present data in a multidimensional fashion that even non-technical users should find intuitive. They should be able to navigate through their business data in a simple way, gaining insights which they simply have not been able to gain using standard approaches ranging from printed reports to report writers to data query tools.

With the advance in networking, telecommunication, the Internet and pervasive electronic commerce on the horizon, today's changing markets are much more competitive and dynamic than those in the past. Business enterprises prosper or fail according to the sophistication and speed of their information systems, and their ability to analyze and synthesize information using those systems in a timely and accurate way.

Ultimately, an enterprise's ability to compete successfully and to grow and prosper may be in direct correlation to the quality, efficiency and effectiveness of its OLAP capability. It is, therefore, incumbent upon IT organizations within enterprises of all sizes, to prepare for and to provide rigorous OLAP support for their organizations.

1.2.   Why Multidimensional Analysis

To understand the significance of OLAP, it is critical to understand the multidimensional nature of so much of today's business data. Multidimensional data analysis is the ability to consolidate, view, and analyze data according to multiple dimensions, in ways that make sense to one or more specific enterprise analysts at any given point in time.

Consider the example of the VP of Sales of a retailing company. He wants to analyze how products are selling across the retail outlets. He wants to be able to spot sales trends, identify sales strategies which are working (and those that are not) and generally learn all he can about how products are selling and what he might be able to do to improve sales and profitability.

The key thing that the VP cares about is sales by product. But for each product he wants to know unit sales, dollar sales, discounts allowed and perhaps certain other key statistics. But he wants to know this information on a daily basis, by region, by salesperson, and by channel. What we have identified is a 6 dimensional model. The dimensions are accounts (often also called variables or measures), products, time, channel, region and salesperson.

One of the key features of OLAP technology is that the user is able to navigate through the data in any way that makes sense, without knowing in advance what the navigation route might be. Our hypothetical VP of Sales first looks at the total sales by region, comparing this month with the same month last year. He notices that month on month sales are flat, despite the fact that he has opened three new stores in the last three months. So the first thing that he does is to drill down to look at sales by store, still comparing this month with the same month last year. It quickly becomes apparent that most of the stores have gained a healthy 7% over last year. He is able to determine this by asking his OLAP tool to show this year's gain as a percentage of last year and ranking the stores based on this derived metric. But the bottom of the ranking shows that certain stores have actually declined. By drilling down on region he is able to ascertain that sales from the new stores appear to be cannibalizing sales from existing stores. On the other hand, his inquiries may have shown that the decline in sales was caused by certain product lines which were selling less well than the competition. In this case he would have navigated the data completely differently to reach his conclusion.

Another good example is financial planning wherein organizations plan from the top down or the bottom up. If the planning is done from the top down the impact of the plan must be projected down to the responsibility center level in order that managers may be held accountable for their plans. If the planning is done from the bottom up then the plans must be consolidated so that top management can agree to the overall plan. In practice most organizations take a hybrid approach. The consolidated plan is reviewed by top management to refine their guidelines, resulting in a further round of planning at the detailed level. This process may go on for many iterations and is also multidimensional in scope. The dimensions include accounts, responsibility centers, time, versions (actual, plan, revised plan etc.). Additional dimensions commonly included are product and customer type. This type of planning model may well have sophisticated business logic embedded in it. Ideally, one should be able to change a key assumption and immediately see the impact on the business model. For example, compensation costs should depend on assumptions about headcount, headcount growth, average salary per department, average salary per job title, etc. Revenue and product profitability depend on assumptions of industry growth rate, market share, product mix and manufacturing costs. Today's OLAP tools should be capable of embedding this type of complex business logic in the multidimensional model and be capable of responding to changing assumptions in real time.

These examples illustrate how valuable and essential it is for the user or enterprise analyst to be able to explore and interact, ideally in real time, with the data in a fashion which takes full advantage of its multidimensional structure.

2. Multidimensional Architectures in OLAP

2.1. Sparsity in Multidimensional Data

In financial and business analysis, multidimensional data is almost never 100% dense. That is, typically only a small percentage of all the theoretical cells in the database are populated. As an example, a financial database for an enterprise with 2,000 accounts each for 50 entities covering 36 time periods with 3 versions has a theoretical *hypercube* size of 10.8 millions cells. The actual number of populated cells can be considerably less. The typical *sparsity* ranges over 95%, or around 500,000 or less in population.

Furthermore, the more dimensions that are added to the hypercube, the greater the sparsity is likely to be. In business terms this simply means that as we add more dimensions each number does not break down into a possible value for each member of the new dimension. If we add a customer dimension containing 10,000 customers to a sales hypercube we increase the theoretical volume of the hypercube by a factor of 10,000. The actual populated volume of the hypercube is unlikely to increase by more than a factor of ten or so, where ten is the average number of customers who buy each product in any month, in any region etc. In general, several millions of populated cells in the hypercube is a large financial or business model.

Sparseness is but one of the characteristics of data distribution. Managing this data sparsity, which is present in all multidimensional data, is one key to providing optimal performance from an OLAP server. The inability to adjust to the sparse data distribution can make fast, efficient operation unobtainable. Business and financial models which appear to be practical - based upon the number of consolidation paths and dimensions or the size of the enterprise source data - may be needlessly large and unbearably slow in performance.

2.2. Multidimensional Architectures

One of the design objectives of the multidimensional server is to provide fast, linear access to the data regardless of the way the data is being requested. The simplest request is a two dimensional slice of data from the n-dimensional hypercube. The objective is to retrieve the data equally fast, regardless of the requested dimensions. In practice such simple slices are rare; more typically the requested data is a compound slice where two or more dimensions are nested as rows or columns. Put another way, the goal is to provide linear response time regardless of where the data is being retrieved from in the hypercube.

A second role of the server is to provide calculated results. By far the most common calculation is, in fact, *aggregation*, but more complex calculations such as *ratios* and *allocations* are also required. In fact the design goal should be to offer a complete algebraic ability where any cell in the hypercube can be derived from any others, using all standard business and statistical functions including conditional logic.

Most OLAP servers in fact achieve fast response to computed results by computing them in advance. This technique can be very effective but will not work well where the size of the fully calculated model is thousands of times greater than the volume of the input data. This may sound unlikely but, in fact this can easily happen, particularly where the number of dimensions is large and the hierarchies in each dimension are deep.

This precalculation technique is also not effective in the case where the input data is being updated in real time such as in interactive budgeting or financial reporting applications. This is because analysts want to see the effect of changes immediately. Forcing a batch mode recalculation of some or all of the hypercube is very disruptive to the process.

Balancing the tradeoffs of supporting complex calculations, providing fast access to data, minimizing data explosion (see below) and supporting real time updates has led to three major architectural approaches to OLAP: ROLAP, MOLAP and RAP. These will be discussed in the following sections.

2.3. Relational OLAP (ROLAP): Multidimensional Views of Relational Data

Relational OLAP combines powerful, flexible query capabilities with a scalable multilevel architecture: RDBMS, OLAP engine, and OLAP client. ROLAP symbiotically depends on and leverages the vastly improved capabilities of today's parallel-scalable relational databases. By blending these components within a scalable, multilevel architecture, ROLAP vendors have scaled their databases well beyond 100 gigabytes in size.

In ROLAP, an analytical server performs direct analysis of relational data in a typical DW configuration. Embedded SQL or ODBC is used to integrate the ROLAP server with the DW. By generating SQL commands against the RDBMS, ROLAP can allow for ad hoc queries, compute aggregates and consolidations and work with timely, constantly changing data.

In order to provide a multidimensional view of data, ROLAP vendors store the data in relational tables: a special way known as a *star join* or *snowflake schema*. The most common form of this stores the data values in a denormalized table known as the *fact table*. One dimension is selected as the fact dimension and this dimension forms the columns of the fact table. The other dimensions are stored in additional *satellite tables* with the hierarchy defined by child-parent columns. The satellite tables are then relationally joined with the fact table to allow multidimensional queries.

The data is retrieved from the relational database into the client tool by SQL queries. However, SQL is an access language to relational databases rather than a design for analysis and calculations, so an OLAP SQL query must be carefully formulated or it can be extremely slow [LEO96].

SQL is not necessarily optimal for multidimensional queries. For example, SQL can perform more complex calculations across rows than across columns. This is not a deficiency of SQL as much as a reflection of the fact that the relational model was invented to overcome a number of problems associated with database management. One of the primary problems was maintaining database integrity and ensuring consistent data updates. By storing the data in relational tables a single piece of data is stored in one and only one place. This ensures that the database is consistently maintained and that transaction updates can be performed in a fast and efficient manner.

Join processing, break row processing, use of the RDBMS to store intermediate results, and Visual Basic queries have been implemented to improve the retrieval process and to support typical drill down, drill across user interfaces. Artificial intelligence algorithms have also been introduced to optimize SQL queries required to retrieve the relational data for OLAP, but this nevertheless imposes more technical knowledge demand on the typical non-technical end user.

It is also argued by ROLAP vendors who provide multidimensional views of data stored in relational tables that the data is stored in an open environment and is therefore accessible and that there is no need to duplicate any data since the transaction data is already stored in a relational database.

In practice, the situation is somewhat different. In order to provide the multidimensional views of the data all vendors that use a relational database require that the data be organized in the star join or snowflake schema described above. This means the data must almost always be duplicated. There are also many other good reasons why the data should be duplicated anyway: performance, summarization and organization of data into distinct time periods and so on.

Thus, the implication that using an RDBMS eliminates the need to duplicate the data is not valid. The vast majority of ROLAP applications are for simple analysis of large volumes of information. Retail sales analysis is the most common one. The complexity of setup and maintenance has resulted in relatively few applications of ROLAP to financial data warehousing applications such as financial reporting or budgeting.

2.4.   Multidimensional Databases

The next two major OLAP architectures, Physical Multidimensional Database OLAP (MOLAP) and Real Time Analytical Processing (RAP), provide their own multidimensional databases. These architectures assume that multidimensional models, because of their unique characteristics of sparsity and the need for potentially complex derived results need an architecture all their own. Although all software vendors are proud of their architectures and all believe they are uniquely efficient (several vendors have actually patented their algorithms), in practice there are some common techniques which are used by many of the vendors. These techniques include mapping out zero values by compression, using indexes of pointers to compressed arrays of values and sophisticated caching algorithms.

Before discussing these two architectures, it is important to understand more about how sparsity causes *data explosion* and its implications.

2.5. Data Explosion

It is not immediately obvious that a fully calculated hypercube is usually dozens of times, and in some cases many thousands of times, larger than the raw input data. Some would argue that this is not a problem since disk space is cheap, at least relatively speaking. Despite disk space being relatively cheap, consider what happens when a 200 MB source file explodes to 10 GB. The database no longer fits on any notebook PC for mobile computing. Consider what happens when a 1 GB source file explodes to 50 GB. The database no longer fits comfortably on typical desktop servers. In both cases, the time to precalculate the model for every incremental data change will likely be many hours. So even though disk space is cheap, the full cost of precalculation can be unexpectedly large.

There is a trade off between the time to precalculate and response time. Many OLAP vendors assume that multidimensional databases precalculate everything or nothing. The optimal approach might be to partially precalculate and only leave the less requested or smaller calculations until run time, as in the case of OLAP applications with more than 1 million cells [PEN97].

With this understanding, we can now review the MOLAP and RAP architectures.

2.6. Physical Multidimensional Database (MOLAP)

The MOLAP approach is to provide a database specifically designed for multidimensional data and then precalculate all derived values. The theory behind this is that precalculating all derived values will result in very fast retrieval times, and that data explosion does not matter since disk space is cheap, relatively speaking. Retrieval times are typically on the order of one second or less, and is one of the reasons for the widespread acceptance of MOLAP.

Since derived values are precalculated and stored, when incremental changes to the data are made, a user must request that the database be calculated again. This means the users must wait, typically many hours, until the calculation is finished. Some MOLAP engines provide the capability to recalculate only those derived values that were affected by the change. This cuts the calculation time on the order of 50%, but still does not lend itself to applications that must change the data frequently.

There are also hybrid systems making use of MOLAP with the ROLAP approach. A relational database is typically used as an adjunct to the multidimensional database to accommodate large database sizes (say over 50 gigabytes), and to store intermediate and precalculation results which are less frequently requested for analysis. Part of the data is stored in the OLAP server and part stored in the relational database. However, both DW and OLAP design technical knowledge as well as business analysis knowledge is required for a successful implementation.

2.7. Real-time Analytical Processing (RAP)

RAP takes the approach that derived values should be calculated on demand, not precalculated. This avoids both the long calculation time and the data explosion that occur with the precalculation approach used by most OLAP vendors. In order to calculate on demand quickly enough to provide fast response, data must be stored in memory. This greatly speeds calculation and results in very fast response to the vast majority of requests.

Another refinement of this would be to calculate numbers when they are requested but to retain the calculations (as long as they are still valid) so as to support future requests. This has two compelling advantages. First, only those aggregations which are needed are ever performed. In a database with a growth factor of 1,000 or more, many of the possible aggregations may never be requested. Second, in a dynamic, interactive update environment, sales analysis being a common example, calculations are always up to date. There is no waiting for a required precalculation after each incremental data change.

One may question whether a multidimensional application of any size can fit into memory. The answer is yes. All multidimensional databases store each number very efficiently, generally 10 to 15 bytes per number. The actual memory requirement in an RAP application depends on the number of input values, rules, randomness of data, dimension ordering, number of open reports, report complexity and so on. A server with 64 MB of memory can typically store about 6 million input numbers or populated cells while a server with 512 MB of memory can store about 45 million input numbers.

It is important to note that since RAP does not precalculate, the RAP database is typically 10% to 25% the size of the data source. This is because the data source typically requires something like 50 to 100 bytes per record and possibly more. Generally, the data source stores one number per record that will be input into the multidimensional database. Since RAP stores one number (plus indexes) in approximately 12 bytes, the size ratio between RAP and the data source is typically between 12% and 24%.

The second reason applications generally fit into memory when using a RAP architecture is due to the very high sparsity previously mentioned. With sparsity typically 99% or greater in models with 5 or more dimensions, the 45 million actual values that a 512 MB server can accommodate represents a model with a theoretical volume of more than 4 billion cells. Few financial and business multidimensional models approach these data volumes. As mentioned earlier, a few million populated cells is a large financial model.

So RAP avoids the long calculation times and data explosion associated with other approaches. This is especially important for dynamic applications where having immediate access to the results of incremental data changes is critical. There are other considerations which deserves attention when choosing an OLAP architecture for a given application.

3.   Oher Considerations

3.1.   Single Hypercube vs. Multicube

Just as in a relational database, where the data is typically stored in a series of two dimensional tables, the data in an OLAP database consists of values with differing dimensionality. For example, consider the case of a bank which wants to analyze profitability by customer and product. Certain revenues may be dimensioned by customer, product, time, geography and scenario. But costs such as back office salaries might be dimensioned by cost type, cost center and time. Thus, a real world multidimensional database must be capable of storing data that uses different sets of dimensions in a single logical database yet presenting a single conceptual view to the user.

It is not acceptable to insist that all data in the model be dimensioned by the same dimensions. Putting data into an element called "no product" because the data item happens not to be dimensioned by product merely serves to confuse the user. Products that cannot support a multicube architecture with the ability to logically relate cubes, force unreasonable compromises on the developer of sophisticated models. Not only does it make the access to the data less logical but it can have serious adverse effects on database size and retrieval efficiency.

In many situations, data from multiple sources lends itself to a multicube architecture. In a large DW implementation, breaking down the data volume to *data marts* using only portions of the multisource data available is often essential to efficiently serve high impact business analysis needs. Data marts are typically implemented across company departments with different nature of business.

Another important benefit of the multicube architecture is the ability to distribute processing at multiple regional cubes (servers) that feed a central, higher-level cube (consolidation) at corporate headquarters. The regional cubes can in turn be broken down further into other business dimensions as necessary. All of this enables the OLAP applications to be more compact and more understandable. Distribution of multiple "megabyte cubes" is more feasible than attempting to distribute a single gigabyte cubes to achieve the same functionality.

In general, a multicube architecture is much more natural for modeling than single-cube modeling products. It allows much cleaner structuring and segmentation of modeling issues.

3.2.   Dynamic Modeling and Ad Hoc Queries

Instant, real-time calculations facilitate dynamic modeling and guarantee up-to-the minute results. There is no need for cumbersome, time consuming batch pre-calculations. RAP which uses a RAM based calculation approach can often deliver results 200 times faster than disk or file-based processes. The ability of RAP to dynamically and speedily recalculate large models in a multiuser environment can provide for true multiuser read-write and instant recalculation of results whenever data changes. This fast recalculation technique in RAP can result in very fast aggregations on read-mostly tables and still yield significant productivity in constantly changing tables.

RAP will also work with virtual memory. Although the performance will suffer relative to using real memory, the application might have to spill over quite significantly before performance drops to the point where RAP is slower than disk-based products.

In contrast, OLAP products that precalculate can require many hours or even days before they can provide access to the most recent incremental update. In RAP, for incremental updates, data are available for analysis as soon as they are loaded. Again, the precalculation approach can take hours or days if large data sets are being exploded, which is not an uncommon practice.

3.3.   Spreadsheets and Websheets

The client interface in OLAP should always appeal to spreadsheet users since it allows easy "browsing" of data in tables and facilitates the building of sophisticated reports. Little additional training will be required of an experienced spreadsheet user. Seamless spreadsheet integration is a very important part of an OLAP product and is especially relevant for financial and accounting people who are often spreadsheet macro gurus.

With the rapid growth of the Internet and corporate intranet, we have now seen the migration of the spreadsheet desktop to the websheet webtop [MCN96]. Web-enabled software such as Java and the Web browser bring to the desktop, now aptly called the webtop, speedy delivery of standard, open-platform, yet customizable decision support systems (DSS) and executive information systems (EIS). For the very first time, key business performance indicators and ratios, cost/expense analysis, product and customer profitability, and financial and management reporting and analysis are truly made available through a widely understood interface such as the Web browser.

RAP, which is specifically designed to calculate large volumes of multidimensional data in real-time, has been used to demonstrate real-time OLAP on the Web. For example, it is now possible to perform a simulation of a foreign currency traders' risk management application making use of live data feeds from on-line financial and data information services. The RAP engine and the websheet is intimately linked with total transparency. This demonstrates the benefits of real-time feedback from a multidimensional database without the need to precalculate to achieve fast response and fast performance.

3.4. Distributed Mobile Environment, Security and Audit Trail

Client-server and nomadic (local, stand-alone) OLAP analysis are both prevalent in today's open-platform and network-centric computing environment. Often it is necessary for enterprise OLAP users to distribute parts of the data and reports to individual department managers or marketing managers. Alternatively, enterprise applications can start in one department with one single stand-alone user and distribute across the enterprise.

Portability of solutions, support of client-server architecture and thin clients such as a typical notebook PC in a mobile operating environment are quite essential in today's OLAP implementation.

OLAP applications should therefore scale from a single-user browsing or stand-alone development to an enterprise-wide implementation. Migration up should be as easy as moving files from the PC's directory to the server's. Supporting a distributed architecture, the same OLAP engine should run on a notebook PC as well as multiple, multiuser servers for all major environments including Microsoft, Novell, and TCP/IP.

For example, this OLAP engine can integrate with operational systems which produces the source data. One can design a system to include a seamless, monthly process to build dimensions on-the-fly, process descriptive textual data, process actual data into the OLAP engine, produce analysis and consolidation reports and upload final results back to source systems.

The client-server architecture is ideal for today's distributed, mobile operating environment. In RAP, for example, the OLAP cubes are resident in the RAM of the Server. When the OLAP Server receives requests from the clients, it finds the data and does any required calculations. Just the requested data and calculation results are sent back to the client. The client is not required to perform any further processing. The client can optionally perform further calculations it needs to in the spreadsheet or report generator etc.

A request from a client for values is by batch, the results from the server are also by batch, thereby minimizing network traffic. The server can alternatively store calculated values in RAM, so that the next request for that data is much faster. Therefore the objective of either a balanced client with programs and metadata for optimal performance or a thin client with the least programs loaded (only for web access, for example) can be achieved.

While end users always demand friendly interfaces and flexible operation environment, IS departments need to maintain control and access security.

Security should be on the server and cannot be bypassed using an API. Users can be granted read, write or no access to tables loaded on the server. Access to individual tables can be further controlled by restricting access across one or more dimensions. Other desirable security functions are automatic audit trails that detail change to the database, such as user identity, automated back-up, recovery and roll-backs. It should be added that security in general has virtually no negative impact on performance.

3.5.　　Value　Added　Intelligence,　Easy　Application　Development　and Maintenance

Increasingly, value added functions such as financial intelligence are added to OLAP tools. Built-in accounting concepts, costing rules, multicurrency translation, and time series intelligence are always helpful as these are always the essential dimensions in financial and complex business analysis. There should be no need to code commonly used rules.

Rapid OLAP application development is generally enabled by a graphical application manager with drag-and-drop interface. There are also the use of predefined industry specific templates for different industries or for common practice in financial and business analysis.

Intuitive rules builders eliminate the need for setting up complex calculation rules and languages. Intelligence can further be built into a rule such that only those cells that need to be calculated will be recalculated.

Application development wizards enable users to build custom applications with minimal IS support. The custom applications built on templates enable immediate "best practice" analysis. For example, finance managers can create reports by performing customer/product profitability analyses that drill down into business data sources without the need to have the IS department do construction or reconstruction.

After an application has been created, a dynamic link between the data and structure can minimize the need for staff to perform manual maintenance. By keeping data and dimensions in an OLAP application in synchronization with source database structure, this dynamic link enables real-time, instant updates and consolidation.

Data import process to OLAP engine must be easy and cost effective. Automated scheduling and data feeds simplify the maintenance of data transfer. Users should be able to automate the maintenance of multiple hierarchies and other tasks without having to write customized code. For example, in financial planning applications, a monthly process can be adapted to maintain dimensions on-the-fly, process descriptive text and general ledger data, produce reconciliation reports, and upload final budget results back to the general ledger.

3.6.　　Agents and Exception Reporting

Intelligent agents and alerts that monitor the query environment, run analyses in the background, and notify the user when a predefined business condition or exception occurs have found their way into the OLAP marketplace. It is not surprising after all in this age of information explosion that even useful information from an OLAP solution can be excessive and should be properly sieved and screened for the ever-busy executive.

Agents can uncover problems at the lower levels of the data hierarchy, so one does not have to go searching through the whole massive database to find the root of the problems. Other features including exception reporting, criteria-based formatting, conditional suppression, intelligent grouping and sorting, what-if criteria suggestions all bring an extra degree of convenience and time savings to the end user.

All these above-mentioned technological advances in OLAP should be on the checklist when one sources an appropriate OLAP solution for one's business analysis needs. Some OLAP architectures are better than others in providing for the fast response, instant information update, real-time calculation on demand, distributed and mobile operation support, tight integration with spreadsheets, web delivery and rapid implementation time which most users are increasingly expecting and demanding today.

4. Conclusions

ROLAP products relying on SQL queries to access data from a relational database are often complex and require much specialist assistance and therefore can be costly to set up and maintain. They do not provide the performance available from the other OLAP architectures. For these reasons, most ROLAP applications are for analysis of large volumes of data where the close integration with the RDBMS is an advantage.

MOLAP products use precalculation to achieve their impressive retrieval speed. This approach works well for static or mostly static data, but the resulting long calculation times make them unsuitable for dynamic applications that require access to data soon after incremental updates. In addition, the data explosion caused by the precalculation approach may make MOLAP inappropriate for large applications with more than five dimensions.

RAP is the optimal architecture for dynamic applications that require frequent input of data or analysis of what-if scenarios. These type of applications include financial reporting and consolidation, budgeting, forecasting, and product profitability. RAP is also the optimal architecture for supporting a mobile or distributed environment. Since RAP does not precalculate, the resulting small data footprint makes it very suitable for notebook PCs and distributing applications via the Internet Web browser and email. Finally, the extreme scalability of RAP makes it well suited for applications with more than five dimensions where MOLAPs would explode the data beyond a manageable size.

References

[COD94] E.F. Codd and S.B. Codd, "Providing OLAP (On Line Analytical Processing) to User-Analysts: An IT Mandate," 1994.

[LEO96] M. Leon, "Vendors Pushing OLAP into Mainstream," *Infoworld*, USA, 11 June 1996.

[MCN96] S. McNealy, "From Spreadsheet to WebSheet," *Netscape Columns*, 20 Nov--2 Dec 1996.

[PEN97] N. Pendse, "Data Explosion," *The OLAP Report*, http://www.olapreport.com/DatabaseExplosion.htm, 1997.

Data Marts and Beyond
The Pragmatic Approach to Enterprise Decision Support

Ray Ruff, Sybase

1. Distributed Data Warehousing: A New Approach

Data warehousing has become a critical competitive edge in the 1990s. But the traditional "enterprise data warehouse" has proven to be costly, slow to implement, and filled with risk. According to Meta Group surveys in 1996, the average enterprise data warehouse project costs $3.2 million to build and takes 24 months to implement. Despite industry hype for a few high-profile successes, the vast majority of enterprise data warehouse projects result in disappointment. According to Earl Hadden & Associates, a well-known data warehouse consulting group, up to 80 percent of current corporate data warehouse projects fail to meet organizational objectives; 40 percent fail completely.

Fortunately, a new, more pragmatic approach is now available: one we call distributed data warehousing. It focuses on application-centered data marts, built rapidly with new cost-effective, scalable database technology. When constructed with a solid enterprise architecture, data marts can provide dramatic returns on investment-without the high cost and risk of centralized enterprise data warehouse projects. This white paper examines the issues in centralized versus distributed data warehousing and how Sybase's distributed data mart approach enables businesses to rapidly develop decision support applications that can grow and change as business needs evolve.

2. The Traditional Approach: Yesterday's Solution to Today's Problems

According to Meta Group, 90 percent of the Fortune 1000 are attempting some form of data warehousing project. Yet despite the huge efforts underway, CIOs still feel that the biggest problem they face is delivering valuable, integrated information to their end users. According to a recent Forrester Research report, more than 70 percent of IT budgets are dedicated to the work that IT departments hate the most: creating user reports and responding to ad hoc user requests for information.

Despite the enormous investment and level of effort, why has data warehousing still failed to deliver rapid information access to the vast majority of business decision-makers? At an average cost of well over $3 million, data warehouse projects are beyond the reach of many departments and businesses.

2.1.   Centralized Top-Down Approaches Are Risky

The traditional view of the data warehouse, originally pioneered by IBM, Teradata, and others in the 1980s, is that of a large, centralized repository of historical corporate information. Enterprises repeatedly express the need for terabyte-class data warehouses, large parallel systems, and enterprise data models. This ideal data warehouse serves as a "single version of truth" for the business, and houses all types of cleansed, transformed, and scrubbed corporate data for development of enterprise decision support applications.

The problem with this top-down approach is that it is highly risky. The lifeblood of IT organizations is the ability to rapidly develop applications that quickly deliver valuable information to business decision-makers. The centralized top-down data warehouses often focus excessively on architecture; they are designed to accommodate a few applications, but are unable to adapt and change as new applications are needed.

Due to the constant need for new reports and summary tables, our centralized Data Warehouse exploded to 7 times the size of our original estimate, drastically increasing the cost beyond our budget. And due to the difficulties of managing user queries, we do not even let users run parallel queries during the day."
Mary McCormick, Manager of I/S, Mervyn's, Computerworld, 7/31/95

2.2.   Long Times to Deliver

A recent IDC study confirms this problem. After studying 62 companies building data warehouses, IDC discovered that the ones building centralized systems with an architecture focus delivered half the ROI and took twice the time to implement as the applications-focused data mart implementations. On average, these projects took nearly three years and several million dollars to go into production. And nearly half the enterprise warehouse projects resulted in a negative ROI or failed projects. ("The Foundations of Wisdom: A Study of the Financial Impact of Data Warehousing," IDC, March 1996.)

2.3.   Unresponsive to Changing User Requirements

Centralization appeals to IT departments' need for control and consistency. But a problem with a top-down approach is that users cannot agree on what they want. Meta Group data warehouse surveys conducted in 1995 and 1996 estimate that nearly half the questions users ask of a data warehouse are ad hoc, exploratory queries. As users get information, they need to explore it in different manners to answer diverse questions. And as additional departments and users come on line to the data warehouse, they generate new and different queries and new requests for information.

"Data Warehousing is a process of discovery. Users rarely know what information they need in advance."
Bill Inmon, Building the Data Warehouse.

IT organizations face the daunting challenge of designing the centralized warehouse to meet wide and varying needs, while constantly building new extracts, queries, and reports to meet users' needs. Time and time again IT groups have built data warehouse projects that users largely ignore, because they cannot respond to users' rapidly changing need for information.

2.4.   High Cost of Parallel Technology

Traditional centralized data warehouse technology is built on a 10-year-old, brute-force approach: parallel technology. Parallel database and hardware technologies solve the problems of batch throughput and very large database (VLDB) processing (load, backup, restore), but do nothing to provide rapid query response to ad hoc queries. Parallelism, by its very nature, uses additional hardware to work on a single query at a time. The overhead associated with sharing the hardware for multiple simultaneous query streams actually works against the need to provide rapid query response to multiple users. In fact, one major parallel database vendor automatically turns off parallelism when more than three simultaneous queries are running on the system.

To furnish ad hoc query performance, parallel databases require the use of summary tables, aggregates, predefined query paths, and complex schemas for adequate performance. These extensions to the database explode database size and dramatically increase the DBA workload to keep the warehouse current and tuned. Data warehousing with traditional RDBMS technology is often called "The DBA Full Employment Act."

The result is that many of today's large data warehouses become "data jailhouses" - large repositories of information that cannot be easily modified for new user requirements and that require support by dozens of database administrators providing care and feeding for the system.

3.   The Pragmatic Approach: Enter the Data Mart

Today, there is a new approach: Data marts, or application-specific data warehouses. The industry is now abuzz with the term data mart:

A data mart is an application-focused data warehouse, built rapidly to support a single line of business application.

Data marts can be complemented by, but do not require, "enterprise data warehouses," which hold enterprise-level transaction data across multiple subject areas.

Data marts should be built with an enterprise data mart architecture to allow consistency and sharing of data and data transformation and movement tools.

Data Marts vs. Enterprise Data Warehouses

Enterprise Data Warehouse	Scalable Data Mart
Single warehouse across the enterprise	Distributed across the enterprise
Multiple subject areas	Limited subject areas
Multiple operational user targets	Division/departmental user targets
Wide problem scope	Limited problem scope
2 years, $3.2 million +	90 days, < $1 million

There are several myths to data marts.

* **Myth #1:** Data marts are small; enterprise warehouses are huge. **Reality:** Single application/subject data marts can often be very large and hold much historical data - tens to hundreds of gigabytes.

* **Myth #2:** Cross-functional analysis requires a corporate warehouse. **Reality:** In a well-designed enterprise data mart architecture, corporate warehouses are not necessarily needed for cross-functional analysis.

* **Myth #3:** Corporate data warehouses are part of an overall decision support strategy. **Reality:** Corporate data warehouses can be useful for physical or logical consolidation and redistribution of data to data marts.

Data marts are application systems. They must be built iteratively and deployed rapidly to be successful. If implemented this way, they can grow in size and in number of users - without sacrificing enterprise data quality, scalability, and flexibility. But how does an IT organization develop a data mart strategy without creating a "Tower of Babel" of inconsistent, patchwork systems?

3.1.   Requirements for an Enterprise Data Mart Architecture

There are four key requirements for an enterprise data mart architecture:

3.1.1.   Flexible Technology for Rapid Implementation.

The platform, RDBMS, and design must support a rapid and iterative implementation. Data marts must deliver results in the first 90 days. Therefore, flexibility to adapt to change is important as the users and IT implementors agree on what the initial application will really look like. The database engine must support a wide range of queries and not force the designer into a fixed design, such as a star schema or rigid multidimensional cube. Many data marts are built from large mainframe normalized databases, and it may not always be cost-effective or business appropriate to implement a star schema.

Data mart database designs must be easy to understand and flexible to reflect users' needs. Rigid schema designs rarely accommodate rapidly changing business environments without very high maintenance costs.

3.1.2.   Scalability to Large Data Volumes and Support for Detailed Data.

Data marts may start small, but as users start to look at information, they begin to ask for more history, more external data, and more detail. Many "quick and dirty" data mart architectures store only summarized data (for example, quarterly sales volume by city), and then expect the user to drill down to operational systems to get detail.

The problem with this approach is that users naturally want to explore data in different dimensions. (Why is a given quarter lower than others? What are my sales by month, or by day, or by product? Where are my best customers coming from? What effects do various promotions have on sales?) If the data mart does not hold the detailed data, these queries are impossible.

To support analysis of detailed data, the database engine and platform must support dynamic aggregation and fast, flexible queries against tens to hundreds of gigabytes of detailed data. 1996 Sentry Market Research surveys show that data marts grow in size, on average, by 56 percent per year.

3.1.3.   Fast, Flexible Query Response.

Data marts are user and application driven. Users need to drill down and explore their data to find the information they need. Often the users are performing ad hoc queries or relying on OLAP query tools, which generate complex SQL statements rapidly. If it is to succeed, the data mart must provide fast response (in seconds, not hours) to any query.

With traditional database technology, IT departments must optimize the database for each query, creating new indexes and summary tables in order to prevent table scans. In a cost-effective data mart implementation, ongoing tuning must be minimal since it will delay answers to users.

Similarly, with multidimensional databases, precomputations are performed along a limited number of dimensions to create a database capable of satisfying user queries. Users will not be able to get rapid responses to questions incorporating dimensions beyond those planned for. And the time and cost for rebuilding the multidimensional cube to support new dimensions are very high.

Finally, data marts must accommodate multiuser query demands without bogging down performance. Parallel processing techniques, while valuable for centralized batch systems, work against data mart workloads because they do not allow large numbers of queries to run simultaneously with high performance.

3.1.4.   Enterprise Data, Transformation, and Refresh Architecture.

Data marts cannot be built in a vacuum. Each data mart must use common data elements, share common data transformation programs, and use common data movement tools to maintain enterprise data consistency and quality. The Direct Marketing data mart, for example, must share customer information with the Sales Tracking data mart to make sure that both are analyzing the same view of customers. And both data marts must be refreshed in a consistent way, as new customers are added.

IT organizations need a robust and reliable data movement architecture to ensure that the data marts are refreshed regularly and consistently, without a huge army of support personnel creating extracts and loading updates.

3.2.   New Database Technology for Breakthrough Performance

High performance can be achieved through the use of vertical data storage (by column, not row) and powerful query processing. Vertical data storage allows queries to only touch the fields or columns they need, dramatically reducing the I/O in a typical user query. As a step beyond traditional indexes or bit-maps, all data and values can be represented in special binary structures, which can be accessed, summarized, grouped, and compared with lightning speed. A comprehensive four-part indexing scheme manages various data types, optimizing query performance for any data cardinality and use.

Unlike bit-mapped indexes, which have been available for many years, one can apply indexes concurrently. In a traditional relational database (even with bit-mapped indexes), queries are limited to one index, followed by a partial table scan to complete each query. Tables scans are eliminated through high-cardinality processing using rapid, dynamic aggregation of relational data, delivers vastly improved query response. There is no need for complex summary tables such as those frequently used with traditional parallel databases or multidimensional databases. Any aggregate needed can be calculated in real time.

4. Pragmatic Evolution: From Data Marts to an Enterprise Data Warehouse

Enterprise data warehouses, while costly, can still provide a valuable function in certain organizations. Enterprise data warehouses will be most successful when built from the bottom up-after implementation of successful data marts.

As businesses build data marts and meet users' application needs, they learn what data elements are most valuable, what data elements need to be most current, and where additional detailed data or external data is needed. Over time, IT organizations will see places to centralize data that can be shared among multiple data marts. This is the true role of an enterprise data warehouse. It becomes, over time, a place to centralize information that multiple users and data marts need.

Our enterprise data mart approach, the enterprise data warehouse is built slowly, in steps - or not at all, depending on business needs. IT teams can develop one data mart at a time, and as the data marts grow, a multi-tiered DSS architecture results-one where data marts and the shared enterprise warehouse can coexist.

4.1. Data Marts in Action at MCI

A good example of this approach is MCI-one of the most successful users of data warehouse technology in telecommunications. MCI customers produce millions of detailed transaction records every day. How can MCI use this information across the wide variety of business applications to develop new products and new price offerings, plan capacity, aid in telemarketing services, and do all this across consumer, small business, and large enterprise customers?

Ideally, a centralized data warehouse would work. But pragmatically, with multiple business units rapidly developing applications, this would not work.

Today at MCI there are three data marts in production, some approaching 100 gigabytes or larger in size. They are used for telemarketing, product profitability, and customer service. Each is a data warehouse application solution in its own right.

Separately, MCI has a project to develop a large centralized transaction data warehouse, which can be used to feed shared transaction information to data marts. But since each data mart has different information needs, each has its own design and uses its own external data that is not needed by other data marts. The data marts have been implemented much more rapidly, cost-effectively, and flexibly than they would have been if MCI had waited for the central data warehouse.

"With Sybase IQ and System 11, we were able to build our data mart rapidly and in a scalable, enterprise architecture," says Scott Barnes, Manager of IS for MCI's Small Business Telemarketing Centers. "If we had to wait for the centralized solution to appear, our group would be out of business."

MCI realizes that over time it needs to share call detail record information across multiple business units. The centralized data warehouse project, while ongoing, has been underway for nearly three years and is still not satisfying all business needs. Someday, it may serve as a centralized data transformation location for these data marts. Because MCI's solution has the scalability and architecture to grow into this multi-tier environment if needed. But today it has generated huge returns by developing applications rapidly.

5. Conclusion: Pragmatic Solutions for Data Warehousing

As this paper shows, the idealistic approach - developing a large enterprise data warehouse - is giving way to the pragmatic approach: distributed data marts. Implemented in an enterprise data mart architecture, distributed data marts provide rapid return on investment at lower risk. They give users the speed and flexibility they need, yet they fit well into an enterprise decision support architecture.

What is Data Mining and how to apply data mining techniques to exploit information from your datawarehouse or data mart

Paul Chik, Regional Project Manager, SAS Institute, Hong Kong

Abstract

Customers are the ultimate company assets. Their behaviour is the most important determining factor of success of your company. Many figures, graphs, tables and reports are requested by management to monitor customers behaviour and movement. All these results produced are based on what has already happened and are passive, that is to say they do not pre-empt to the future market trend and demand. They are merely an image of yesterday. However, past knowledge about customers' historical behaviour is no longer enough to satisfy the insatiable appetite of Management and analysts quest for future knowledge. Therefore a whole new dimension of investigation of future knowledge about customers behaviour has prevailed. It is called Data Mining. While most Data Mining provided by many other organizations mainly focus on reporting the figures and numbers, very little has been done on making predictions based on either some classification rules and business facts. Here at SAS Institute, while many tools are already available to produce reports based on historical information, there are also a lot of statistical and scientific research and forecasting tools which can produce predictions and business knowledge that management and analysts would like to know. This presentation will focus primarily on what is the SAS Data Mining SEMMA methodology and the tools available within the SAS System. Examples and areas of practical application of Data Mining will also be discussed.

Overview of Data Mining

To convert the value of the data warehouse or data mart into strategic business information, many companies are turning to data mining, an emerging technology based on a new generation of software. Data mining combines techniques including statistical analysis, visualization, induction, and neural networks to explore large amount of data and discover relationships and patterns that shed light on business problems. In turn, companies can use these findings for more profitable, proactive decision making and competitive advantage.

Data mining was designed for exploiting massive amounts of data. This process can be more efficient if you first define what the business problem is, then determine the amount of data you will need to solve the problem. By taking this bottom up approach to data mining and involving upper management in the understanding of business problems and the potential Return of Investment, the process will be much more acceptable and the goals attainable. We define data mining as the process of selecting, exploring, and modeling large amount of data to uncover previously unknown patterns for a business advantage. As a sophisticated decision support tool, data mining is a natural outgrowth of a business' investment in data warehousing. The data warehouse provides a stable, easily accessible repository of information to support dynamic business intelligence applications. As the next step, organizations employ data mining to explore and model relationships in the large amounts of data in the data warehouse. Without the pool of validated and scrubbed data that a data warehouse provides, the data mining process requires considerable additional effort to pre-process data. Although the data warehouse is an ideal source of data mining activities, the Internet can also serve as a data source. Companies can take data from the Internet, mine the data, and distribute the findings and models throughout the company via an Intranet.

Although data mining tools have been around for many years, data mining became feasible in business only after new hardware and software technology advances became available.

Hardware advances, for example, reduced storage costs and increased processor speed, paved the way for data mining's large scale, intensive analyses. Inexpensive storage also encouraged business to collect data at a high level of detail, consolidated into records at the customer level.

Software advances continued data mining's evolution. With the advent of the data warehouse, companies could successfully analyze their massive databases as a coherent, standardized whole. To exploit these vast stores data in the warehouse, new exploratory and modeling tools, including data visualization, neural networks, and decision trees, were developed. Finally, data mining incorporated these tools into a systematic, iterative process.

SEMMA

Data mining is often seen as an unstructured collection of methods, or as one or two specific analytic tools, such as neural networks. However, data mining is not a single technique, but an iterative process in which many methods and techniques may be appropriate. And, like data warehousing, data mining requires a systematic approach.

Beginning with a statistically representative sample of the data, you can apply exploratory statistical and visualization techniques, select and transform the most significant predictive variables, model the variables to predict outcomes, and affirm the model's accuracy.

To clarify the data mining process, we have mapped out an overall plan for data mining. This step-by-step process is referred to by the acronym SEMMA: Sample, Explore, Modify, Model and Assess.

Step 1: Sample

Extract a portion of a large data set big enough to contain the significant information yet small enough to manipulate quickly.

For optimal cost and performance, SAS Institute advocates a sampling strategy, which applies a reliable, statistically representative sample of the full detail data. Mining a representative sample instead of the whole volume drastically reduces the processing time required to get crucial business information.

If general patterns appear in the data as a whole, these will be traceable in a representative sample. If a niche is so tiny that it is not represented in a sample and yet so important that it influences the big picture, it can be discovered using summary methods.

Step 2: Explore

Search speculatively for unanticipated trend s and anomalies so as to gain understand and ideas.

After sampling your data, the next step is to explore them visually or numerically for inherent trends or groupings. Exploration helps refine the discovery process.

If visual exploratory does not reveal clear trends, you can explore the data through statistical techniques including factor analysis, correspondence analysis, and clustering. For example, in data mining for a direct mail campaign, clustering might reveal groups of customers with distinct ordering patterns. Knowing these patterns creates opportunities for personalized mailings or promotions.

Step 3: Modify

Create, select, and transform the variables to focus the model construction process.

Based on your discoveries in the exploration phase, you may need to manipulate your data to include information such as the grouping of customers and significant subgroups, or to introduce new variables. You may also need to look for outliers and reduce the number of variables to narrow them down to the most significant ones.

You may also need to modify data when the mined data change. Because data mining is a dynamic, iterative process, you can update data mining methods or models when new information is available.

Step 4: Model

Search automatically for a variable combination that reliably predicts a desired outcome.

Once you prepare your data, you are ready to construct models that explain patterns in the data. Modeling techniques in data mining include neural networks, tree based models, logistic models, and other statistical models, such as time series analysis and survival analysis.

Each type of model has particular strengths, and is appropriate within specific data mining situations depending on the data. For example, neural networks are good at combining information from predictors which support nonlinear associations with a target.

Step 5: Assess

Evaluate the usefulness and reliability of findings from the data mining process.

The final step in data mining is to assess the model to estimate how well it performs. A common means of assessing a model is to apply it to a portion of data set aside during the sampling stage sometimes known as validation data. For a model to be considered successful and useful, it should work for this validation sample as well as for the training data used to construct the model.

Similarly, you can test the model against known data. For example, if you know which customers in a file had high retention rates and your model predicts retention, you can check to see whether the model selects these customers accurately. In addition, practical applications of the model, such as partial mailings in a direct mail campaign, help prove its validity.

Illustrations

We have completely adopted the SEMMA methodology and incorporated it into the framework of data mining processes.

Let us now consider two scenarios which address common issues that are facing business today, i.e. how to strengthen the vendor/customer relationship most effectively and proactively. We demonstrate below how the flexibility of our data mining tools can be applied to each of these three business problems.

Scenario 1: Credit Card Fraud Detection

The data used to detect fraudulent use of credit card consists of many transaction records for a large number of customers. A number of these transactions are known to be fraudulent, since some credit cards are stolen. In the data being used for the study, each record contains a variable of the data of the card was reported to be stolen.

The goal of the study is to discover a method of predicting whether a new transaction is from a stolen card to catch thieves red-handed, rather than discovering the fraud after the fact. Because of this, the predictive method must work with transactions that are not known to be from the stolen credit cards. In the eventual proactive application of this method, this information will not be known.

For this reason, the analyst chooses to put some transactional data aside in his database for subsequent testing of the prediction scheme.

Sampling

Depending on the ratio of 1:5 of stolen to unstolen cards in the total transaction base, the analyst might decide on sampling 20,000 stolen cards and 100,000 unstolen cards. He assumes that this provides enough details to represent both categories of credit cards accurately.

Exploration

The next step is to explore the data from this sample. The analyst creates some plots to get a first impression about the data. For a number of stolen cards, he plots the amount of purchases against the date of purchase. The analyst looks for interesting features, for example, whether purchases after the theft are more expensive or more frequent.

He connects the pints for one customer (in order to see which points correspond to the same customer). He aligns for one customer plots horizontally by subtracting the date of the theft from the transaction date, which results in the number of days that passed since the date of the theft. This plot might reveal something unexpected. Suppose that for many cards, the number of purchases did not increase enough to readily distinguish transactions with stolen cards from transactions with unstolen cards. Perhaps knowing the types of products being bought would help.

To find out, the analyst sorts the products by the proportion of times a product was brought with a stolen card, for all customers in the sample. Now he applies a color spectrum, such as green-blue-red, to the products so that the product bought with the highest percentage of stolen cards is associated with red. Does the plot reveal predictive clues?

Instead of coloring just by product, the analyst decides to incorporate information about the region and venue of purchase. He lets a program find a scoring function that best explains the proportion of fraudulent purchases in the various product-region-venue categories, and colors a transaction based on the scoring function.

Modification

The analyst could continue exploring in this way, but there are so many possibilities, that eventually he requires an automated search to find a predictive relationship. He begins to prepare for the modeling process. The plots have provided some understanding of how transactions differ after a card is stolen and they have also given the analyst an idea as to how far back before the date of theft he needs to look to detect this difference. For example, he has determined that the data set input into the modeling process would only need to contain information on each transaction for the previous three months. Therefore he only considers data from, the last three months, and only the specific number of variables he needs to simplify the modeling process.

Modeling

Neural networks and logistic regression (a regression explaining a variable with two values,, in this case fraudulent transaction or not), are appropriate modeling techniques. Neural networks search over a wide variety of candidate relationships, whereas logistic analysis can come up with a more restricted but mire interpretable prediction. The result of these modeling techniques is a scoring function that estimates the probability that a transaction is fraudulent.

Assessment

The analyst wants to convert the scoring function into a rule that decides whether a transaction should be questioned as a fraudulent. He chooses a probability threshold, 0.8, for example. If the scoring function assigns 0.85 as the probability that a transaction is fraudulent, then the rule classifies the transaction as fraudulent and some investigate action ensues.

Before implementing this rule, the analyst wants to know how good it is. He applies his rule to the transaction in the sample and looks at the misclassification rate - the proportion of transactions incorrectly classified. Actually, he looks at a plot of misclassification rates versus all possible thresholds - and chooses his threshold based on that plot.

When the rule is applied to new transactions, the misclassification rate will be higher than the rate on the study sample. To get a more reliable estimate, the rule is applied to customers in the database excluded by the study sample.

The model is first implemented for a test period of one month to see how well it performs in practice. Then after some adjustment of the scoring function the system is used in production on a routine basis. It turns out that the systems classifies 87% of the credit card fraud correctly (tested six moths later when the final outcome is known). The automatic system is a significant saving in manpower opposed to the previous manual checking and also allows a faster response to any transactions detected as fraudulent.

Scenario 2: Customer Retention

For the customer retention study the insurance analyst gathers data that contains the length of time a customer holds his policy, what kind of policy it is (house insurance, car insurance or life insurance), demographic data on customers and geographically related data with information such as average household income, distribution of house ownership, how long customers have been living at their current residence, and whether or not the insurer has an agency at the particular geographical region.

Initially the insurance analyst is interested in determining the probability that a customer will keep his policy for at least two years and what controllable variables influence the lifetime of the policy.

For initial exploration of the data, she plots the probability that the customer will subscribe for at least two years. The plot might reveal something unexpected. For example, there might be a small drop in the curve after one year. She separates the customers by type of policy, and simultaneously plots each group. It turns out that the small drop seen for all policies is largely due to a large drop of car insurance policies returned after one year. Competition studies reveal that this might be the result of competition from the new direct insurers who offer very competitive prices. Information about the competition is merged with the current internal database and analysis continues.

The analyst chooses now to use stepwise variable selection in a survival model to discover what variables significantly influence retention. The relative important of the variables would be related to the coefficients the model assigns to them.

She can then stratify the customers based on the important controllable variables, and plot the probability of longevity for each stratum. Assessment of the model reveals that types of policies and the new direct insurance are indeed significant factors that help to explain customer retention, but overall the model only 40% of the customer retention.

The result is not satisfactory. The analyst notices that there is a large range in the number of customers per geographical unit in which the insurer operates. She suspects that this might be related to the lack of offices in areas with low customer penetration.

Therefore the analyst steps back a little to undertake more exploration. This time she plots the data geographically over a map and reveals that indeed there are quite a number of regions which are not well covered by agencies.

Based on this analysis the insurer might adopt a strategy: increase the number of agencies in those regions that has a high withdrawal rate after one year, or open up a direct insurance line service to compete with the start-up competition on the same ground.

Conclusion

Data Mining

Customer-related information is a competitive advantage. Increasing understanding of this issue, together with technological advances in data storage, generate an ever increasing amount of operational data.

This trend is common to all industries, but decision makers in industries such as retail, consumer goods manufacturing, insurance, banking and telecommunications are most actively searching for efficient ways to exploit this data to business advantage.

Traditional techniques such as OLAP are too specific in the initial phase of roaming the vast amounts of data collected, they do not inform about the general tendencies hidden in the data.

Data mining is the appropriate set of technologies to exploit patterns of information from massive customer-focused databases.

Data mining is a process, which can rarely be fully automated. Applications of this set of technologies have to be adjusted to the specific business interest.

Data Mining and Our View

We define data mining as advanced methods for exploring and modeling relationships in large amounts of data.

Data mining is a technology, not a ready-made solution to a business problem. Therefore data mining has to be embedded in the present corporate-wide information delivery solution.

Data mining is NOT the isolated usage of one or two esoteric techniques but a very practical methodology: SEMMA - Sample, Explore, Modify, Model and Assess. This methodology helps to get data mining processes established even with limited analytical expertise.

Data sources for data mining may be diverse. RDBMSs and data warehouses are data organizations of choice. Data needs to be organized according to the subjects of study: customers, products, services and so on.

A comprehensive solution for data mining, from data access through every phase of SEMMA is a must.

For the best reesults, our Data Mining solution can be linked to data warehouse architectures..

Data Mining complements analytical query and reporting tools, such as OLAP and EIS techniques, that are well suited to find specific answers to specific business questions.

Data Mining:
The software that finds pattern never seen before

Samson Tai, Business Intelligence Solutions, IBM Greater China Group

Abstract

Data Mining can provide a well spring of information that companies can maximize in order to make better informed and effective decisions. This paper discusses what data mining is and the common algorithms that are used in today's commercial data mining applications. Business examples will be given to illustrate each of the data mining operations in order to demonstrate how they extract the hidden knowledge in the data.

1.   What is data mining?

Data mining is the data-driven extraction of information from large databases. It is the process of automated presentation of patterns, rules or functions to a knowledgeable user for review and examination. Here the human plays an essential role in the paradigm because it is only he, the analyst, who can decide whether a pattern, rule or function is first interesting, second relevant and third useful to the enterprise.

In business and in the press, data mining is hot. As with most waves that flash through our culture, care must be taken to separate the fact from the fantasy. Data mining is a useful tool, a new approach which combines discovery with analysis. Data mining is not a newly discovered branch of mathematics embodied in software that will, when hooked-up to a large and problematical database, inexplicably and inevitably reveal the business insights contained in the millions of records stored therein. Yet still it is important. It is an area that will increasingly become mandatory for competitive businesses.

2.   Why data mining now?

A number of factors have combined to bring data mining to the attention of the business community. They are:

1.   A general recognition that there is untapped value in large databases
2.   A consolidation of database records tending toward a single customer view
3.   A consolidation of databases, including the concept of an information warehouse
4.   A reduction in the cost of data storage and processing providing for the ability to collect and accumulate detailed data

5. Intense competition for a customer's attention in an increasing saturated marketplace
6. The movement toward the de-massification of business practices.

De-massification is a term from Alvin Toffler. During the industrial revolution economies of scale led businesses to mass manufacturing, mass marketing and mass advertising. The information revolution is providing the capability to custom manufacture, and to market and advertise to small segments and ultimately to the individual. This is de-massification and it is a strong force in business today.

2.1. Business as usual

Every important problem already has significant resources being applied to it. How can a companies improve their decision making with the data that they have?

2.1.1. Answer standard questions

Business operations today are supported by regular reports which are the output from canned database queries. What are sales in Detroit? What are the trends underlying the sales figures? Are our new products being better received in urban or suburban stores? Reports with cross-tabs form the basis of most executive decision making. The queries are crafted interactively with the user to ensure that the information is structured effectively. These reports are built to answer continuing standard questions.

2.1.2. Answer new questions: Hypothesis testing

More unstructured are ad-hoc database queries. An analyst has a hypothesis: "more short sleeve shirts are sold in the West than the East". He causes a database query to occur, gets a report back, and either proves or disproves his hypothesis. Another form of hypothesis testing is regression modeling. This form of standard statistics always begins with a hypothesis, sales of short sleeve shirts increase linearly with average temperature. A model is built and tested to see how well the data fits this hypothesis. Technically, what is done is an attempt is made to disprove the null hypothesis (i.e. to prove that any fit to the model is not by chance). This is the mainstay of most predictive modeling and has been extremely effective, but it does require that the modeler come up with the idea, that the hypothesize the form and shape of the relationship.

2.1.3.   Segmentation

True mass marketing, where an advertiser picks names randomly, and expects a response proportional to the number of pieces of mail that are sent, is rarely done today. Instead segmentation is used to divide the potential customer base into demographic sub-groups; usually this means that census data is used. For example, all addresses in zip code areas with higher than average age and income might be selected to mail nursing home insurance applications. Most segmentation that is done is biased segmentation. That is, the analyst believes, he hypothesizes, that by slicing the database by median age and income in a zip code, he has separated the population into homogeneous groups relevant to his mailing problem.

The above mentioned methods are commonly used in today's business to identify the information hidden in the data. Under this scheme, the decison maker is required to hypothesize the desired information. Due to the complexity of the stored data, this kind of verification driven type operation is not sufficient for the decision making. It must be complemented with the ability to automatically discover important information hidden in the data and then present it in the appropriate way. The corresponding systems are called the discovery-driven data mining systems. In the discovery-driven data mining systems, the decision maker does not need to make a hypothesis beforehand. There are different kinds of data mining operations which in combination can be used to solve different kinds of business problems.

3.   Data mining Operations

There are four major data mining operations:

- Creation of prediction and classification models. This is the most commonly used operation primarily because of the proliferation of automatic model-development techniques. The goal of this operation is to use the contents of the database, which reflect historical data, i.e., data about the past, to automatically generate a model that can predict a future behavior. For example, a financial analyst may be interested in predicting the return of investment of a particular asset so that he can determine whether to include it in a portfolio he is creating. A marketing executive may be interested to predict whether a particular consumer will switch brands of a product of interest. Model creation has been traditionally pursued using statistical techniques. The value added by data mining techniques in this operation is in their ability to generate models that are comprehensible, and explainable, since many data mining modeling techniques express models as sets of if... then... rules.

- Link analysis. Whereas the goal of the modeling operation is to create a generalized description that characterizes the contents of a database, the goal of link analysis is to establish relations between the records in a database. For example, a merchandising executive is usually interested in determining what items sell together, i.e., men's shirts sell together with ties and men's fragrances, so that he can decide what items to buy for the store, i.e., ties and fragrances, as well as how to lay these items out, i.e., ties and fragrances must be displayed nearby the men's shirts section of the store. Link analysis is a relatively new operation, whose large scale application and automation have only become possible through recently developed data mining techniques.

- Database segmentation. As databases grow and are populated with diverse types of data it is often necessary to partition them into collections of related records either as a means of obtaining a summary of each database, or before performing a data mining operation such as model creation, or link analysis. For example, assume a department store maintains a database in which each record describes the items purchased by a customer during a particular visit to the store. The database can then be segmented based on the records that describe sales during the "back to school" period, records that describe sales during the "after Christmas sale" period, etc.

- Link analysis can then be performed on the records in the "back to school" segment to identify what items are being bought together. Deviation detection. This operation is the exact opposite of database segmentation. In particular, its goal is to identify outlying points in a particular data set, and explain whether they are due to noise or other impurities being present in the data, or due to causal reasons. It is usually applied in conjunction with database segmentation. It is usually the source of true discovery since outliers express deviation from some previously known expectation and norm. Deviation detection is also a new operation, whose importance is now being recognized and the first algorithms automating it are beginning to appear.

4.   Data Mining Techniques

While there are only four basic data mining operations, there exist numerous data mining techniques supporting these operations. Predictive model creation is supported by supervised induction techniques, link analysis is supported by association discovery and sequence discovery techniques, database segmentation is supported by clustering techniques, and deviation detection is supported by statistical techniques. To these techniques one has to add various forms of visualization, which even though does not automatically extract information, it facilitates the user in identifying patterns hidden in data, as well as in better comprehending the information extracted by the other techniques.

4.1. Supervised Induction

Supervised induction refers to the process of automatically creating a classification model from a set of records (examples), called the training set. The training set may either be a sample of the database or warehouse being mined, the entire database, or a data warehouse. The records in the training set must belong to a small set of classes that have been predefined by the analyst. The induced model consists of patterns, essentially generalizations over the records, that are useful for distinguishing the classes. Once a model is induced it can be used to automatically predict the class of other unclassified records. Supervised induction methods can be either neural or symbolic. Neural methods, such as backpropagation, represent the model as an architecture of nodes and weighted links. A variety of neural supervised induction methods can be used such as backpropagation, radial basis functions, etc. Symbolic methods create models that are represented either as decision trees, or as if ..then.. rules. Decision trees are generated using algorithms such as id3, and cart. Rules are generated by algorithms such as IBM's RMINI, the public domain algorithm foil, etc.

For example, credit card analysis is an application for which a supervised induction is well suited. A credit card issuing company may have records about its customers, each record containing a number of descriptors, or attributes. For those customers for which their credit history is known, the customer record may be labeled with a good, medium or poor labels, meaning that the customer has been placed in the corresponding class of good (medium or poor) credit risk. A supervised induction technique producing symbolic classification models may generate the rule stating If the customer's income is over 25,000, and the age bracket is between 45 and 55, and the customer lives in XYZ neighborhood then the customer is good. A supervised induction technique is particularly suitable for data mining if it has three characteristics:

1. It can produce high quality models even when the data in the training set is noisy and incomplete.
2. The resulting models are comprehensible and explainable so that the user can understand how decision are made by the system.
3. It can accept domain knowledge. Such knowledge can expedite the induction task while simultaneously improving the quality of the induced model.

Supervised induction techniques offer several advantages over statistical model-creation methods. In particular, the induced patterns can be based upon local phenomena while many statistical measures check only for conditions that hold across an entire population with well understood distribution. For example, an analyst might want to know if one attribute is useful for predicting another in a population of 10,000 records. If, in general, the attribute is not predictive, but for a certain range of 100 values it is very predictive, a statistical correlation test will almost certainly indicate that the attributes are completely independent because the subset of the data that is predictive is such a small percentage of the entire population.

4.2. Association Discovery

Given a collection of items and a set of records, each of which contain some number of items from the given collection, an association discovery function is an operation against this set of records which return affinities that exist among the collection of items. These affinities can be expressed by rules such as "72% of all the records that contain items A, B and C also contain items D and E." The specific percentage of occurrences (in this case 72) is called the confidence factor of the association. Also, in this association, A, B and C are said to be on an opposite side of the association to D and E. Association discovery can involve any number of items on either side of the association.

A typical application that can be built using association discovery is Market Basket Analysis. In this application, a retailer will run an association discovery function over the point of sales transaction log. The transaction log contains, among other information, transaction identifiers and product identifiers. The collection of items mentioned above is, in this example, the set of all product descriptors, or SKU's. Typically, this set is of the order of 100,000 or more items. The set of products identifiers listed under the same transaction identifier constitutes a record, as defined above. The output of the association discovery function is, in this case, a list of product affinities. Thus, through association discovery the market basket analysis application can determine affinities such as "20% of the time that a specific brand toaster is sold, customers also buy a set of kitchen gloves and matching cover sets."

Another example of the use of association discovery is in an application that analyzes the claim forms submitted by patients to a medical insurance company. Every claim form contains a set of medical procedures that were performed to the given patient during one visit. By defining the set of items to be the collection of all medical procedures that can be performed on a patient and the records to correspond to each claim form, the application can find, using the association discovery function, relationships among medical procedures that are often performed together.

4.3. Sequence Discovery

In the transaction log discussed above, the identity of the customer that did the purchase is not generally known. If this information exists, an analysis can be made of the collection of related records of the same structure as above (i.e., consisting of a number of items drawn from a given collection of items). The records are related by the identity of the customer that did the repeated purchases.

Such a situation is typical of a Direct Mail application. In this case, a catalog merchant has the information, for each customer, of the sets of products that the customer buys in every purchase order. A sequence discovery function will analyze such collections of related records and will detect frequently occurring patterns of products bought over time. A sequence discovery function could also have been used in one of the examples in the previous section to discover the set of purchases that frequently precede the purchase of a microwave oven. Another example of the use of this function could be in the discovery of a rule that states that 68% of the time when Stock X increased its value by at most 10% over a 5-day trading period and Stock Y increased its value between 10% and 20% during the same period, then the value of Stock Z also increased in a subsequent week.

Sequence discovery can be used to detect the set of customers associated with frequent buying patterns. Use of sequence discovery on the set of insurance claims can lead to the identification of frequently occurring medical procedures performed on patients, which in turn can be used to detect cases of medical fraud.

4.4.   Conceptual Clustering

Clustering is used to segment a database into subsets, the clusters, with the members of each cluster sharing a number of interesting properties. The results of a clustering operation are used in one of two ways. First,
for summarizing the contents of the target database by considering the characteristics of each created cluster rather than those of each record in the database. Second, as an input to other methods, e.g., supervised induction. A cluster is a smaller and more manageable data set to the supervised inductive learning component.

Clusters can be created either statistically, or using neural and symbolic unsupervised induction methods. The various neural and symbolic methods are distinguished by (1) the type of attribute values they allow the records in the target database to take, e.g., numeric, nominal, structured objects, (2) the way they represent each cluster, and (3) the way they organize the set of clusters, i.e., hierarchically or into flat lists.
Once the database has been clustered, the analyst can examine the created clusters to establish the ones that are useful or interesting using a visualization component.

Statistical methods represent a cluster as a collection of instances. It is difficult to decide how to assign a new example to existing clusters since one must define a way for measuring the distance between a new instance and the instances already in the cluster. It is also difficult to predict the attributes of members of a cluster. One must identify the attribute's value by applying a statistical procedure to the entire data set.

Neural clustering methods such as feature maps, represent a cluster as a prototype with which they associate a subset of the instances in the data set being clustered. Symbolic clustering methods, e.g., AQ11, UNIMEM, COBWEB, operate primarily on instances with nominal values. They consider all the attributes that characterize each instance and use artificial intelligence-based search methods to establish the subset of these attributes that will describe each created cluster.

Clustering differs from other data mining techniques in that its objective is generally far less precise. Such techniques are sensitive to redundant and irrelevant features. This problem can be alleviated by permitting the user to direct the clustering component to ignore a subset of the attributes that describe each instance, or by allowing the analyst to assign a weight factor to each attribute; increasing the weight of an attribute increases the likelihood that the algorithm will cluster according to that attribute. The importance of attributes, especially numeric-valued attributes, can be established using univariate and bivariate statistical methods.

4.5. Visualization

Visualization provides analysts with visual summaries of data from a database. It can also be used as a method for understanding the information extracted using other data mining methods. Features that are difficult to detect by scanning rows and columns of numbers in databases, often become obvious when viewed graphically. Data mining necessitates the use of interactive visualization techniques that allow the user to quickly and easily change the type of information displayed, as well as the particular visualization method used (e.g., change from a histogram display to a scatter plot display, or to Parallel Coordinates). Visualizations are particularly useful for noticing phenomena that hold for a relatively small subset of the data, and thus are "drowned out" by the rest of the data when statistical tests are used since these tests generally check for global features.

The advantage of using visualization is that the analyst does not have to know what type of phenomenon he is looking for in order to notice something unusual or interesting. For example, with statistical tests the analyst must ask rather specific questions, such as "does the data fit this condition" Often, the analyst wants to discover something unusual or interesting about a set of instances or an attribute. However, he must ask very directed questions, such as "is the distribution skewed?" or "is this set of values consistent with the Poisson distribution?" No general statistical test can answer the question "is there anything unusual about this set of instances" there are only tests for determining if the data is unusual in a particular way. Visualization compensates for this; humans tend to notice phenomena in visually displayed data precisely because they are unusual.

5. Practical data mining

Data mining is not a simple process. It is not a plug and run toolset. It can be aided by excellent tools, but it requires both human data mining expertise and human domain expertise.

There are six basic steps for effective data mining:

1. The first step in a data mining project is to understand what problem you are addressing. Ill-defined projects are unlikely to perform satisfactory value. Not only must the business objectives be clear, but the operational environment of any expected resulting system must be laid out.
2. Once the problem is well-defined, the data must be selected. All these algorithms have in common a need for substantial databases. If we are to let the data speak, we must have some meaningful sample. Data selection consists of selecting the time span, geography, and product set to be addressed. It also requires a selection of the relevant variables from an often large possible set of stored data elements.
3. The next step, determining how to represent the data elements to the data mining algorithm, is just as critical. Will muffins and pound cake be grouped together into baked goods? Will age be represented by category (e.g. 40-45), or value (e.g. 41)? Will quantity used be represented by dollar amount or item count? The way we answer these questions may well determine if the project will succeed or fail.
4. Run the appropriate data mining algorithm, or combination of algorithms. This is often an iterative process, going back to step three or even step two, if the results are not good.
5. Analyze the output of the data mining run. This usually involves the domain expert. Each industry has evolved salient and customary ways of presenting analyses. The data mining output has to fit into this framework to be readily absorbed and accepted by the people who will use the results. Visualization is often important in this step as well.
6. Present the results to operational managers so that the insights generated can be integrated into the companies processes. Depending on the results this may require delivering either output data files or installing data mining software.

6.   Conclusion

Data mining enables organizations to take full advantage of the investment they have made. By identifying valid, previously unknown, and ultimately comprehensible information from large databases decision-makers can take advantage of unique opportunities.

Because of the complexity of the business decisions that need to be taken, a variety of data mining operations must be performed on the stored data. These operations range from predictive model creation and database segmentation, to link analysis and deviation detection. While not every data mining application will require the use of all operations, newer applications, especially in the marketing area, necessitate the cooperative use of several data mining operations.

Due to the diversity and complexity of the data stored in the data warehouses, a single data mining technique is not sufficient for addressing every problem within a particular operation. For this reason, it is important that several data mining techniques have to be used by the data analysts in order to perform the data mining operations for the real-world problem.

112

About the Speaker:

Samson Tai has over 10 years experience in the I/T industry and is currently the I/T Architect of IBM's Business Intelligence Solutions, Greater China Group. His key focus is to help companies leverage their customer data to improve the business processes. His work mainly on the area of business intelligence discovery and information infrastructure development. Specifically, some of the recent projects included data warehousing design and database marketing analysis.

Samson Tai has a Master degree in Business Administration and a Bachelor Degree in Computer Science and is a frequent speaker in the subjects of data warehousing and data mining.

A Data Warehouse is For Life
Not Just for Christmas

"Owning a Data Warehouse; Your Responsibilities.
Best Practices From Experience"

Peter Hall, Region Program Director, Hewlett-Packard

So you're going to put in a data warehouse. Finally succumbed to all the seductive stories of 400-600% returns on investment, and eager to analysis your own business in hope of discovering some interesting and valuable relationships, such as the often quoted US drug store that discovered a direct correlation between the sale of disposable nappies and six packs of beer. Or the discovery in a part of Mid-West USA where they found a direct relationship between the sale of mattresses and chainsaws, and thereby cleaned up by offering the bed and saw combo pack.[1]

Ideally your organisation has a committed business unit, eager to work directly with a strong IT team that is similarly committed to implementing data warehousing so as to finally allow the organisation to get some real value out of the data that you have spent the rest of your time and money on getting into your organisation. That is the essential difference between all your transaction systems and the data warehouse. The goal of transaction systems has been to capture or get the data in. The goal of the data warehouse is to now get the data out to those who need it to facilitate the important analysis and decisions impacting the organisation; its profitability and ultimately its competitiveness.

Whilst your organisation has probably spent many millions and millions of dollars on your transactions systems, (the systems that everyday take new orders, update back orders, record financial transactions, book airline seats, and dispense money out of ATMs), the amount invested on getting the data out has probably been almost irrelevant, and the results have probably been reflective of this. It is predicted that over the next several years, many organisations will see a change in their spending patterns that would suggest that eventually the amount invested on "getting the data" out could come close to half of your overall IT expenditure.

But what are your responsibilities as the owner of a data warehouse? You could ask your parents, but given the infancy of the IT industry, and in particular the recency in

---

[1] The former is put down to the fact that when males are required to go down to the drug store to pick up a pack of disposable nappies, that they often decide to grab a six pack of beer as well. In the Mountain areas of the USA, a lot of cabins are built as week-end retreats, and it appears that two of the essential items that all new cabins need are a bed and a chainsaw.

the growth in large scale data warehousing, it is unlikely that your parents were ever owners of a data warehouse, and thus would offer little advice.

1.   Ask a Publisher

However, if your parents where editors or publishers of magazines, or newspapers, then they could well teach you a lot about data warehousing. Publishing, and being a publisher is a terrific analogy of the roles and responsibilities of the owners of the data warehouse.

Like every quality publication, it is the editors duty to assemble on the copy table all the inputs and stories. To assess them for completeness, quality, consistency, style, and theme. If there are any deficiencies or problems, the editor must ensure these are fixed or overcome, and consider what impact any delays may have on the publication deadline. Finally, when all is in order to the point that the publisher is satisfied to put their professional name behind the publication, they release it to their readers, who rely on them to have done this prior work.

The readers or users of your data warehouse will expect nothing less of you. The data warehouse will be where the corporate data is "published". People will rely on it. They will use it to make decisions, and to watch the trends in the business. They will constantly dissect it to look for changes, major or subtle. They will expect it to be complete, accurate, and timely. As they will be following trends and patterns, they will expect consistency in terms of the basis that the data is loaded and accepted.

2.   Dancing to A Different Beat

These rhythms and issues effecting how we manage a data warehouse are different to the traditional responsibilities we have had as managers of transaction systems. For example, when you want to be able to do a withdrawal of money from a bank branch in your neighbourhood, all you care about is if that branch is on-line, and able to do that small single inquiry and transaction. That is, check the balance for available funds, and if okay, then release the funds, and record the deduction. For that transaction, it doesn't matter at all if for some reason branches on the other side of the country are currently not on-line.

For the data warehouse however, you manage everything on a global level. Data has to have been captured from all branches and laid onto the data warehouse like an additional blanket being put on to a bed. Each layer adds to the depth, and each layer needs to be complete. The data items captured need to be consistent. The quality and completeness of the data will ultimately be the measure of usefulness of the data warehouse that will determine the value and reliance put on it by its users.

It is often felt that data warehouses are only for "strategic" value, used occasionally by senior executives to get a perspective on the health and trends of the business. Successful data warehouses however are often much more operational than expected. Line managers often find that the data warehouse is the "only single place" that they can get a total view of their business, or their customer. They come to expect the data to be available everyday, and rely on it being up to date. In every sense of the word, the data warehouse can become "operational", and as critical to the daily running of the business as the transaction systems.

As the owners, this means that much thought needs to be given to the ongoing operation and administration of the Data Warehouse environment, (which of course is unlikely to stop at just one). In designing your systems, it is necessary to consider important infrastructure issues, management issues, user access, and ongoing development, enhancement, growth, in fact all the usual factors that continue to keep IT professionals employed.

For example, the system should be designed around the time it will take to load the data, not the query times. In a transaction system, the focus will be on designing a system that can support a large number of users, often needing less than 1-2 second response times for thousands of transactions per second. On the other hand, the data warehouse must be designed around the time available to complete its single daily transaction; feeding the data in from all the relevant sources, checking it for completeness, loading it into the data warehouse, indexing it, building summaries, and then ensuring it is ready for publication the next morning. (As the types of inquires allowed of a data warehouse are unpredictable, it is in fact a fallacy to expect to design around achieving sub-second response times).

3. Election Night

Every night can become like an election night. As soon as the polls are closed, the individual transactions are all collated, loaded, counted, summarised, and the results published in the morning.

The available time to complete this will determine important decisions about network bandwidth and infrastructure, as well as hardware design, databases, and other software and operational considerations. If for example it is determined that there is only an eight hour window available each night to load the data warehouse, then we need to think about whether we should design the system to complete the task in four hours, just in case for some reason a problem causes a delay or results in the need to restart the process. How much data can be moved from the source systems to the data warehouse systems in what sort of time? Where is the data coming from that feeds the data warehouse or the many data warehouses? What is the agreed definition of the data items? What pre-processing has to be done to ensure the data is scrubbed and indexed? What pre-processing of summaries needs to be completed, prior to publication (if any)? What sort of access will the users require, and what tools will they be using?

4.   Learning from Experience

These and many other questions all need to be asked to ensure a suitable design is developed for the "whole of life" of the data warehouse, not just its early implementation or acceptance testing. Much of the work done by our Professional Services Practise focuses on these and many other issues. Our consultants work through all these considerations to ensure a quality and successful implementation, that has the capacity and flexibility to grow and serve the organisation for many years.

To give some more detail and better explore these issues, it is worth looking at our the background of own experiences. We gained considerable practical experience from when we started our own internal Data Warehouse program in 1986. Over the course of the last 11 years we have evolved ourselves from a reactive Decision Support environment to a carefully planned Enterprise Data Warehouse environment.

Due to this internal knowledge we began a Data Warehouse Consulting program, (the Open Warehouse Practise in our Professional Services Organisation), in 1990 focused on delivering Data Warehousing to our customers. Our experience and program has helped us work with over 220 customers to assist them in building data warehouses.

This experience we has shown that there are really two main categories of issues:

1. Architectural Issues
2. Project Issues

Once organisations accept and adopt Data Warehousing, one of the most prevalent architectural problems that arises is unplanned growth. Data Marts and Data Warehouses tend to spring up with no co-ordination and planning. This can lead to two main problems.

1. An unplanned extraction process that fosters duplication in the actual extraction programs. This wastes CPU time and can lead to different results dependent upon the ensuing transformation process.
2. There will not be a common agreed upon definition for the meaning of the operational data and there won't be an agreed upon best source for data elements that exist in multiple locations. Semantic integrity will not have been addressed.

Isolated Data Warehouses and Data Marts can behave as independent islands, executing multiple extractions from the same sources. This results in duplication of effort, and is quite common in an unplanned environment.

A proliferation of Data Marts within the business and with no comprehensive architecture in place can result in an environment where it is difficult for users to access the many disparate Data Marts and understand their contents without a lot of knowledge and help.

With a little planning, an architecture can be implemented to overcome these obstacles. One common extract can be designed and executed against the operational environment and a hub can be used to manage user access to the various Data Marts and Data Warehouses.

In a carefully designed environment, one extract and transformation process against all relevant operational sources can be piped into a Standard Data Archive (SDA). This solves the first obstacle.

This SDA should have the following characteristics:

- Can be flat files or an RDBMS.
- Will contain clean data.
- Will contain data in an agreed upon format and meaning.

The SDA can now be used to populate Data Warehouses or Data Marts.

5.   The Need For Some Intelligence

Some mechanism is needed to manage a diverse environment of Data Warehouses, Data Marts, and Multi-Dimensional Databases. To accomplish these goals the product that we use is the HP Intelligent Warehouse (IW).

This product was developed internally for our own Data Warehouse environment when we determined that commercially available products with this functionality had not been created.

The product has the following characteristics:

- **Logical view** - this feature allows the implementor to create a logical business view over the entire physical environment, effectively shielding the user from different databases, table joins, different levels of summarisation and complex SQL. RDBMS database views can quickly become unmanageable in a complex Warehouse environment. Using these logical view decreases view management to the bare minimum.

- **Partitioning** - for those Relational Database Management Systems that don't support partitioning, this tool can be used to partition large Warehouses, typically along some time value such as months or years.

- **ODBC driver** - The ODBC driver allows any ODBC compliant client to plug into the IW managed environment. Thus the users aren't tied into one database client tool.

- **Security** - Security and access is managed to all the underlying databases from one central point, obviating the need for hundreds, and even thousands, of GRANT commands. Also, security is provided down to the row level, which is a capability unavailable in most Relational Database Management Systems.

- **Metadata** - Metadata is stored for the entire Warehouse environment.

- **Advisor** - Statistics about usage in the warehouse environment is collected, stored, and displayed (in graphical format). Statistics are managed relating to query usage, partition usage, and summary level usage. Using the Advisor can give the implementor clear data on which summary levels are needed and which aren't being used at all.

- **Summary level management and aggregation navigation** - is aided enormously by this tool. Any Warehouse environment will use summarisation of data for performance reasons. It is difficult for users to navigate through the different summary tables and it is also difficult for the implementors to predict exactly which summary levels are needed.

- **OLAP Server** - Since IW keeps metadata about the Warehouse environment, it can be used to easily create and populate two popular Multi-Dimensional Databases (MDDs), Arbor Essbase and Oracle Express. MDDs only store aggregated data, when the analyst needs detail data, the MDD must drill through to the RDBMS to obtain the detailed data. IW intercepts these queries and rewrites them to be efficient against the underlying RDBMS environment.

- **Metadata Browser**- which significantly aids the user in understanding the data and formulating reports.

6.   GE Appliances: A Case Study

GE Appliances, a US $6 billion division of GE Corporation, makes an interesting case study.

The IW was used at GE Appliances to create one single logical Warehouse out of the numerous Subject Areas pertinent to their business. The Warehouse provides analysis of sales and profit-margin data, quality of products, warranty and service data, transportation efficiency and cost, and the performance of field technicians.

It was relatively easy to add new Subject Areas into the Warehouse since the logical views could integrate the new data elements into the existing views without impacting the current user environment.

Another large benefit of building this Warehouse came from the process of validating and cleaning up the operational data. Inconsistencies in the Warehouse data have been tracked back to the operational systems and has led to improved data integrity at the operational level.

7.   Knowing Your Subject

Many businesses that are starting off in Warehousing have a difficult time identifying potential Subject Areas and then ranking them according to their value in the organisation. A methodology that facilitates these processes is required. As an example, I will describe the one developed and used by us.

To begin, organisations are given a task list that guides them through the preparation for an initial workshop. The organisations assemble relevant information in order to brief the consultants about their business.

Next, key managers and business users brief us about their :

*   Business
*   Products
*   Jobs.

This session is presented with enough detail so that we can understand the structure and nature of the business.

Interviews are then conducted with the organisation in order to examine the factors that influence or are important to their business. Investigating these issues allows the team to compile a list of potential Subject Areas.

After the list of Subject Areas has been compiled, it is necessary to run a workshop to investigate and rank the various categories of each Subject Area. These categories fall under two groups, business and technical.

Once the various categories have had values assigned to them, each Subject Area can then be numerically ranked. To facilitate the ranking process, a spreadsheet, that has been created to cover the categories in the Subject Areas, is used.

If some of the categories can't be ranked due to insufficient information, then there will be the need to go back to the appropriate source to answer the questions.

The end result, and main deliverable, of this workshop is a report including :

- The findings from the business interviews.
- The list of potential Subject Areas.
- The valuation and information uncovered relating to each category in each Subject Area.
- A relative ranking of the Subject Areas.
- Recommendations for a first Subject Area.
- Next steps.

8.   Find the Links

Sometimes Value Chains can be created to help understand Subject Areas and the how they fit together in a business.

A Value Chain is a sequence of events that occurs in both the supply side and the demand side of a business. The supply side of a business consist of those processes that occur from purchasing raw materials through producing a finished product. The demand side of the business consist of those processes that are necessary to market, distribute and sell the products to customers.

By constructing and modifying the Value Chain, the designers can understand how Subject Areas and dimensions interrelate for reporting purposes. This will be invaluable in planning for an Enterprise Data Warehouse.

Another issue that arises quite frequently is the use of an Operational Data Store (ODS) along with a Data Warehouse for data analysis.

The ODS resembles the Data Warehouse in many ways.

- It is integrated from one to many operational sources.
- It is subject oriented.

But in other ways the ODS is very different.

- It is volatile; it is updated on a regular basis which may vary from as little as immediate updates (when the operational data changes), to hourly or daily updates. The Data Warehouse, on the other hand, is non-volatile.
- It is current valued; data in the ODS is up to date. There is usually no archival data found in an ODS, a situation opposite of the Data Warehouse.

- The data in the ODS is detailed since it is used for decision support by the operational community. The Data Warehouse, on the other hand, contains various levels of summary data as well as detailed data.

There is another fundamental difference between the two methods of Decision Support.

The use of the Data Warehouse is for long term and strategic goals whereas the use of the ODS is for immediate and tactical goals.

An ODS and a Data Warehouse can logically coexist in a business environment. Many times the ODS will populate the Data Warehouse with closed transactions.

We built an integrated ODS and Data Warehouse solution for a large pharmaceutical company that wanted to analyse and improve their Order History Life Cycle.

The ODS was used by the Customer Order Support group for the following purposes.

- To answer all questions generated by customers pertaining to their orders.
- To flag orders in the fulfillment pipeline that could turn into potential problems in relation to late delivery or incorrect quantity.

The ODS was populated and updated nightly with open orders only.

In comparison, the Data Warehouse was used by business analysts for the following purposes :

- To investigate all aspects of the Order Life Cycle for time efficiency
- To investigate all aspects of the Order Life Cycle for quality

The state of an order throughout the entire process was captured and performance is compared on a daily basis. The Data Warehouse contained only closed orders, over a 2 year period.

Another environment where ODSs have been used frequently is the financial industry where Risk Management is important to every serious business.

An example of an integrated ODS and Data Warehouse solution was implemented in a project for the Canadian Imperial Bank of Commerce (CIBC). The ODS was used for current analysis of risk exposure. The Data Warehouse was used for historical analysis of risk trends.

One of the major benefits of this project was the consolidation of financial data from over 300 legacy applications residing on over 20 source systems. The Prism Warehouse Manager was used as an extraction and transformation tool for this project.

9.   Avoid The Bumps And Use A Map

Once you have decided to go ahead and start building an actual Data Warehouse, you will find it is best to use a proven methodology in order to:

- Decrease risk.
- Reduce the time spent on the project.
- Cover all aspects of the Warehouse development.

The one I will describe is our "Open Warehouse Implementation Road Map" which is the basis for our methodology and takes organisations from the Warehouse Definition stage to full Enterprise roll-out.

The Warehouse Definition consists of a workshop and investigations. The following areas are investigated and analysed.

- Business objectives, problems, and critical success factors.
- User requirements; in the form of data, reports, and analytical environments.
- Architectural requirements; software, hardware, management infrastructure, and data.
- The operational environment; source systems, applications, databases, and outside data.
- Capacity planning; sizing requirements.

The output of the workshop is:

- A project plan.
- An architecture.
- A project proposal.

There are many issues and challenges related to the Warehouse Definition phase, which will require careful consideration.

To start with, business sponsorship is key for your Data Warehouse projects. These projects should not be undertaken from an exclusive IT perspective. Business unit buy-in is essential for a co-operative effort to occur with a minimum of friction and effort. Also, a powerful business sponsor will be essential to make tough decisions and facilitate problem solving within the business unit.

This approach results in Warehouses being built in an iterative fashion, one Subject Area at a time. With this in mind, it is essential to identify a first Subject Area for the Data Warehouse. Having a Subject Area identified before the Warehouse Definition workshop begins will also increase efficiency. It is extremely difficult to run

Definition workshops for multiple Subject Areas at the same time. It takes to long and doesn't make sense when an iterative approach to Subject Area addition is taken.

Return On Investment (ROI) for Data Warehouses can be a tough subject. Companies often find this a difficult area to quantify before a Warehouse project even begins because only projections can be attempted at this point. The good news however is that many companies that have installed data warehouses have found that they are able to clearly measure the impact, (as you will be able to use the data to support distinct decisions, and then measure the result), and that their returns are significantly high. [2]

Analysis paralysis is that state where the designers and implementors over analyse everything to the point where no progress is made. We see this from time to time and it can be the death of an otherwise sound project. It is useful to keep one main thought in mind; you cannot build a perfect Data Warehouse - it is virtually impossible to predict exactly how the users will use the Warehouse one year down the road. This occurs because the Data Warehouse is non-deterministic in nature. By comparison, you can create an OLTP system with all the requirements firmly in mind because these systems support a deterministic operational process.

Identifying the needed skill sets for a project is only difficult if you have never down it before. The definition workshop will identify all necessary skill sets.

A large multinational high tech manufacturer provides us with another case study. They were not untypical in having many possible opportunities such as better potential marketing to their installed base, more cost effective management of product recalls, and generally an improved understanding of their customer and product.

Their existing infrastructure presented its own problems. The required data was spread across various operational systems, platforms, and file formats. Reports were collated by hand from extract files, which was of course a very laborious task which caused unacceptable delays and potential errors.

The benefits offered by a Data Warehouse included the ability to integrate product data to reflect the product life cycle (manufacturing, testing, order fulfillment, shipping, and repairs), improve reporting time and accuracy, and widen the usage of installed base intelligence within the company.

A five day workshop was undertaken to consolidate and analyse the requirements. This produced a report outlining the architecture for the Phase 1 project, a draft project plan, and a project costing proposal. All of these were of course important to

---

[2] There is an excellent report from The International Data Corporation (IDC) titled "The Foundations of Wisdom: A Study of the Financial Impact of Data Warehousing" that should help the implementors justify their Data Warehouse projects by looking at some of the experiences of others.

enable the business to then make the decision to go to the next step. In fact, this workshop was necessary to allow the project to go to the approval stage.

The people that were involved in this particular workshop were:

- The business sponsor and numerous end users
- The IT project team: manager, source system specialists, DBAs, and reporting specialists
- Two Data Warehouse consultants

10.   Now You Have The Map, Let Us Take The First Step

Your initial Warehouse creation and deployment should be on a limited basis. It is meant to be completed quickly and show value immediately. In fact it is important that it does this. It will also be the foundation for full deployment and roll-out.

The flexibility offered by this particular Data Warehouse Implementation Road Map is very important. Sometimes the deployment stage is implemented with full functionality (data, users, management infrastructure, automation, etc.) in mind. The final choice is left up to the organisations. The more cautious and less risky approach is of course limited deployment.

The Warehouse deployment is iterative in nature. Quick iterations and subsequent refinements due to user feedback and testing will lead to the best results.

As you deploy the first Phase of your Warehouse, you will find that there are many issues. Firstly, data audits must be accomplished for the following reasons.

- All the relevant data sources and elements that support the Subject Area in question must be known before data modelling begins. This will ensure that the modelers have the best chance of including the right data into the Data Warehouse.
- The meaning of the data must be known and agreed upon by all parties involved.
- The best source for all data elements must be determined. Sometimes, the same data element exists in multiple systems and the cleanest or original source must be determined.
- The quality of the data must be known. Abysmally poor quality data must be identified and rectified before inclusion into the Warehouse. Because data cleanup is so costly, many companies now use the Data Warehouse to facilitate data cleansing. But this strategy will only work on data that isn't extremely poor since bad quality data will have no analytic benefit.

If the original scope of the project was thorough and correct, avoid scope creep, it can cause the project to slip in major ways. If scope expansion is being forced upon the design team, then make a careful analysis of the cost in dollars and time that the "enhancement" will incur. Many times hard data on added cost and time will deflect scope creep.

Some business rules are complex and twisted in ways that defy logic. Unfortunately, it is seldom possible to change the way a business conducts itself. This type of problem can lead to strange schema designs and divergence from ideal dimensional models. If odd business rules impact schema development and subsequent database performance, document and educate all relevant parties as to why this event has occurred.

Dimensional modelling is key for Data Warehouse design. You will fail if you use standard ER design principles with normalisation in mind. We recommend reading Ralph Kimball's excellent book titled "The Data Warehouse Toolkit" for a clinic on dimensional modelling of Data Warehouses.

All the Data Warehouses that we have built have been dimensionally modelled although some may have varied from the ideal due to strange business rules. Additionally, we have replaced numerous failed Data Warehouse efforts at customers sites that had highly normalised schemas.

Business user sponsorship and a business champion are just as important at this phase as they were for the previous phase. If you run into any business and user obstacles these people will be essential for success.

Remember that development is iterative in nature. Iterations are followed by feedback and testing that lead to more iterations.

Of all the Warehouses that we're cognisant of, roughly 50% - 60% of the effort will be spent on the data audit, extraction, and transformation process. This will also be the most cost intensive part of the project from a labour perspective. We have also found that the cost of cleaning up truly poor data can run into the millions of dollars!

The full deployment stage is the second phase of the implementation of a Production Warehouse. This is the more cautious, risk adverse, approach, where you complete the deployment as a second phase, rather than attempting to do this in one step.

Because the deployment is often likely to extend across the whole Enterprise, we also recommend breaking the project down to a third phase to complete the full Enterprise Wide Warehouse deployment, usually along geographical, organisational, or subject boundaries.

There normally aren't as many issues at Phase 3 compared to previous phases but the issues are very large in magnitude.

The sheer scale of data size and user numbers can be staggering.

Distributed management of numerous relational and multi-dimensional databases as well as hundreds or even thousands of users can entail a major effort in planning and resources.

11.   A Vendor's Own Case Study

Hewlett-Packard was faced internally with these issues roughly 6 years ago. The IW product was used, to ease the transition into and the management of this environment.

A feature of the product is that it can be used to facilitate a global Enterprise Data Warehouse through the use of what we call IW hubs.

As an example, HP currently have a large (660 GB) Order History Data Warehouse located at corporate headquarters in Palo Alto, California that is managed by the IW. The European headquarters has European Order History in a Data Warehouse stored locally in Geneva, Switzerland. Instead of duplicating the global Order History data in Geneva, the European Order History Data Warehouse uses IW's virtual view to present the global Order History data from California as if it were local. An Asia-Pacific hub is currently being completed for addition to this global environment.

12.   Three S's Of Data Warehousing

Some principles that can help when considering how to make your data warehouse successful can be summarised by the Three S's of Data Warehousing:

1. **Simplicity**: Keep the data warehouse projects simple in design. Particularly for the early efforts, don't attempt a grand scale project to build the ultimate enterprise data warehouse to satisfy any and all users in your organisation. There are simply too many data sources, and too many diverse user needs and types to make this an achievable goal. The phased approached discussed in this paper is proven.

2. **Standards:** Make all your technology and component selections from those that are based on standards, and avoid proprietary technologies, even those that promote themselves as more specialised to meet the needs of data warehousing. By using popular technologies, such as UNIX based servers, capable of being built into either small or massive configurations, you give yourself the best flexibility and cost advantage. There is a greater wealth of experience and software development going into supporting these environments, and so you will find yourself in a large and successful club of users with a wealth of knowledge to share.

3. **Skills:** Seek help. Work with experienced organisations that understand not only the data design issues, but also the other important considerations that ensure the

ongoing successful implementation, administration, acceptance, and continuing value that the data warehouse needs to fulfill. Ensure they are up to date on important emerging trends, such as providing Internet based access to corporate data warehouses, without threatening corporate security.

Our OpenWarehouse program is based on all these principles. It includes important data warehouse middleware software, Intelligent Warehouse (discussed in this paper), that significantly enhances the ease of administration and performance improvement of heterogeneous data warehouses, that can be running on many different platforms and database technologies, whilst helping to achieve the most important of all aspects of the data warehouse, which is; making it easy for the users to access.

Ultimately it will be the ongoing ease of access, on a regular and reliable basis, that will enable your users and the organisation to get their own incredible return on investment.

After all, the return on the investment made in the data warehouse should continue for many years, and not just to help you capitalise on the Christmas holiday spending!

References:

[GRA96]   Graham, Stephen, "The Foundations of Wisdom: A Study of the Financial Impact of Data Warehousing", IDC (Canada), 1996

[KIM96]   Kimball, Ralph, "The Data Warehouse Toolkit. Practical Techniques for Building Dimensional Data Warehouses", Wiley, 1996

About the Speaker:

Peter Hall is responsible for Hewlett-Packard's Enterprise Computing Program within Asia/Australasia, including HP's data warehousing programs which are marketed under the name HP Open Warehouse. Peter has fifteen years experience within Hewlett-Packard, having held key responsibilities within Hewlett-Packard's Sales & Marketing teams, predominately in Australia. Peter has worked with many customers moving to Open Systems in industries as diverse as Manufacturing, Retail, Financial Services, Government and Telecommunications. Peter holds a Bachelor of Business Degree (Accounting) from Phillip Institute of Technology (Australia).

Mr. Peter Hall
Region Program Director
Enterprise Computer
Asia/Australasia
Hewlett-Packard Company
31-41 Joseph Street, Blackburn VICTORIA 3130
Australia
Phone: +61 3 9272 2031, Fax: +61 3 9272 2726
E-mail: peter_hall@hp.com

Data Warehouse Key Components & Process: Using a Rational Approach to Build Your Data Warehouse

Dale Mietla, NewTHINK, Inc., Marvin Miller, DEC, George Kong, DEC

Abstract

For decades computer systems have been limited in what they could achieve and how they could achieve it by computer technology itself. Over the years technology advancement have see use move from a world of batch processing to a world of online processing , Client/Server and now, Data Warehousing - all promising to improve your bottom line.

You can call it the search for the holy Grail, but then it all boils down to making information available in a useable form to everyone who needs it in the enterprise, quickly. The key word here is quickly. Today, huge volumes of data can be cataloged, indexed, combined and analysed to provide information about group behaviour, uncover hidden relationships about seemingly unrelated facts and coordinate activities of a sales force around the world.

However, building a Data Warehouse requires a completely new approach to application, hence solution, development that not only requires technical knowledge, but also in-depth knowledge of the company's business processes and requirements. It is also different for every single company and the adage that "you can't buy a Data Warehouse, you have to build it" is so true. Once you started, it is a never ending process of re-building, adding and enhancing.

Most companies miss the obvious point of selecting the best products and services for their needs in the race to implement a data warehouse. In the attempt to gain a competitive advantage, they focus on selecting the latest, the fastest, or the largest products. The use of a rational process to define the business problem and solve it are usually overlooked or ignored.

The success of the Data Warehouse poses a great deal of management problems too from how to manage user requirements and expectation while keeping pace with the implementation of new technology to satisfy user demands - but still deliver under budget constraints.

This paper organizes the various technology choices which are available for data warehousing and addresses the need for a process to implement the data warehouse application. The paper contains a concise roadmap that illustrates the relationship of software and hardware products, and service providers. The roadmap is a set of illustrations that explain the interaction of technology choices in the process of building a data warehouse. As this paper is very short, it will only give a brief overview of the process and hopefully, an insight to what is required when building a Data Warehouse.

1.   Key Components

1.1.   Data Warehouse Products - Software and Hardware

The purpose of the data warehouse system is to analyze corporate data. The knowledge gained from the analyses is used to guide organizations. This intent is fundamentally different from operational systems, whose purpose is to keep the organizations running each day.

Each system has different usage characteristics and generally requires different hardware and software configurations in order to achieve maximum performance.

In general, the data warehouse system is tuned for a smaller community of users that generate a small number of transactions. Because the data in the database is analyzed, it is rarely updated during transactions; instead the data is repeatedly read and combined in different ways. The transactions however, are very large and sometimes require scanning entire tables.

Operational systems on the other hand, are tuned for a large community of users, with a high volume of relatively simple transactions. These transactions update the individual records in the database, so that the data is always current. As such, the database is organized to quickly retrieve individual data items and update only the pieces information that change.

One way to understand the products which comprise a data warehouse system is to follow the flow of data from operational systems to the data warehouse system. A successful data warehouse system must be stocked with data from operational systems. The data in the data warehouse system usually contains a deeper history than the data in operational systems. Often, three to five years of data is stored in the data warehouse. The data must be accurate, without duplications or inconsistencies. The selected data must be moved to the data warehouse system and stored in a database management system.

Current database technology for data warehousing offers a variety of choices, from Multi-Dimensional Database Management Systems (MDBMSs) to Relational Database Management Systems (RDBMSs) such as Informix OnLine Dynamic Server, Oracle7 Server, or Sybase System11. Due to recent advances, these database systems to support vast amounts of data, provide rapid data retrieval, and offer various combinations of data. Please see Figure 1.

Building the Data Warehouse

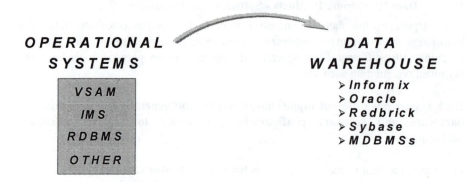

Figure 1: Building the data warehouse from data in operational systems

The actual movement of data from the operational systems to the data warehouse system is done by a group of software products that bridge the gap between the older data access methods, such as VSAM, IMS, IDMS, and others and transport the data into the RDBMSs and MDBMSs of the 1990s.

These software tools usually execute a series of steps to select, match, filter, cleanse, and copy the selected operational data into the data warehouse system. Please see Figure 2.

Stocking the Data Warehouse

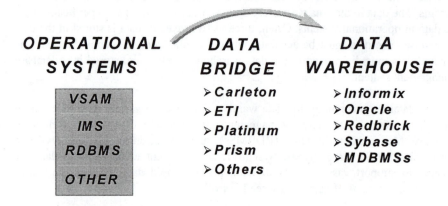

Figure 2. Stocking the data warehouse via data-bridging tools.

Portions of the operational data may be duplicated, since the data is stored in several sources. These sources grow over time as new OLTP applications are developed. This overlap can present itself as similar names for data items (CUST, CUST_NAME, etc.) or as partial overlapping fields (PART_NUMBER, ASSEMBLY, SUB_ASSEMBLY, etc.)

The data-bridge software products need a method to keep track of data items, so that the items are correctly combined in the data warehouse system. This requirement can be met by using a data dictionary, known as *metadata*.

Metadata acts as a traffic policeman for data coming into the data warehouse system, including tracking changes to field names, time-stamping when the datasets were loaded into the data warehouse system, and tracking versions of both the operational and the data warehouse system field names.

The next group of products in the roadmap are the view tools. Because the analytical function is so critical to the success of the data warehouse project, a large number of these products are available. Basically, they provide two important functions:

1) Generate sophisticated queries of the data warehouse; and
2) Present the results in a variety of graphical formats.

These view tools are the primary contact that end users have with the data warehouse system. They must be flexible, easy to understand, and provide the user with a variety of choices for generating the query, presenting the results, and keeping track of the flow of the analytical session. This is because most analytical sessions are based on an "ad-hoc" approach, where the outcome, and even the process of arriving at the outcome, are unknown.

Most data warehouse queries answer a specific set of questions that relate to an organization. For example, a retail store chain would analyze market baskets, shelf-space allocation, or the effectiveness of targeted marketing programs. A healthcare provider is interested in fraud detection, the efficiency of various reimbursement plans, or tracking the usage of various medications.

Some analyses are saved for repeated use. They can be thought of as data warehouse applications for the end-users. Note that these applications are not written (compiled, debugged, etc.) by traditional Management Information System (MIS) departments, but are built by the end-users to answer repetitive questions like "What are the latest sales trends as of today?" or "Rank the effectiveness of my largest suppliers".

The viewing tools must also use metadata so that the data items are used consistently and the results can be matched to existing operational data. These points are illustrated in Figure 3.

Using the Data Warehouse

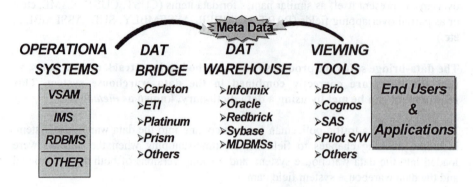

OPERATIONAL SYSTEMS	DATA BRIDGE	DATA WAREHOUSE	VIEWING TOOLS	
VSAM	➤Carleton	➤Informix	➤Brio	End Users
IMS	➤ETI	➤Oracle	➤Cognos	&
RDBMS	➤Platinum	➤Redbrick	➤SAS	Applications
OTHER	➤Prism	➤Sybase	➤Pilot S/W	
	➤Others	➤MDBMSs	➤Others	

Figure 3 :Metadata provides consistency and matches data items from multiple sources.

The previous points address the requirements of data warehouse software products. Once these requirements are met, the roadmap is complete from a software perspective. However, equally important is the need to have a hardware system that can support the extreme demands of data warehouse environments. Because of the vast volumes of data stored in a data warehouse system, traditional 32-bit computers have limitations that reduce the size, performance, and scalability required for data warehouse projects.

Specifically, 32-bit systems are limited to files and file systems which are 2 GB or less in size. This means that data must be partitioned or segmented into smaller groups so that the 32-bit system can handle it. This creates multiple operational problems for backup, recovery, design, and maintenance, especially when data warehouse projects are frequently approaching 1 TB in size.

The next step in computer architecture is 64-bit computing. 64 Bit Systems run fully adapted 64-bit RDBMSs with essentially no constraints for growth, usage, or design of data warehouses. In addition, 64-bit RDBMSs have the added benefit of outperforming their 32-bit predecessors, because of the economies of scale provided in 64-bit architectures.

Hardware systems can be thought of as the foundation for a data warehouse system. They must support rapid growth as more and more data is added to the data warehouse, and they must be able to handle increasingly complex queries from a growing user community. These requirements: more users, smarter users, and more data can cause traditional 32-bit systems to either collapse, provide extremely slow performance, or limit analyses to sizes that they can handle. Not a desirable group of choices to pick from.

Supporting the Data Warehouse

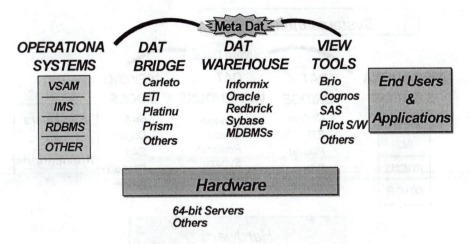

Figure 4: 64-bit systems meets the changing needs of the data warehouse.

1.2.   Data Warehouse Services

The previous section described the products required to build the data warehouse. The final portion of the data warehouse roadmap focuses on the services required to build the data warehouse. Most data warehouse installations require outside assistance to build the total solution.

Outside help is usually required for several reasons:

1) Data warehouse projects are large efforts, which usually require several months or longer to design, create, and maintain.

2) The projects require a wide variety of skills, from database design to data modeling, to user viewing tools.

3) The existing MIS staff is often overburdened with application development and the management of the operational systems.

4) Data warehouse expertise is rare and seldom part of an organization's existing MIS departmental skill set.

Typically, a systems integrator supports, manages, and delivers a data warehouse project. In fact, most MIS departments have worked on other projects with systems integrators. Most data warehouse system needs can be met by the larger systems integrators, provided that the integrator has experience with data warehouse systems. Please note Figure 5.

134

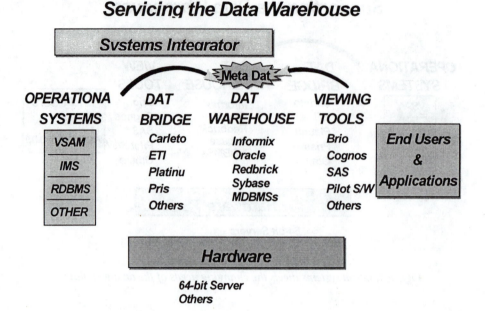

Figure 5: The systems integrator services the data warehouse.

However, there is an additional service provider that is extremely useful for most data warehouse projects. Independent data warehouse consultants have carved out a valuable niche for themselves over the past two years. They actually provide the "grease" to keep the entire project running smoothly. At times these consultants are contracted by the Systems Integrator.

The added value of the independent consultants is that they address the needs of the end users in the *language* of the end users, instead of in the language of computer technology.

Data warehouse projects are built for use by the end users so that the business can be analyzed efficiently. Once the analysis is completed, the new knowledge needs to be put into practice in order to improve the functioning of an organization. Therefore, end users become implementers.

There are different perspectives of the data warehouse component roadmap, depending on who views it:

- End users view the roadmap starting at the right-hand side of the page. They see the viewing tools primarily and, possibly, some portions of the database engine.

- MIS departments and system integrators view the roadmap as starting at the left side of the page. They see the operational systems, the data-bridge software (due to its impact to the operational systems) and, probably, the database engine.

The point is that the two views do not naturally have any common ground for discussion, design, development, or testing. The two views start from different perspectives and different goals.

Successful data warehouse projects require a focus on the solution by both MIS and end users at every stage. The independent consultants can bridge this gap and create the common ground where solution sharing can occur. These consultants are trained to listen to end users, develop a set of requirements that are business based (not technology based), and translate them into traditional MIS requirements.

Please note the completed roadmap shown below:

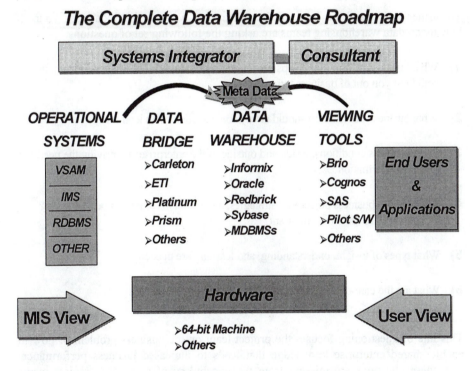

Figure 6: The completed data warehouse roadmap.

The completed roadmap offers the reader a chance to organize the various technology options into categories which explain their function, purpose, and relationship to each other. Products and services are two fundamental requirements in any data warehouse project.

The next section presents the process for analyzing, designing, and implementing the information technology components of the data warehouse roadmap.

2. Data Warehousing Process

2.1. The Time is Right for a Process

We are in the initial stages of data warehousing maturity. This stage can be characterized by marketplace excitement and hype, preoccupation with solutions and technologies, and many project failures. We can clearly see this today as we read about star schemas, bit-mapped indexing, OLAP, VLDB, and so on. In fact, a recent industry publication conducted a survey to find out who has the largest database. Survey respondents bragged – and everyone focused on the wrong set of issues. Unfortunately, and maybe unknowingly, credibility was given to "bigger is better".

To further understand the "state of the art" in data warehousing today, ask yourself how many data warehousing teams are asking the following set of questions:

1) What business information keeps you in business today? What business information could put you out of business tomorrow?

2) What business information should always be one click of an icon away?

3) What business conditions, inside and outside of the enterprise, are driving the need for business information?

4) What are the business objectives, strategies, and problems that must be addressed? Which ones are the most important?

5) What types of insight, understanding, and learning are needed?

6) What are the elements of information that can fulfill these needs?

This line of questioning focuses the project team on the business problem of how to enable shared enterprise knowledge that leads to increased business performance. Yet, these questions are missing from the vocabulary of many DW project teams today. This is a significant problem because the issue of where value is added is left undiscussed. This vacuum is usually filled by discussion about data mining, parallel architectures, and moving all the data into the warehouse.

It is now time to move from the excitement and fascination about data warehouse technology to an understanding of the real business and technical issues that are central to data warehousing. It is also time to move from "trial and error" projects to development efforts that address the engineering complexities inherent in building a data warehouse. A well-defined data warehousing process can help organizations make the transition to a higher level of maturity and more predictable results.

2.2.   What Is a Process?

First of all, a process is not a methodology. A methodology is a *theoretical* set of concepts and practices for producing a specified result – in this case, a functional data warehouse. In other words, if the theory defined by methodologists is properly applied on a project, the desired outcome will, in theory, be produced. Methodology "binderware" continues to adorn shelves as ready evidence to the QA audit team that a methodology exists.

A process, on the other hand, is an *applied* set of concepts and practices for producing a specified result. This is a subtle but important distinction. A process is the product of real projects, not a product of methodologists. It is acquired knowledge that contains the combined best practices of project teams for producing a solution. Processes commonly exist in automated form and are an integral part of the project team's infrastructure.

A well-defined data warehousing process helps project teams:

• Understand the critical business and technical issues of data warehousing;

• Create project outcomes and evaluate their quality;

• Apply a process workflow (tasks) and set of techniques for developing a data warehouse solution;

• Understand roles and responsibilities of team members; and,

• Determine the project schedule and level of effort.

A process that provides guidelines, pitfalls, strategies, hints, examples, lessons learned, and other types of practical tips is considerably more useful to project teams than a detailed "cookbook" task structure that encourages blind adherence. A good process energizes the creativity and thinking of the project team, instead of stifling it.

Once an organization has accepted the need for a data warehousing process, the next key challenge is how to define and evaluate a process. The two most common approaches are "acquire and adapt", or "build your own". In either case, the process consumer must take full control and ownership of the data warehousing process for it to be accepted and used.

The following 12 kernels of data warehousing are provided as a guideline for organizations defining or evaluating a process. The 12 kernels are the "essential blocks of development activities" that must be present in a data warehousing process to completely address the business and technical issues for developing a data warehouse. The 12 kernels themselves do not constitute a process and, therefore,

138

cannot be applied without adding more detail. Rather, they define a high-level framework or architecture of a process.

The figure below presents a workflow view of the data warehousing process, showing each kernel and its primary dependencies on other kernels. The diagram does not explicitly depict sequence.

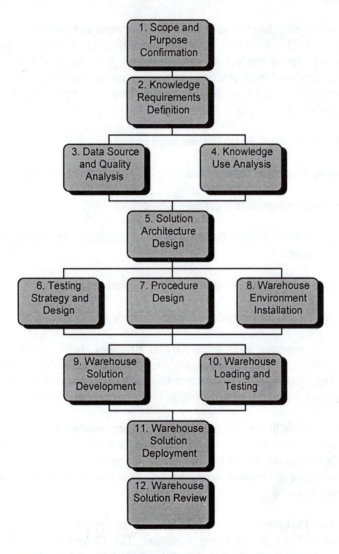

Figure 7: NewTHINK's 12 Kernels of Data Warehousing

The following paragraphs provide a description of each kernel and some of the key issues addressed by each (the issue lists are not exhaustive).

2.3.   Scope and Purpose Confirmation

Before the project can move into high gear, it must be positioned (given context) by explicitly defining the project boundaries from a business and technical perspective. Project team members and key stakeholders must have a shared vision of the project and its results. Central issues to be addressed include:

- What business value is to be added by the project? How do you spell "SUCCESS"?

- What will form the basis for competition in the enterprise's industry in the future?

- What business drivers does the project address? Which ones are most important?

- What part of the business operations is affected? Which processes, subjects, locations, and organizations?

- Who are the key stakeholders and what are their expectations?

- Who are the consumers and producers of knowledge? What types of knowledge do they need?

- What technology standards are in place that constrain the project?

- What are the funding, schedule, and resource constraints?

- What is the relationship between the project and other data warehousing solutions or projects?

2.4.   Knowledge Requirements Definition

Information is understanding about events of the past. Knowledge, on the other hand, is insight that enables prediction and creation of events in the future. The focus of data warehousing must be on the development of knowledge, not just the reporting of information.

In this kernel, the project team works with business customers to define the knowledge requirements for the data warehousing solution. Dialog takes place in a natural business language, with plenty of visualizations to help team members understand the requirements and business customers to feel confident that their requirements are understood. Central issues to be addressed include:

- What are the business objectives, strategies, and problems that require measurement and analysis? What opportunities and challenges are driving the need for knowledge?

- What types of insight, understanding, and learning are needed? Which ones are historical versus predictive in nature? Who needs this knowledge? Where? How often?

- What are the elements of knowledge that can lead to insight, understanding, and learning? Where can these elements be acquired?

- What are the business rules that govern the elements of knowledge?

- What types of analytical methods will be used to develop knowledge?

- How is the result of these analytical methods to be visualized?

- How is information about knowledge requirements represented as metadata?

Note: Star schema versus relational schema is not an issue here. These are storage structures that should be considered in the solution architecture. The knowledge models created in this kernel are for a business audience.

3.   Data Source and Quality Analysis

As the knowledge requirements are being defined, the project team must map these requirements to the discrete elements of internal and external data sources. In many cases, the mapping will be to data fields in existing OLTP systems. The team must also address one of the most difficult problems in data warehousing – how to handle "dirty" data. Central issues to be addressed are:

- What are the potential internal and external sources for knowledge? What discrete facts (data) must be leveraged from these sources?

- Which sources are closest to the point of data entry?

- How often are the sources updated? How volatile are they? How current are they?

- What are the business rules that constrain each discrete fact of data? Which business rules are inconsistent with the business rules of knowledge?

- How uniformly have the business rules been applied in the data sources? What percentage of the data is "dirty"?

- Which sources will actually be used for satisfying the knowledge requirements?

- How is information about the selected sources represented as metadata?

4.   Knowledge Use Analysis

As the knowledge requirements are being defined, the project team must also understand the usage metrics (e.g., size, volume, frequency) for the requirements. Scalability is a very important issue in data warehousing. The metrics on knowledge usage, which relate to scalability, must be visible and understood early on. Central issues to be addressed are:

- What is the estimated size of each element of knowledge?

- How many instances are contained in each knowledge set?

- What analytical operations are performed? Which sets of knowledge are involved? How often are the operations performed?

- How often is each knowledge set refreshed with new data from internal or external sources? What are the sizes of the source data sets?

- How often are instances removed from each knowledge set? What are the criteria for removal?

- How is information about knowledge usage represented as metadata?

5.   Solution Architecture Design

The project team, using its understanding of the knowledge requirements, usage, and data sources, designs the data warehousing solution. The solution architecture is a specification containing four of the key components of data warehouse solutions presented earlier in this article (i.e., data bridge, data warehouse, view tools, hardware). Central issues to be addressed are:

- What existing standards and infrastructure (i.e., hardware, software, network) constrain the solution? How does the project team leverage existing infrastructure to shorten the development cycle time?

- What data warehousing tools are currently in use that should be considered?

- What classes of business customers must the solution support? Where are they located? What levels of security must be provided?

- What view tools (e.g., query, reporting, analytical, visualization) should be provided?

- How is access to metadata provided to business customers? How is metadata kept consistent with the data in the warehouse?

- What is the data architecture of the solution? What storage structures (e.g., star schema, relational schema) and indexing methods should be used? How is the data summarized, partitioned, and distributed?

- What is the application architecture of the solution? What programs and logic are needed to extract, transform, cleanse, and load the operational data? How is the application logic partitioned and distributed?

- What is the technology architecture of the solution? What hardware, systems software, and networks support the solution? How is the technology distributed to support the data and application architectures?

6.   Testing Strategy and Design

As the solution architecture is being defined, the project team must develop strategies, procedures, and data for testing the data warehousing solution. The four key components of the solution should be addressed in the test strategy and design. However, the data bridge component is likely to require the most testing. Central issues to be addressed are:

- What is the potential business impact on the enterprise (e.g., decisions made, actions taken) from use of the data warehouse? What degree of testing rigor must be applied?

- What degree of data correctness must exist? How is data correctness proven?

- How are data bridging programs tested? How is the correctness of extraction, transformation, cleansing, and loading logic proven?

- How are view tools tested? How is the correctness of their results and visualizations proven?

- In what sequence will the components be tested? What procedures and test data will be used?

- Who will do the testing? How will the test results be reported and evaluated?

- What tests must be completed successfully for system acceptance?

7. Procedure Design

As the design of the solution architecture unfolds, the project team must also focus on procedures that are required to operate and administer the data warehouse. Automated and/or manual procedures must be designed for availability, security, performance, and storage management. Central issues to be addressed include:

- What are the procedures for backup and recovery?

- What are the procedures for data refresh and archival?

- What are the procedures for monitoring and tuning data warehouse performance?

- What are the procedures for data warehouse security?

- What are the procedures for extending and scaling data storage?

8. Warehouse Environment Installation

Before development of the data warehouse solution can be kicked off, the hardware, system software, and network must be installed and/or made available to the project team. Each infrastructure component should be thoroughly tested and certified. Testing and certification of the environment can save the implementation team time in isolating problems during the development of the solution.

9. Warehouse Solution Development

The project team builds the data warehousing solution according to the specifications of the solution architecture and design procedures. The project team should expect to spend most of its effort on the data bridge component of the solution architecture.

10. Warehouse Loading and Testing

As the project team assembles components of the data warehousing solution, an independent testing team must prove the correctness of the solution. The testing strategy and design is used to guide the testing team as they construct test data, test the data bridge components, load the data warehouse, and test the view tool components. Business customers should be included in testing the view tool components and conducting the final acceptance test before the solution is deployed.

11. Warehouse Solution Deployment

The accepted data warehouse solution is installed, tested, and made available at the targeted sites. The extraction and load processes are executed to bring the data warehouse to production status. Documentation for end users and the operations staff is packaged and issued. Training is conducted to help end users understand the potential of the solution and become comfortable with the functionality of the view tools.

12. Warehouse Solution Review

With the solution deployed, the project team archives important project documentation and data, and conducts a final meeting to discuss the project process and results. Central issues to be addressed during the discussion include:

- What was the quality and completeness of the solution? How satisfied were business customers with the solution?

- What portion of the original scope was "thrown overboard" and should be moved into a subsequent project? What improvements should be made to the current solution?

- How well did the development process work? What improvements should be made to the workflow and techniques?

- How well did the project team work together? What improvements should be made to roles, responsibilities, and allocation of workload?

- How well did the development tools work? What workarounds or utilities should be implemented to increase usability or functionality?

13. Iterative Application of the Process

It is a well known fact that implementing a data warehouse is an iterative process. Consequently, the above process should be performed iteratively under the control of a process that determines the sequence and scope of each project, as illustrated below. DW Scope and Iteration Management is an ongoing process that employs estimating and release management techniques to implement the data warehouse vision through a series of process iterations. Other ongoing processes, such as configuration management, change control, process and project management, and architecture management, must also interface with each iteration of the data warehouse process.

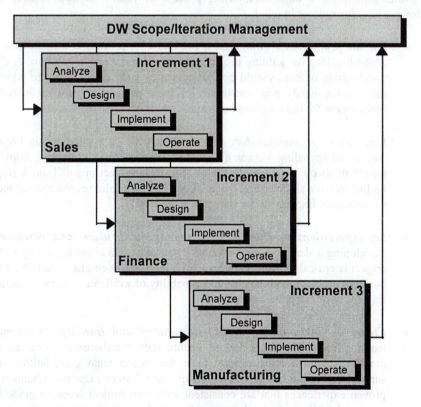

Figure 8: Data Warehouse Process Iteration

14. Concurrent Engineering Can Shorten Cycle Time

To shorten cycle time, the data warehousing project team should be a multi-disciplined team of managers, business customers, analysts, solution architects, and implementers. A concurrent engineering team is a key ingredient in shortening the implementation cycle. For example, involvement of solution architects during the analysis of knowledge requirements enables solution tradeoffs to be discussed early in the project cycle. Unfeasible or expensive options can be discarded before the consume considerable resources. Solution architects also can begin positioning the solution architecture earlier in the project. Likewise, involvement of business customers and analysts during the design and implementation can speed up the resolution of issues relating to the requirements. In addition, business customers and analysts can be invaluable resources during testing.

15. Keys to Project Success

Before implementing a data warehousing process in your organization, keep the following keys for success in mind:

- *Use the process as a guide, not a cookbook*. A process is a framework (a generalization) for guiding project teams from problem to solution. A data warehousing process should be customized by each project team to address the specific needs and constraints of their project. A process is not a replacement for thinking and innovation.

- *Keep the scope manageable.* An enterprise-wide data warehousing project may sound appealing, but can quickly become a sinkhole, collapsing from the weight of its own complexity. Think "big picture", act in small quick steps. Its fine to have an enterprise-wide vision. But, use solid release management techniques to implement the vision "step by step".

- *Set expectations up-front between management, users, and developers.* Developing a shared vision between key stakeholders at the beginning of the project is critical to project success. An honest and open discussion about the business problem, and the cost and capability of available solutions can help set expectations on the right path.

- *Create an environment for experimentation and learning.* Much more learning must take place before mature data warehousing processes are practiced in most organizations. Give the project team great latitude and support during the first few iterations of a new process. Use consultants with proven experiences that are consistent with your project scope to guide the team and facilitate technology transfer. At the end of each iteration, make sure the team's learning is captured in the data warehousing process so that subsequent teams can benefit.

16.   Conclusion

Data warehousing can be a valuable analytical tool and a competitive weapon. It can also be a large waste of time, resources, and money. The difference between these two outcomes is having clearly focused goals from the beginning of the data warehouse project and following a rational approach in building the data warehouse.

Using the goals of the project as a guide, your company can select the technology best suited to your needs, using the data warehouse component roadmap described in this article. Using a coordinated project plan including the process of definition, analysis, design, and deployment with MIS staff and key end users will result in a successful data warehouse implementation, on time and within budget.

About the Authors:

Dale Mietla is Director of Consulting Services for NewTHINK, Inc., where he helps clients visualize the elements of knowledge that define the data warehouse and the architectures and processes that deliver the data warehouse. He has over 17 years of experience with emphasis in the areas of enterprise architecture, business and information modeling, application design, and development processes and technologies.

Marvin Miller is a Senior Consultant for Digital Equipment Corporation, where he works closely with data warehouse companies and customers on large scale data warehousing opportunities. He has over 20 years of experience in the computer industry, including large scale system design, performance benchmarks, and application migrations.

George Kong is the Asia Pacific Enterprise Marketing Manager for Digital Equipment Corporation, based in Singapore, where he has responsibilities for selling and marketing Data Warehouse solutions. He has over 13 years of experience in the computer industry, spent in England and Asia, which includes designing and implementing Client/Server solutions while specialising in Middleware technologies (while working for IBM in Singapore), large system and application migrations and EIS/DSS application development for ICI in England. George can be reached at: konggeorge@mail.dec.com or gkong@singnet.com.sg.

Successful Data Warehousing:
Driving Value from your Meta Data Initiative.

Cass Squire, Director of Professional Services, Prism Solutions, Inc.

Abstract

This document was created to help data warehouse developers derive business value from a practical, incremental approach to implementation of a meta data initiative. The approaches in this document have been compiled based on input from Prism consultants and system engineers, representing years of warehousing expertise.

Introduction

The concept of meta data is not a new one. Unfortunately, it has not been widely implemented in the data warehouse industry. The problem with meta data is not the recognition of its importance in the warehouse environment. Industry analysts, warehouse tool vendors and customers all agree that it is vital. Rather, the problem is twofold. First because meta data is an intangible thing, it is difficult, if not impossible, to start building. Second, it is extremely challenging to measure the return on investment (ROI) of meta data.

The goal of this document is help an organization define, build, and most importantly, implement a meta data initiative. Included will be: the definition of meta data, what it is and why an organization should have a meta data initiative, detailed questions to ask during the definition stage, practical suggestions for when and how to get started, and meta data use cases. By building a meta data initiative, meta data becomes tangible.

The way we look at the ROI of implementing meta data needs to change. Separating meta data from the warehouse environment and attempting to measure the ROI on its own is impossible. When we go to the library, we expect to find both the card catalog and the publications it describes. There is no value in having only a card catalog, and certainly the value of the publications is increased when we have a way of determining what publication will fill our needs, and where it is located in the stacks. In short, the ROI should be measured across the warehouse environment as a whole, which comprises both the data and the meta data.

Several assumptions are made in this document:
- A warehouse environment can include an enterprise data warehouse, distributed or departmental warehouses, departmental data marts, and/or personal data marts.
- There is a dedicated meta data architect. As good as the card catalog is, a library still needs a librarian. This is the role that the architect must fill.

What is Meta Data

By definition meta data is "data about data."

To understand meta data's vital role in the data warehouse, consider the purpose of a card catalog in a library. The card catalog identifies what publications are in the library and where they are physically located. It can be searched by subject area, author or title. By showing the number of pages, publication date, and revision history of each book, the card catalog helps you determine which books will satisfy your needs. Without the central card catalog information system, finding books in the library would be a cumbersome and time-consuming chore. The card catalog is the bridge between the users of the library and the publications contained in it. Meta data is the bridge between the users of the warehouse and the data contained in it. Most meta data already exists in the organization in various forms such as spreadsheets, CASE tool data models, word processor documents, warehouse queries and reports, and source data acquisition and transformations.

In order for meta data to be used effectively, it needs to be stored in an Information Directory. Meta data must have four attributes:

1. **Integrated** business (logical), technical (physical) and operational meta data for all subject areas.

2. **Historical** meta data representing the changes in the warehouse environment.

3. **Customizable** meta data to address the varying needs of both business and technical users.

4. **Iterative** development and maintenance of the meta data.

Meta data can be classified in two ways:

A. **Static** meta data either doesn't change or does so only in very rare and special occasions. Examples of static meta data would be the logical warehouse data model, business rules and definitions, and historical meta data.

B. **Dynamic** meta data changes on a periodic or frequent basis. Examples of dynamic meta data would be the operational meta data concerning the load of warehouse tables such as number of rows added and last refresh date, and usage meta data such as access of the warehouse tables.

There is no right or wrong answer about what meta data is in a particular organization. Meta data captured by one organization may not be important (or applicable) to another organization. Indeed, meta data needs across an organization will differ. To better understand which meta data should be captured in the development process, it is best to look at why meta data is needed.

Why Meta Data is Needed

Meta data fulfills the role of the card catalog in a data warehouse. By defining the contents of a data warehouse, it helps you locate relevant information for analysis. By managing the structure of the data over a broad spectrum of time, it provides context for interpreting the meaning of the information.

By explaining the meaning of the data, meta data increases the:

- **Efficiency** of data analysis to answer business questions.

- **Productivity** in designing, building, maintaining and rolling out the warehouse.

- **Integrity** of data acquisition, transformation and analysis.

Each subject area (or iteration) in the warehouse environment is developed to solve a specific business need. As more and more subject areas are developed, the importance of a meta data initiative becomes apparent.

The Importance of a Meta Data Initiative

A meta data initiative is an organization's guide for determining what meta data is, and how will it be managed on an ongoing basis. The initiative should address the following:

What are the goals for meta data in the organization?

What meta data is required to meet the goals?

What are the sources of the meta data?

How will the meta data be maintained, and who will maintain it?

What are the meta data standards in the organization?

How will meta data be accessed/viewed?

What meta data tool(s) will be used?

A meta data initiative thus defines the who, what, when, where, how and why of the meta data needs of an organization. Meta data questions initially will be raised by the meta data architect on the data warehouse team. These include: what meta data is to be captured; how and where will it be maintained; who needs to view the meta data and how they will view it; what warehouse reports and queries exist; who are the data stewards; and what are the business definitions of the business rules, transformations, and warehouse entities and attributes (warehouse tables and columns). A wider audience than the data warehouse team must be sought by the architect to answer these questions. This is a good indicator that an initiative is needed for the current and subsequent iterations of the warehouse.

How to Develop a Meta Data Initiative

The architect can start a meta data initiative using the business questions outlined in the iteration scope document. Once these have been reviewed, then the source of the meta data needed to answer these questions can be determined. For example: What source meta data is required to perform impact analysis? A meta data initiative should encompass a:

- **Strategic** definition of an organization's meta data needs, and

  an implementation plan for the

- **Tactical** meta data requirements for each iteration.

Similar to the warehouse, it is impossible to satisfy everyone's needs for meta data in the first iteration. By taking an tactical approach to building the meta data initiative, many difficult questions are answered. It is easiest to get started by defining the use cases that the tactical implementation is trying to solve. For example: Who is the target audience for the meta data, what do they need to see, and what delivery mechanism will be used.

Meta Data Use Cases

Impact Analysis

One of the most common uses of meta data is to perform impact analysis. In this case, the technical user needs to determine the impact on the entire warehouse environment when a change occurs to the legacy or operational source. Changes may be needed in the data acquisition, transformation and /or summarization process.

The starting point is a search engine that will allow searching for all uses of the source data. Once this has been determined, the user will be able to track the data through the transformation process that resulted in the atomic (detail) and summarization tables. Special consideration needs to be taken for "black boxes," where a transformation is performed and the meta data is not automatically captured or is incomplete. It is best to plan for the "black box" scenario when designing and implementing the meta data. Adequate description/comments allow the user to continue performing impact analysis through the "black box."

For example: It has been determined that the source field CUST-LAST-PURCH in the VSAM Customer source system is not being maintained correctly. A decision has been made to either devote the resources to properly maintain the VSAM Customer system, or to choose the CUST_LAST_PURCHASE column from the DB2 Customer Information system. The first step is to use the search engine to find all instances where the source field CUST-LAST-PURCH was used in data acquisition. Once data acquisition has been determined, then specific analysis can be performed on the various transformations that might have occurred (record selection, trigger selection, business rules, DB lookups, etc.). This will allow the technical user to follow the data forward into the warehouse, including summarizations. The technical user will also be able to perform the analysis required to determine the impact of changing the source from a flat file source (VSAM) to a relational source (DB2).

Source Data Analysis

Another common use of meta data is to perform source data analysis. In this case, the business analyst is trying to determine the legacy or operational source for a piece of data. The user will be concerned with a warehouse table and/or column. He or she will need to understand how the column(s) were summarized if this is a summary table, what transformations took place to create the data loaded into the column(s) in the atomic-level table, and what source data was used and how was it acquired.

For example: A business user needs to determine the source for the Customer Last Purchase Date (logical name) column in the warehouse. The user will first need to determine what the physical name of the column is, such as CUST_LAST_PURCH_DATE. Using the search engine or standard drill-down navigation, the user walks back through the transformations (record selection, trigger selection, business rules, DB lookups, etc.) resulting in the ultimate source data. Once the source data has been determined, the user understands which source system was used and what business assumptions were made in data acquisition, transformation and summarization process.

Summary Table Analysis

In this case, the user may be either a technical user who is determining which tables should be summarized, and/or a business analyst who is trying to determine if he/she should be querying summary data or atomic-level data.

The technical user is concerned with the type of analysis being performed on the atomic-level data, and whether there should be summary tables. The business user will be looking at the summary table meta data to determine which atomic-level data was summarized, or will look at the atomic-level data to determine if there are any summary tables that will answer the required summary query.

Example 1: A technical user needs to decide if a summary table should be built for the PRODUCT table. This table includes the column PROD_LINE (physical name) and, depending on the queries performed, general performance improvements may be seen by providing a summary table by product line. The first step is to review the query descriptions stored in the meta data. The search engine could be used to find all queries containing the column PROD_LINE. A determination can be made that if a sufficient number of queries are summarized across product lines, then a summary table might improve productivity.

Example 2: The business user of a data mart needs to determine what is the atomic-level of data for the column Product Line (logical name). Using the Search engine or simple meta data drill down, the user will determine the base atomic table and the summarizations that took place. The user can view the meta data describing the queries and reports that already exist at the atomic-level for the column/table before creating a new one.

Historical Data Analysis

In this case, a business analyst may need to determine how the data has changed over time and when those changes occurred. This analysis would reveal what the meta data (and thus the data) looked like at a certain point in time compared to how it looks today. It is important that the historical analysis allow for either simple changes in the data, and versions of the data which would indicate a significant business event such as a new iteration, change of business process or acquisition/divestiture of subsidiary.

For example: A business user may need to determine why the results of a query are different than anticipated, such as regional sales totals on the Quarterly Regional Sales query. First the user will need to see the meta data description of the query. Second, using simple drill down, the user needs to be able to determine what warehouse column(s)/table(s) are being used in this query. It would also be helpful to know which business data steward is associated with the regional sales subject area, and the technical steward associated with the warehouse tables within the regional sales subject area. The user should be able to determine if the warehouse table(s)/column(s) being used have been versioned and when. The user then changes views to the prior version to determine how the table(s)/column(s) changed, which will explain why the query results are different than expected.

Who is Responsible

In this case the user may be a technical user attempting to determine who the lead business analyst is for a business subject area, or a business user who must determine who the lead warehouse developer is for a particular warehouse table. The technical user may have questions about the business goals of a particular transformation that the lead business analyst would understand. The business user may have questions about why particular source was or wasn't used to acquire the data, or why a transformation was (or wasn't) performed and how.

For example: In the prior Historical Data Analysis example, what if the tables have not changed or the change does not explain the different results? The business user will need to contact the warehouse developer or technical steward who is familiar with the table(s) in question. By contacting the steward, the business user has a contact who can quickly review the technical changes in the data acquisition and transformation of the atomic and/or summary tables used by the Quarterly Regional Sales query. Perhaps the regions have been realigned so that the data acquisition business rule includes New York in the Northeast region, where it was part of the Mid-Atlantic region in the prior quarters. This represents a change in the data that can be determined by looking at the business rule. This is an example of the three-tiered architecture for meta data access, where the business user is tier three and the technical steward is tier two. The three-tiered architecture is explained later in this document.

By no means is this a complete list of meta data use cases in the warehouse environment. The lines of when and how meta data is used will blur in most environments. Take for example a site that has implemented multiple data marts without a central meta data Information Directory. It will be next to impossible to understand what warehouse tables exist, how the source data was acquired and transformed, what queries and reports exist, and who the data steward is for each piece of data. Meta data must be stored in a central Information Directory that will answer the requirements of the various use cases encountered in an organization.

Requirements of a Central Meta Data Information Directory

There are five categories of requirements: Historical, Iterative, Integrated, Customizable and Open.

Historical

An Information Directory must be able to represent the changes in the data warehouse over time. The following requirements are essential for an Information Directory to maintain a historical perspective of the meta data:

- Version control bound to the data warehouse version
- Tracking of non-version changes in meta data
- Effective dates (from and to dates)

Iterative

An Information Directory that supports iterative development is one that grows as the data warehouse initiative grows. The following requirements are essential for iterative support:

- Supports rapid business subject development
- Supports mart development and management
- Grows with the data in the warehouse
  1. Levels of summary
  2. Data redundancy
  3. Data versions

Integrated

An integrated Information Directory stores meaningful meta data. The following requirements are critical for an integrated Information Directory:

- Stores business, technical and operational meta data
- Store meta data relationships to answer questions for many types of users

Customizable

An customizable Information Directory supports changes in the meta data requirements. The following requirements are important for customization:

- Ability to ceate views to meet many user needs
- A flexible information model that allows new meta data objects/relationships to be added to the existing model, and can be extended to support the import of existing meta data constructs from external sources
- Ability to handle changing warehouse technology

Open

An open Information Directory shares all meta data externally and makes it accessible to all users. The following requirements are important for the Information Directory to be open:

- Supports exchange via industry-standard interfaces
- Shares model-level information with a wide variety of tools

Practical Steps to Follow

While this is not a complete list, the following are practical steps that can help the meta data architect develop and implement a meta data initiative. As was previously stated, most meta data already exists in the organization in the form of spreadsheets, CASE tool data models, source transformations, MS Word documents, etc. Every implementation of meta data is as unique as it is diverse. By remaining flexible, the architect will find that the process will become easier and more effective over time.

1. **Review the iteration scope document.** The scope document contains the goals and processes for implementing the iteration. This is the meta data architect's success criteria. What must be understood are what business questions the implemented subject area is answering.

2. **Determine who is involved in the iteration.** These are the people who can help the architect understand what meta data will be required to answer the business questions identified in the prior step. They include the iteration developers, the data modeler and the business analysts.

3. **Educate the people involved.** Meta data is only as good as its source. By educating others on the importance of the meta data, the source will be more complete and robust. This will make integration and management an easier process.

4. **Identify the who, what, when, where, how and why.** Some of these questions are answered by the meta data initiative document, so this is a good starting point.

   Other questions will arise during (or even after) the iteration. Examples of these are:

   - Who maintains the source meta data, who needs to see the meta data, and who is responsible for the data.
   - What are the meta data standards, what are the sources of meta data, what meta data management tool(s) will be used, what are the change procedures of both the data and the meta data, what history will be kept, what summarization levels are needed, what are the archive procedures, what collection strategies will be used to gather the meta data, and what meta data delivery tool(s) will be used.
   - When will the data be updated, when does meta data change to reflect

changes in the data, and when do we make meta data available to the users.

- Where are the sources of meta data, where are the warehouse tables (detail and summary) physically located, and where should the meta data physically reside.

- How will the meta data be sourced, how will it be maintained, how will it be integrated, and how will meta data be delivered to the desktop of the various users.

- Why each of the tools are selected, why does data change in the organization, and why will standards be needed.

5. **Define what meta data standards will be needed.** Naming, updating and versioning standards are needed before work begins in acquiring and transforming the data into the warehouse. Existing standards documents can be leveraged to help in defining the meta data standards.

6. **Determine what meta data tool(s) will be used.** This process is both driven by and supports meta data development, integration, management, rollout and delivery. It is likely that more than one tool will be required. Choose the tools that best support the key qualities meta data should possess (Integrated, Historical, Customizable and Iterative) and why it is needed (Efficiency, Productivity and Integrity).

7. **Identify how meta data will be accessed and viewed by the users.** Remember that there are many users of meta data. Technical users need to see the source data acquisition and transformations, business analysts need to see more descriptive meta data in business terms, and the architect needs to see everything in order to manage it. This is the start to customizing the meta data. The architect will also need to determine how to deliver the meta data. In most organizations, a three-tiered delivery approach works best:

- Tier 1 is the meta data architect. The architect has full read/write capability to all meta data. This includes the responsibility of building, maintaining and implementing the meta data Information Directory.

- Tier 2 is selected business analysts and warehouse developers who need read capability of a customized view of the meta data. This tier is typically limited to those members of the iteration team (technical and business analysts) responsible for the subject area implemented. These users can be classified as "super users" or "technical users" and will have a variety of tools on their desktops, including a dedicated meta data navigation tool.

- Tier 3 is the vast majority of users, requiring read-only access to a highly customized (limited) view of the meta data. They typically have only one desktop tool, such as spreadsheets, decision support systems, multi-dimensional tools, executive information systems and/or Web navigation tools.

The advantage to a three-tiered approach is that it allows the second tier to be the point of support for the third tier. The architect then only needs to provide support to the smaller second tier.

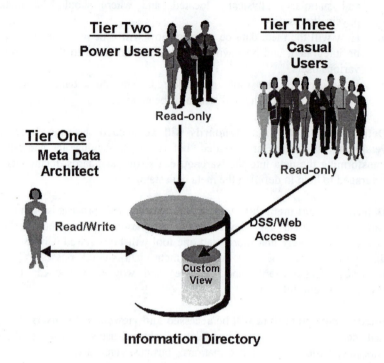

Information Directory

8. **Create a feedback loop.** Working with the users of meta data will help ensure its effectiveness. Develop the first iteration of the meta data, and review it with the appropriate tier two users. Expect and encourage their feedback, and most importantly, implement it. As much as possible, have the tier two users make the changes to the meta data source. This reduces the amount of work for the architect, as well as allows the users to take ownership of the meta data. Implementing standards is very important here.

Conclusion

The importance of a meta data initiative is clear. By planning for the implementation of the meta data and the data together, there is a much greater success rate in the data warehouse iteration.

About the Author

Cass Squire

Currently the Director of Professional Services for Prism Solutions Asia operations, Mr. Squire has assisted over fifty companies in the design, development, and implementation of their data warehouses. Those companies encompass virtually all industries in areas such as marketing and sales, customer, product profitability, risk analysis, logistics, and purchasing.

With twenty years of experience in both the public and private sectors (with special emphasis in information systems architecture and data warehousing), Mr. Squire is an expert in the issues surrounding requirements analysis, networking, security, database and applications systems design, user training, implementation, and maintenance. He began using Information Engineering techniques for data-oriented design of large scale systems in 1981. His first data warehouse was built in 1985 based on Bill Inmon's architecture concepts.

His industrial experience includes banking, transportation, logistics, public utilities, and government (defense and civilian agencies).

Email: csquire@prismsolutions.com

Building a Data Warehouse:
Its Methodology and Returns on Investment

Danny Lau, SAS Institute Ltd., Hong Kong

Abstract

The successful implementation of a data warehouse can be an extremely complex process, requiring significant planning, patience, and persistence. This paper addresses many of the challenges and issues that were encountered during the development of data warehouses. It explores the definition and purpose of data warehouses, the returns of investment, and presents my company's Data Warehouse Model. Finally it introduces the Rapid Data Warehouse Methodology.

What is Data Warehouse?

Data Warehouse vs. Transactional System

Online Transaction Processing Systems (OLTP) have the primary role of capturing business transactions, and the data relevant to them. The OLTP system is primarily concerned with adding, updating, and deleting data. This data represents "actual events", and is at a very atomic level. OLTP systems are typically implemented with hierarchical or relational database management systems, and are accessed using structured query language (SQL). They are typically single platform (usually mainframe) based, and managed by a central corporate information systems entity. In summary, their primary function can be thought of as getting transaction data into the information system quickly and accurately for clerical usage.

Since these systems must support huge volumes of adds, updates, and deletes (thousands per second in many systems – think about an airlines reservation system), they are very performance oriented. This performance orientation often involves utilizing a database schema that is entity-relationship based, and highly normalized. This type of schema provides a framework to support explicit data relationships, enforce referential integrity, and limit redundancy, to increase data access speed for single record operations.

The purpose of the data warehouse is to provide information for managerial decision making that is distinct from, and does not interfere with the performance requirements of the OLTP systems. This is usually done by re-engineering OLTP system data around business subjects and making it easily available to the managerial community in a separate repository. This subject-based modeling allows a more logical view of the data from a business users perspective.

Before being loaded into the data warehouse, data must go through a transformation or integration process. In brief, integration ensures data fields are populated, data is correct, not out of range, and not duplicated. Data warehouse data are not updated with the frequency of transaction data, therefore they are non-volatile (not updated in real time). The data warehouse typically gets updated on a weekly, monthly, or bimonthly batch update cycle from the OLTP system. Since the data are non-volatile, the data warehouse does not need to employ the overhead aspects of the traditional RDBMS, such as locking, referential integrity checks, transaction logging, checkpoint/rollback, and so on.

In contrast to the OLTP system's "actual events", the data warehouse organizes data into dimensional slices of time to produce quantitative results of events at some time interval. In essence, the purpose of the data warehouse is to get data out of the system, and turns it into information. This analysis-driven, time variant data are often pre-summarized into levels usable for decision support, negating the need to summarize atomic level data in query operations.

Data Warehousing and OLAP

Online Analytical Processing (OLAP) involves using a multidimensional database model, and appropriate access and analysis tools to quickly pull data from the warehouse, and turn it into meaningful information. OLAP's goal is to provide Fast Analysis of Multidimensional Information.

There are currently two primary methods for implementing OLAP from a model/product perspective. The first method is composed of building subject-based models using a traditional relational database product. This approach is termed ROLAP, or Relational OLAP. The second method uses a new type of multidimensional database or "cube", and is termed MOLAP for Multidimensional OLAP.

ROLAP and The Star Schema

The Star schema is often employed when the ROLAP approach is taken. Relational tables are used to model the subject of interest. The schema utilizes implicit modeling of relationships instead of the explicit models of the entity-relation schema. It is currently one of the most popular subject-based models, involving a "fact" table that holds numeric information about a particular subject. Because it holds large volumes of numeric factual data about the subject, the fact table is typically the largest table in a subject-based schema. This "fact" table is surrounded by accompanying "dimension" tables which describe attributes of the "facts".

Dimension tables are typically much smaller since they provide descriptive data. In order to process a query against a subject-based schema, the keys of the surrounding dimension tables required to fulfill the query, are acquired and driven against the fact table. While introducing some increased data redundancy, the Star schema provides greater flexibility and simplicity in query generation. This is possible because the data redundancy allows the Star schema to utilize fewer tables to model a subject, requiring fewer joins to be made.

Another popular subject-based schema is the Snowflake schema. The Snowflake schema, with its variations, could remove data redundancy in the Star schema by de-normalizing the tables. This is done to reduce storage requirements, but at a performance cost.

MOLAP and the MDDB

The multidimensional database (MDDB) is used to represent the subject-based organization of the data warehouse when the Multidimensional OLAP or MOLAP approach is taken. The MDDB is a database structure that stores data into a multidimensional format like a "cube". This "cube" allows data to be stored in an array-like fashion. It becomes visually obvious that now one can "slice" through the cube to quickly find facts. The physical structure and indexing systems of cubes are designed to facilitate this "slicing and dicing" approach to data access.

Data and Information Marts

Both subject-based tables (ROLAP), and the MDDB (MOLAP), are also used to create "Data Marts". A Data Mart is a body of decision support data (DSS) for a department that has an architectural foundation of a data warehouse. The primary difference is that the data mart is usually at a more refined level (aggregated, summarized, or subset). Data Marts can reduce the processing load on a data warehouse, and they provide faster query response. They can be thought of as a departmental, "mini" data warehouse.

Some departmental entities also wish to store information in a finished output format (for example reports, graphs, programs, and so on). Some storage structures are built to specifically store this output (or the output from an application) in a viewable format. These structures have been dubbed "Information Marts". They are useful for storing finished information of standard reports, graphs, multimedia, and applications that are widely used.

Why Build A Data Warehouse?

Quantitative Business Benefits

In an independent detailed study of 62 organizations with data warehouse implementations, International Data Corporation (IDC) found that a staggering average three-year return on investment of 401% was realized by organizations building data warehouses. Over 90% of the organizations reported a three-year return on investment in excess of 40%, half reported returns of greater than 160%, and one quarter showed returns greater than 600%. These figures varied widely by type of business, but the overwhelming evidence was carefully weighed by benefit categories. This clearly spells out quantitative benefits to data warehousing!

Qualitative Business Benefits

In addition to the quantitative benefits, there are several qualitative benefits that are harder to measure, but no less dramatic. The first of these is a large one – providing standardized, clean, value-added data to create information from disparate sources.

Another benefit includes better managing the customer relationship or customer opportunity. Information about customers is being used in increasing ways to directly market to individuals. This information is being successfully used to acquire and retain customers, and gain or increase their usage of products and services. In addition, the data warehouse is making data available across corporate organizations for better understanding and usage between often non-integrated functions, such as marketing and sales. In companies where there are critical windows of time to make decisions, data warehouses provide the needed information quickly. Finally, most managers are relatively surprised with knowledge gained from the data warehouse, hidden trends discovered, and previous false assumptions exposed. This surprise is especially felt when control of processes and performance is gained through measurement. That measurement is only possible by turning raw data into useful information.

Turning Data into Information

In order to compete in the business world, fast & accurate decision making is essential. The data warehouse provides access to corporate and organizational data to support cost-effective decision-making. It provides the immediate, on-demand, high-performance response that quick decision-making requires, with clean, consistent data. The difficult process of cleansing and verifying data can also used to justify efforts to clean data in upstream transactional systems, to save doing it downstream where it is more costly, and provide cleaner transactional systems. This provides more and higher quality data for competitive business benefit.

A major strength of data warehouses is that they support ad-hoc queries, or unplanned explorations of data. A data warehouse gives business users the freedom and ability to analyze data in different ways, rather than being constrained by a limited set of predefined reports. With its architectural advantages and integration of capable exploitation tools, the data in the data warehouse can be separated and combined by means of every possible measure in the business.

The SAS Data Warehouse Model

A comprehensive data warehouse solution provider should provide a data warehouse model that addresses the entire scope of warehouse management, organization, and exploitation. It also supports by a broad array of products needed for successful warehouse implementation.

Warehouse Management

The warehouse Management process involves creation and administration of a data warehouse. The Management process consists of several sub-processes supported by and implemented with the tools and products available through the solution provider. These sub-processes include data extraction, data transformation, data loading, job scheduling, and metadata management. The data extraction process should support Multiple Engine Architecture with SQL Pass-Through facility for DBMS legacy transactional systems, and other data repository.

Data transformation is supported through the validation, scrubbing, integration, structuring, denormalization, reduction, and date/time variance processes on the data. The data loader permits full transfer or changed data-only transfer from legacy systems to the data warehouse. User-written processes are also supported. The job scheduler utilizes built-in tools or interfaces to third party products.

To provide access to the data warehouse, it is necessary to maintain some form of data which describes the data warehouse. This data about the data is called Metadata. There are two basic views of metadata. The business metadata and Technical metadata. Business metadata is of more interest to end users of the data warehouse - data definitions, attribute and domain values, data timeliness, data coverage, business rules, data relationships, and so on. Technical metadata is used by a data warehouse administrator to know when data was last refreshed, how it was transformed, and other details important for managing the data warehouse. Metadata resides at all levels within the data warehouse. Metadata is the "glue" which holds all the pieces together in warehouse environment. The Metadata Manager also permits metadata to be built from its own or external dictionaries.

Warehouse Organization

At the heart of the data warehouse model is the Warehouse Organization. It utilizes its own database engine, repository, and the accompanying metadata system. This system should be ODBC compliant, and supports file creation, management, population, backup, data inventory services, query processing, and update processing. It also supports a relational data model to provide abstracting of data elements independent of application logic. The Management and Organization portions of the model are ideally under a single interactive management interface acting as a warehouse administrator. The warehouse administrator interface provides data warehouse support staff with a consolidated front-end interface from which to manage, schedule, and maintain the extracting, cleansing, and loading programs for the data warehouse. It also provides metadata management facilities, for expanded metadata beyond what is found in the traditional file definition or data dictionary.

The solution software should support distribution of application logic across diverse hardware platforms:

- Compute server functionality enables the most efficient utilization of distributed computing resources - including hardware, software, and data - to execute an application.

- Remote data services enable access to data stored in a remote environment, the data being transferred to the processing machine. Remote compute services can be exploited to distribute the data management services themselves in a client/server environment, enabling optimal use of hardware resources across the organization's enterprise-wide systems.

Warehouse Exploitation

The Warehouse Exploitation portion of the data warehouse model includes an array of extremely powerful and flexible reporting, analysis, and statistical tools. These tools include point and click interfaces to mine, visualize, and present data. They also include OLAP tools for interactive multidimensional analysis, interactive query tools, and client/server development tools for custom interfaces. Geographic information system capabilities are provided, and it also supports Web access to data, reports, and graphics. In addition, the Warehouse Exploitation toolset includes excellent statistical modules for analysis and modeling.

The SAS Rapid Data Warehouse Methodology

A rapid data warehouse methodology has been developed to ensure a disciplined, iterative, approach in the management and implementation of data warehousing projects. This methodology consists of five distinct phases, designed to enable successful business and technical implementation of the data warehouse. These five phases are the Assessment, Requirements, Implementation, Training, and Review phases.

Assessment Phase

This phase is to determine whether a realistic need or opportunity to develop and implement a successful data warehouse exists. It is composed of two primary stages. The first stage is a Project Definition stage, which defines key subjects or business areas that could benefit from a data warehouse. In this phase several critical success factors are evaluated. These include:

- Choosing the highest corporate sponsor for the project
- Choosing a high-level interdepartmental team from business and IT to carry out the project
- Gaining resources commitment for the project
- Determining project ownership (who is ultimately responsible & will direct)
- Determining evaluation criteria for the project
- Ensuring unity between team members
- Determining the first project module to implement and grow from.

In the first stage the core members work with the business unit members to define the data warehouse subject(s) to be implemented, provide the evaluation criteria for success, and the business unit resources needed for the project. The second stage of the Assessment Phase involves performing an initial assessment of the IT infrastructure, to validate the ability of the computing environment to accommodate the demands and requirements of the data warehouse. This is conducted by the core members in concert with the IT personnel. The outcome of the Assessment Phase is a formal document recommending whether or not to proceed with the project.

Requirement Phase

Once the Assessment Phase is completed and a decision is made to build a data warehouse, the Requirements Phase begins. In the Requirements Phase, the sources of data for input to the warehouse are identified. A logical model of the data warehouse designed, the data transformation process and information delivery needs are documented, a data refresh strategy is built, gaps between needs and IT constraints are identified, and a project schedule is completed. This is in two stages. The first stage is a Requirements Gathering stage where information is collected about a business unit's information needs through in-depth interviews with the business unit members. The components of the IT environment that currently services that business unit are then examined through interviews with the IT members. The second stage is a Reconciliation stage where a gap analysis is performed between business unit requirements and IT infrastructure capabilities. The outcome of the Requirement Phase is a comprehensive Requirement Definition Document containing the logical and physical models, gap analysis, infrastructure diagram from OLTP extraction through warehouse data usage, transformation requirements, warehouse refresh strategy, scheduling tools used, and warehouse construction timeline.

Implementation Phase

Once the Requirement has been set, a physical model is built to implement the logical model that has been designed. This is done in three stages that match the data warehouse model addressed above. The first stage is the Management stage, where transactional data are extracted, and transformed into the data that will load the warehouse. The transformation process is composed of several sub-processes: validation, scrubbing, and integration. In the validation process, invalid, missing, out-of-range, and duplicated data are identified. The scrubbing process corrects that data problems identified in the validation process by re-coding or removal. The integration process brings data variables to consistent meanings, values, and measurements. The scheduling interfaces are written, and all relevant metadata captured.

The second stage is the Organization stage. In this stage that data are actually loaded into the warehouse, the data structures are indexed, and views to them are created. Metadata is captured and loaded.

The last Implementation Phase is the Exploitation stage, in which the graphical user interfaces are developed for the analyses, reports, graphs, and so on, that will be used for the data warehouse. At the conclusion of the Implementation Phase the warehouse and its access mechanisms are built and ready for personnel to be trained in its use.

Training Phase

The Training Phase follows implementation, and consists of two major activities. The first is to create a high-level training document covering the data warehouse and the applications used to exploit it. The second activity is to provide training to warehouse users and the warehouse administrator (if not already part of the project team).

Review Phase

Once the Training Phase is complete and the system has been turned over to the end-users for production operation, an evaluation of the project's success or failure is necessary to quantify its impact on the organization. These findings should be documented for future reference in expanding or building other data warehouses.

Summary

Successful data warehouse implementation requires appropriate knowledge of data warehousing concepts, project management, modeling, methodologies, and the appropriate solution software usage. The ideal solution provider should has developed a comprehensive approach to successfully implement effective data warehouse for its clients. This approach involves the use of the data warehouse model, which includes the abilities of the data warehouse software, and utilizes the rapid data warehouse methodology. The rapid data warehouse methodology provides a structured, iterative approach for successfully managing and implementing data warehouse projects. Usage of this disciplined methodology will help practitioners to achieve data warehousing success.

Semantic Layer for Data Warehousing

Semantic Layers Enable Users to Make Business Decision based on their Databases while Shielding the Underlying Database Complexity from the Users

Yuen Wai Shing, Senior Consultant, Business Objects Greater China

Abstract

In every mature RDBMS and Client/Server market in the world like Hong Kong, users are simply not satisfied with the data available from their operational IT systems. In order to gain or retain their competitive edge at forefront of their furiously changing market, they are desperately demanding for a manageable way to freely access the data stored in their corporate databases so that they can analyze their business and make timely and smart business decision.

However, it is a general rule that the bigger the database, the more difficult it is to analyze and understand data. It is crucial for a decision support system to have a rich, meaningful and intuitive semantic layer that provides end-users a business representation of data and allows them to easily query and analysis data using their everyday business vocabulary.

The notion of a business representation was introduced in 1990 with the purpose to insulate users from the technical complexity of database schemas and SQL syntax. The semantic Layer maps database tables and columns to objects grouped into classes. It offers many features that address the needs of both the end-users and designers: Ease of Use, Ease of maintenance, Correctness, Performance, Openness, Security Control, etc.

In this paper, we will see how the "Semantic Layer" actually works and what is the benefit of using a semantic layer on the top of a data warehouse. In addition, we will study what "Semantic Layer" technology is available in the market and what are the pros and cons of these approaches.

1.   Introduction

In every mature RDBMS and Client/Server market in the world like Hong Kong, users are simply not satisfied with the data available from their operational IT systems. In order to gain or retain their competitive edge at forefront of their furiously changing market, they are desperately demanding for a manageable way to freely access the data stored in their corporate databases so that they can analyze their business and make timely and smart business decision. This is the primary reason to implement a data warehouse in an organization.

However, it is a general rule that the bigger the database, the more difficult it is to analyze and understand data. It is crucial for a decision support system to have a rich, meaningful and intuitive semantic layer that provides end-users a business representation of data and allows them to easily query and analysis data using their everyday business vocabulary. It shields the end user from the technical complexity of the database technologies.

2.   Overview Of The Semantic Layer

The necessary features of the semantic layer includes - Ease of Use, Ease of maintenance, Correctness, Performance, Security and Resource Control.

2.1.   Ease of use

- Objects (business terms) are grouped into meaningful classes or sub-classes so that users can locate objects easily
- Support dimension hierarchy (e.g. country, then region, then city, and so on) to guide end-user to perform data drilling analysis
- Support predefined conditions to help users to build query easily without understanding the underlying database data values

2.2.   Ease of maintenance

- Support inheritance of universe definition. Easy to build universes from existing semantic layers and easy to propagate the changes in base semantic layers to the derived semantic layers.
- Provides check-in and check-out features to facilitate workgroup development

2.3.   Correctness

- Automatically detect loops (where two tables are linked by more than one path) in database schema and create contexts and aliases to resolve loops to guarantee correct query results.
- Support generation of multiple SELECT statements in a single query to avoid the duplicated data or missing data caused by chasm trap.

2.4.   Performance

- Support aggregate aware objects that are smart enough to make use of the aggregate tables built by database designer.
- Support short-cut joins to reduce the time of joining by skipping some unnecessary joining paths.

2.5.   Resources and Security Control

- Allow setting parameters in the semantic layer definition to control on system resources consumed by end-user queries. Resources control parameters specify

such limits as number of rows to be returned from the database, execution time of queries and maximum size of long text fields
- Restrict the usage of objects to prevent users from creating inefficient queries
- Support personalizing universes by setting object restrictions and row restrictions for a particular group or user

3.   Ease Of Use

3.1.   The Structure of The Semantic Layer

A semantic layer usually maps the data stored in data warehouse to "objects" with meaningful names. And then the end user can select the objects in the semantic layer to perform query and analysis in their familiar business terms. There are two basic types of objects: relatively simple labels, such as "customer" or "product," and the key business indicators that you use to measure the performance of your organization such as "sales revenue," and "average quantity." Related objects are grouped into logical "classes" in order to help end user to locate the objects within the semantic layer easily when they perform query and analysis.

Figure 1.1 shows a typical example of semantic layer built with a Decision Support System. This semantic layer is used by the end user to perform query and analysis on the performance of a resort chain. There are two basic types of objects: the cubes are the dimension objects which are usually a column or combination of columns that represents a logical piece of information to the end user. The circles are the measure objects which convey numeric information to measure the performance of your organization. Related objects are grouped into logical classes. For example, all the objects related to resort (the country of the resort, the resort name, service lines within a resort and the services provided by the resort) are grouped under the "Resort" class. Whenever the end user think of a piece of information related to the resort, they just open the "Resort" class and they can locate the object easily. It is not necessary, and usually not recommended, to group the objects according to database structure. The objects should be grouped according to the views of the end user. For example, the country of the resort (the "Country" Object) and the name of

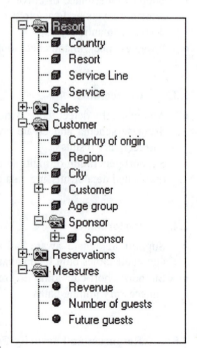

Figure 1. 1

the (the "Resort" Object) may come from different database tables. But they are grouped into the same "Resort" Class because the end user thinks they are related. It is very important for the Information Technology Department to conduct a detailed analysis on the end user's view on the data before the semantic layer is designed. Even though the IT Department may have a strong understanding on the database structure, they may not be able to come up with a meaningful semantic layer until the end user are consulted.

Because the semantic layer is used by the end user to perform detailed analysis on the data in the data warehouse, the end user must have a very clear understanding and a complete grasp on all the objects within the semantic layer. And so the number of objects within a semantic layer is usually not more than 100. If there are several hundred or even several thousand of objects within a semantic layer, the end user just cannot manage the semantic layer and cannot perform intelligent analysis on the data in the data warehouse.

3.2.   Support Dimension Hierarchy to Aid Data Drilling

The primary reason of implementing a data warehouse is to build a company-wide view of information for end-users to perform reporting and data analysis effectively. The two most common analysis methods provided by Decision Support Tools are "slice and dice" and "data drilling." "Slice and dice" means cutting (or grouping) the measures (e.g. sales revenue) by some dimensions (e.g. fiscal year, product categories, customer profiles, etc.) to identify trends and exceptions by viewing business information from different perspectives and at varying levels of detail. "Data drilling" means exploring a different level of information. For example, if you are looking at sales performance by countries, you can perform a "drill down" to explore the sales performance by city within a selected country. Or if you are looking at the sales performance of a particular quarter, you can perform a "drill up" operation to move to a higher level in the data hierarchy in order to get a more global view of the sales performance in the whole fiscal year. Data hierarchies is essential to enable this type of data drilling analysis. Hierarchies are simply an ordered set of dimension Objects; Objects with the highest level of detail are placed at the top of the list. For example, a Hierarchy based on geography could include the dimension Objects "Country", then "Region", then "State", and then "City". It can be easy to get "lost" when end users are drilling within a large data warehouse. By having data hierarchies, Decision Support Tools can have the intelligence to guide the end user through the whole process of data drilling. The Decision Support Tools can inform the end user what will be the next level of dimension for drilling up and drilling down.

3.3.   Support Predefined Conditions

In order to allow end users to build queries easily, it is essential to have predefined condition objects within the semantic layer so that users can use them to restrict the results of a query. Predefined condition objects are particularly useful if there are common, frequently used data selection criteria and the criteria are very tedious. For example, a predefined condition object may restrict only the sales transactions of a particular store with sales amount greater than a lower limit within a particular date range to be returned from data warehouse. End users simply select the pre-defined condition object from the semantic layer when they build a query. They are not required to understand the underlying technical details. Several condition objects can be combined together using the "And" or "Or" operators under different precedence specified by users.

4.   Ease Of Maintenance

4.1.   Inheritance of Semantic Layer Definition

It is natural to have different semantic layers for a data warehouse since different groups of users may have different views of the information stored in the data warehouse. And it is also common that these different semantic layers share some common components. For example, the semantic layers for the Account Department and the Marketing Department may both contain the objects about customer information. Where there are some changes in the database structure about the customer information within the data warehouse, all the semantic layers which access the customer information must be changed accordingly. This poses a big maintenance issue. Using the concept of inheritance of semantic layer definition, we can reduce the maintenance effort significantly.

The designer of the semantic layer first puts the common components such as classes, objects, pre-defined conditions into a "Base Semantic Layer". And then new semantic layers (called the "Derived Semantic Layer") can be created by inheriting the components from the Base Semantic Layer. We can put additional classes and objects into the Derived Semantic Layer according to the needs of different users. We can even inherit the components for a Derived Semantic Layers from more than one Base Semantic Layer. Whenever there are any changes to the database structure of the data warehouse or the layout of the semantic layers, we only have to change the corresponding Base Semantic Layer and the changes will be propagated to the Derived Semantic Layers. Maintenance effort for semantic layer is much reduced.

4.2.   Checkin/Checkout Mechanism for Group Development

There must be some lock features for the semantic layers to ensure only one designer can update or modify a semantic layer such that no collisions occur. When a designer wants to modify a semantic layer, there must be some mechanism to lock the semantic layer so that no one else can modify it. End user may still be able to use the locked semantic layer to make queries. After the designer has finished the modification to the semantic layer, he has to unlock it and make it available to other designer.

5. Data Correctness

Data warehouse provides a company-wide view of information for end users to perform data analysis and make decisions based on the analysis results. And so it is very important to ensure that the data returned by a query are correct. However, because of complex database structure of the data warehouse, the semantic layer must have some mechanism, such as loop resolution and generating more than one SELECT statements for a single query, to adapt to the complex database structure in order to guarantee correctness of result.

5.1. Loop Resolution in Database Schema

The ideal database schema for data warehouses is Star Schema with one fact table joined with several dimension tables. But in reality, the database schema employed within a data warehouse may include normalized schemas, multi-star schemas, normalized schemas with aggregates, etc. Real-life databases often contain loops, that is there are more than one joining path to join two different tables. When several valid paths exist between tables, there are times the Decision Support Tools cannot determine which path to take to generate the result for a query. Look at the example in Figure 3.1. There are two joining paths between the CUSTOMER table and the PRODUCT table. Customers purchase products by inserting a sales order through the SALE joining path. Customers can also loan products by inserting a load record through the LOAD joining path. When an end user picks the customer name object and the product name object from the semantic layer and expects the decision support tool to return a list of products purchased by each customer, the decision support tool may wrongly pick the LOAN joining path and return a list of products borrowed by the customers. The end user who has got wrong result from the decision support tool may make wrong decision based on the wrong result. It is surely not the intention of building a data warehouse.

174

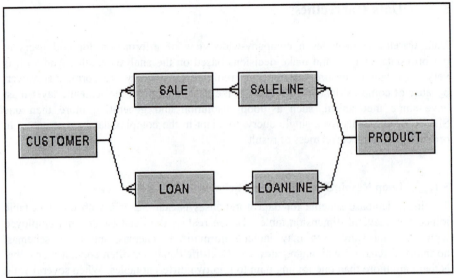

Figure 3. 1

In order to ensure data correctness for queries, the semantic layer must have some methods to resolve the loops in the database schema. The two most common ways of resolving loops in schema are "contexts" and "alias."

In the above example, two contexts may be created within the semantic layer to resolve the loops. The first context may be called the "SALE" context which only includes the joining paths from CUSTOMER table to PRODUCT table through the SALE and SALELINE tables, but excludes the path through the LOAN and LOANLINE tables. Then second context may be called the "LOAN" context which only includes the the joining paths from CUSTOMER table to PRODUCT table through the LOAN and LOANLINE tables, but excludes the path through the SALE and SALELINE tables. When an end user picks the customer name object and the product name object from the semantic layer to construct a query, the decision support tool will determine that there are more than one joining path between the two tables and will pop up the list of contexts for the end user to choose the joining path. And correct query results can be guaranteed.

Another method of resolving loop is to insert alias for some common look-up tables. In the example shown in Figure 3.2, COUNTRY table is a common lookup table for the customers and the products. A loop is formed in this normalized database schema.

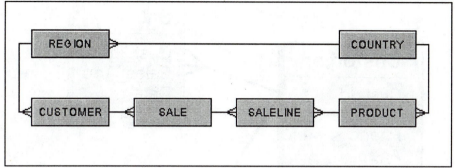

Figure 3. 2

In order to resolve the loop, an alias, CUSTOMER_COUNTRY Table, may be created in the semantic layer (as shown in Figure 3.3). The loop is broken after introducing the alias. The alias does not physically exist in the data warehouse. It still refers to the COUNTRY physically. But it helps to resolve the ambiguity of the SQL statement derived from the semantic layer.

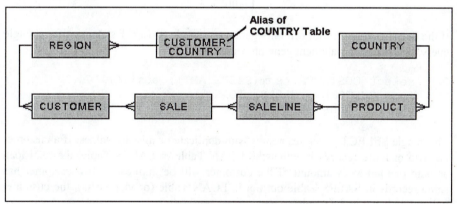

Figure 3. 3

5.2. Multiple SQL Generation for a Single Query

Another essential feature for decision support tool to ensure data correctness is the ability to generate more than one SELECT statement for a single query. Look at the example in Figure 3.4. There is a many-to-one-to-many relationship. A customer can have more than one sales order and more than one load record. CUSTOMER Table has a joining path to SALES Table and LOAN Table. But there is no direct relationship between SALES Table and LOAD Table. To generate a list of total sales amount and loan amount for every customer, end user may just select the "Customer Name" Object, "Sales Amount" Object and the "Loan Amount" Object from the semantic layer.

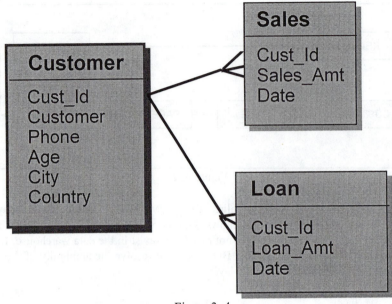

Figure 3. 4

If the decision support tool can only generate a single SELECT statement for a single query, the SELECT statement generate would be:

```
select CUSTOMER, sum(SALES_AMT), sum(LOAN_AMT)
from CUSTOMER, SALES, LOAN
where (joins on CUST_ID)
```

This single SELECT generates results with duplicate or missing values. If a customer has two or more records in either the LOAN Table or SALES Table, the total loan amount or total sales amount of the customer will be duplicated. If a customer has some records in SALES Table but not in LOAN Table (or vice versa), the customer will not be listed in the result.

To ensure correct query results, the decision support tool should be able to generate multiple SQL statements for a single query. In this case, the decision support tool should generate two SELECT statements. The first SELECT statement performs a joining between the CUSTOMER Table and the SALES Table to get the total sales amount for each customer. The second SELECT statement performs a joining between the CUSTOMER Table and LOAN Table to get the total loan amount for each customer. The results of these two SELECT statements are then merged together by the decision support tool. Using this method, there will not be any missing data nor any duplicate data.

6. Performance Consideration

The semantic layer is the bridge between end users and the data warehouse. End users use the semantic layer to construct their queries and the decision support tools uses the semantic layer to convert the queries into SQL statements. Although the data access is performed by the data warehouse, the structure of the SQL statements generated with the semantic layer also attributes to the performance of the queries. To optimize the performance of the queries, the semantic layer should be able to adapt to the special features in the data warehouse schema such as aggregate tables with pre-aggregate figures and short-cut joins.

6.1.   Aggregate Aware Objects

It is well known that decision support queries have to scan through a huge volume of records in data warehouse in order to get the results. For performance reason, it is a common practice for the data warehouse designer to store some pre-calculated summary figures in some aggregate tables and refresh the aggregate tables in a periodic basis. If the user wants sales performance for a particular year for instance, the answer can be retrieved directly from the aggregate table if one has been defined, and does not have to be calculated from the detailed transaction records on the fly. This is obviously much quicker, and in real life databases, these techniques can speed up certain queries by a hundred times or more. The measure objects within the semantic layer should be aggregate aware. That means the semantic layer is smart enough to determine which is the most suitable aggregate table from which the figures are retrieved.

Below is an example of aggregate-aware object. The ORDERS Table contains the sales transaction records. The sales quantity breakdown by year in the ORDERS Table is summarized periodically and is stored in the AGGREGATE Table. An aggregate-aware object called "Total Revenue" can be defined to make use of the aggregate table to speed up queries. The definition of the "Total Revenue" aggregate-aware object is the formula

@Aggregate(sum(orders.quant), aggregate.quant)

which provides two alternate paths for retrieving sales quantity. If end user is retrieving the sales quantity breakdown by year, the aggregate-aware object "Total Revenue" is smart enough to get the summarized data from AGGREGATE Table. There is a significant improvement in response time to make use of the aggregate table rather calculating the sales quantity summary from scratch every time. If end user is retrieving the sales quantity breakdown by other dimension than year (e.g. by product), the "Total Revenue" object will retrieve the sales quantity breakdown from the ORDERS Table.

	Year	Product	Quantity
	1995	Product A	10
Orders	1995	Product	40
table	1995	Product C	20
	1996	Product A	20
	1996	Product B	50
	1996	Product	30

Aggregate table

Year	Quantity
1995	70
1996	100

Total Quantity = @Aggregate(sum(orders.quant) aggregate.quant)

Figure 4. 1

6.2. Support Short-cut Joins

Sometimes we may not completely follow the formal master-detail relationship defined in the data warehouse for table joining in order to speed up queries. We may define some shortcut joins which link two tables already joined to other tables. In this type of join, the link between the tables bypasses one or more other tables in the formal master-detail relationship. The advantage of such short-cut join is that it can reduce the time of joining by skipping some unnecessary joining paths.

Let us look at the example in Figure 4.2. There are CUSTOMER Table which stores the customer records, ORDER Table which stores the purchase orders made by the customers and the ORDER_DETAIL Table which stores the items within an order. The formal joining paths according to the master-detail relationship are shown as solid lines between the tables. Let us say that end users frequently issue queries to determine the total sales amount breakdown by each customer without knowing the exact order numbers. We can define a short-cut join in the semantic layer which joins the CUSTOMER Table and ORDER_DETAIL Table directly and skips the ORDER Table. If the end users just pick the "Customer Name" Object and "Sales Amount" Object from the semantic layer, the decision support tool will be smart enough to make use of the short-cut join to join these two tables directly rather than following the traditional joining paths which involve the unnecessary ORDER Table. Performance can be improved significantly.

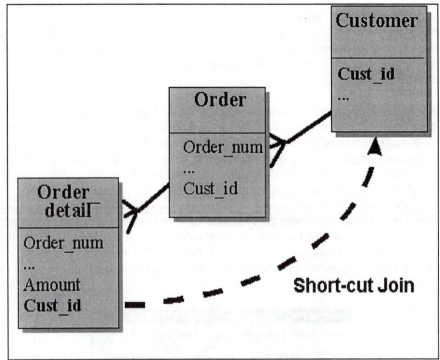

Figure 4. 2

7.   Security And Resource Control

Decision Support Tools give end users the autonomy to perform query and analysis on the data in data warehouse. However, the Information Technology Department must remain certain degree of security and resource control for the data access from the data warehouse to prevent the autonomy to become unmanaged.

7.1.   Security Control

The semantic layer should support personalizing the security by setting object restrictions and row restrictions for a particular group or user. In this way, the designer can design a single semantic layer for a large group of users and every group or user will have a different set of access rights to the data in the data warehouse.

Let us look at anmplementation of semantic layer security. The Information Technology Department can set 3 different controls on semantic layers: Object Restrictions, Row Restrictions and Table Mapping. For example an object restriction can be applied on the semantic layer to restrict a particular group or user from accessing the "Customer Age" object which is considered to be confidential.

Similar to the object restrictions, access to certain subset of records can be restricted when a particular group of user accesses the data from data warehouse through the semantic layer. In this way, the designer only creates a single semantic layer and every user will access different sets of records according to the personalized row restrictions.

Some semantic layer implementations support Table Mapping feature which maps a table to another table in the underlying database structure when end user access the data through the semantic layer. By using this table mapping feature, designer only has to maintain a single semantic layer but different users or groups can access different set of tables, view, or synonyms through the same semantic layer. Figure 5.1 shows an example of a table mapping within a semantic layer. If the end user Albert can only access the customer records stored in Customer_View_A Table, the designer can define a table remapping to map the Customer Table to Customer_View_A. Whenever the end user Albert access the customer information through this semantic layer, the access is redirected to the Customer_View_A Table. Different groups of users have a different views of data, but still maintain a consistent semantic layer for the whole of the organization.

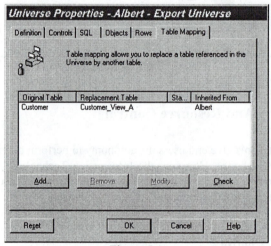

Figure 5.1

7.2. Query Resource Control

In a decision support system, end users are allowed to construct their own queries using the objects in semantic layer. There are chances for the end users to construct a query which returns a huge set of results and jeopardizes the performance of the data warehouse. The end user may not be even aware of the volume of data to be returned when he construct the query. The semantic layer should include some control parameter settings that act as safeguards against excessive query returns or execution times.

Figure 5.2 shows an example of parameters settings to control the resource consumed by a query.

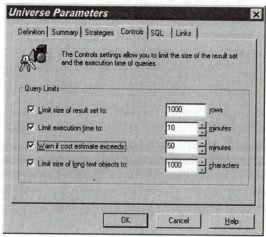

Figure 5. 2

The following configurable controls are indicated::
- Maximum Size of Result Set: limits the number of rows that can be returned in a result set and only returns a partial result set if this limit is exceeded.
- Maximum Execution Time: limits the amount of time a query can run for and only returns a partial result set if this time is exceeded.
- Warning on Cost Estimate: provides a warning message to a user if a query will exceed specified time parameter BEFORE a query is run.
- Maximum size of long text objects: to restrict the size of long text field to be returned.

Different groups of users can be assigned with a different sets of control parameters so that we can have maximum flexibility in resource allocation.

In addition, you may define some object property to prevent end users from constructing inefficient queries. For example, if a database column is not indexed and the end user select the corresponding object to construct the sorting order and selection criteria, the query will perform a sequential scan on the whole table. The execution time will become very long if the table is really large. To prevent end users from constructing inefficient queries, the object which is not indexed can be specified not to be used in selection criteria or sorting.

8.   Conclusion

Today's database, because it lacks of business context, is the preserve of the few in most organizations. Management depends on the computer literate to prepare and massage this data before it can be effectively used. A data warehouse transforms disparate data into information that is consistent across the whole organization and make the information accessible by everyone easily through the use of semantic layers [Devlin 1997]. And it is very vital to make sure the semantic layers provide the features mentioned above.

Data warehousing has been around for 10 years. The scope of data in the warehouse is clearly set to expand over the next few years. With the advances in hardware and database technologies, it is very likely that the data warehouse will span across organization with users and data sources from more than one company, the data access and semantic layers will be distributed around the network (probably through Internet and mobile network). It is vital that data warehouse and decision support system vendors has to respond to these needs.

This paper was written by Mr Yuen Wai Shing, Senior Consultant, Business Objects Greater China in May, 1997.
The book "Data Warehouse from Architecture to Implementation" written by Barry Devlin and published by Addison Wesley in 1997 was used as a reference for this paper.

Moving Data Warehouses to the Net
An overview of concept and strategy

Vincent Boudville, Director of Consulting Services, Infosis Software (HK) Limited

1.   Introduction

Global competitive pressures are driving businesses towards new and improved services and products, increased productivity, decentralized decision making and reduced time to market. This has led to increased demand by business users for access to corporate data in order to make better decisions and is fueling the rapid growth of data warehousing.

Although the deployment of data warehouses has tremendously helped provide the infrastructure necessary for easy access to information, many organizations are not reaping the full benefits of their data warehouse investment due to the inability to easily access, utilize and disseminate information beyond core business users. Overall success has been limited primarily by the following key factors:

1.1   Client/Server Infrastructure

Establishing and maintaining LANs and WANs is both expensive and time consuming, inhibiting broad deployments of decision support solutions. However, without this infrastructure, users cannot access data and thus will not realize a return on their data warehouse investment.

1.2   Fat-Client Based Solutions

Many of today's client/server data access tools are client-centric and thus face scalability issues when handling complex reporting requirements and large numbers of users. Thus, end-user decision support solutions often "hit the wall" when scaling up to meet diverse user and enterprise decision support requirements. In addition, supporting client-based tools becomes expensive and time consuming when distributing new releases and/or modifying metadata or associated business views of the backend database information.

1.3   Limited Access to Information

Access to data warehouses is usually limited to a core set of users. The true value of this information utility is only achieved when its resource is utilized across and between organizations. Thus, there is a need to be able to disseminate this information across more users including partners, suppliers and customers, as well as the requirement to support mobile users.

2.   The Case for Intranet Decision Support

The Internet and internally-deployed intranets provide the necessary infrastructure for overcoming the problems of deploying widespread information by utilizing the World Wide Web (WWW) for decision support delivery. Compelling reasons for using this vehicle include:

2.1   Low-Cost Deployment

With Web-enabled decision support solutions, all it takes is a standard browser to view and request information, thus making the Web a very cost-effective deployment platform for access to information. Furthermore, as decisions are made to empower additional users with access to corporate database information, the Web requires little incremental cost to do so.

2.2   Ubiquitous Access

The platform independence of Web browsers lets organizations deploy Web-enabled solutions independent of whether users have a PC, Unix, or Macintosh client. This means that an organization can support all of its users, whether they are employees, suppliers or customers, independent of their client environment. In addition, these users can view and request information – anytime, anywhere – via the Internet.

2.3   Manageable Environments

Due to the server-based nature of the Web, updates to applications take place on the server without having to update hundreds or thousands of client applications. For example, with Web-enabled decision support, organizations can add or modify reports or business views of the backend data without needing to update individual client versions.

2.4   Future Growth

Evidence of the Internet's value as a decision support dissemination platform is already beginning to surface. The Data Warehouse Institute at their January 1997 conference reported that the Web browser will result "in two orders of magnitude growth in the number of users to be supported and a corresponding explosion in the growth of the number of data warehouses and data marts deployed."

2.5   The Time has come

In essence, the Web as a decision support delivery platform not only overcomes the initial obstacles inhibiting widespread use of data warehouses and data marts, it is beginning to emerge as the "killer application" or catalyst for widespread data warehousing utilization and growth. Thus, the Internet and data warehousing are highly complementary solutions that leverage each others strengths, with the Internet being an ideal vehicle for accessing and disseminating information from within the data warehouse itself.

3. Web Reporting: New Opportunities for Information Deployment

The Internet can be viewed as another vehicle for disseminating information. Similar to viewing within a client/server decision support tool, printing, or emailing, the Web simply offers another mechanism for distributing information.

3.1 When is the choice for the Net wrong?

Many organizations initially see the Internet as an opportunity to replace their client/server decision support tools with Web-enabled solutions. However, these implementations generally target different audiences. Client/server decision support tools target high ROI users within an organization who require full query and reporting capabilities. These users typically require richer functionality and better performance for building their reports and benefit from rich output formatting capabilities for viewing. Thus, they require a more sophisticated environment than a standard browser. Client/server decision support tools will continue to be the right choice for business users requiring a more robust solution for access and analysis of information.

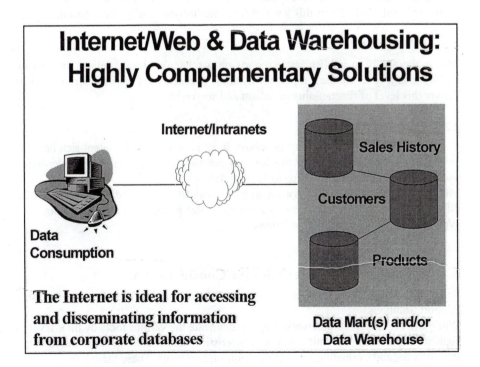

3.2   When is it right?

However, for certain users the Web offers a low-cost and feasible platform for disseminating corporate database information to a much broader audience. These users typically have a requirement to view information and are not impacted by the limited functionality of today's browser environments. For example, with Web-enabled deployment organizations can make reports available for organizational personnel who may require secondary access to this information on a less frequent basis. The Web also allows suppliers, partners and customers to benefit from such organizational information regardless of whether or not they have the standard corporate decision support tool and/or access to the corporate LAN or WAN.

4.   A Framework for Web-Enabled Decision Support

There are wide variations in tools for building and deploying intranet decision support solutions. The META Group (Stamford, CT) offers a useful model for mapping the sophistication levels of Web-enabled tools. They classify these tools into one of three approaches:

4.1   Web "Like"

This is the ability to publish static information in HTML format that can be read by browsers. Tools that deliver this level of functionality are usually client-based.

4.2   Web "Lite"

This is the ability to publish static reports on a scheduled basis, deliver on-demand reporting, and/or to initiate a report for dynamic execution via the browser. Tools that deliver this level of functionality are client and server-based.

4.3   Web "Live"

This is the ability to deploy all of the above in an interactive and content-rich browser environment. Tools that deliver this level of functionality are client and server-based and have some component written in Java or ActiveX.

META's classification serves as a useful framework for understanding and segmenting different approaches. It can serve as a useful model for initially classifying potential Web-enabled decision support solutions.

5.   The Key Characteristics for Consideration

Some of the Key Characteristics to Consider When Selecting Web-Enabled Decision Support Solutions.

While META Group's framework can help delineate the various tools by their level of sophistication, there are other key characteristics that should be considered when investigating and evaluating intranet decision support tools. These include:

5.1   Complete Web-Enabled Solution

Look for a solution that handles all aspects of implementation – from designing and building reports, to deployment, administration and management of Web applications. Depending upon their resource and skill-set base, organizations may also want to consider those solutions that require no programming or scripting. This even applies to any CGI scripts that may be required – the tool should generate these automatically as well.

5.2   Support for Internet Standards

Web-enabled decision support tools, where applicable, should support the standards of the Internet such as HTML output, hot-linking capabilities, and CGI scripts. These tools should also extend HTML's output capabilities by taking advantage of JPEG or GIF output formats (for greater content richness) and should be beginning early deployment of Java applets or ActiveX controls (for interactive and content rich environments). In addition, all Web-enabled solutions' vendors should have a strategy for the future as emerging technologies and standards mature.

5.3   Server-based Processing: UNIX and NT Platforms

When evaluating Web-enabled decision support technology, server-based processing is the key according to many industry experts and analysts. META Group believes that those vendors lacking server-based processing, such as many of the popular client-centric query and reporting tools, are going to be at a distinct disadvantage when it comes to delivering complete Web-enabled decision support. Without processing on the server, users will lack the benefits of automated scheduling and on-demand reporting. This also pertains to the requirement for server-based processing on UNIX and NT platforms as, in addition to scalability options, they are both prevalent in most medium-to-large organizations.

Be cognizant of vendor hype in this area. Many partial implementations (e.g., scheduling on the server) are being incorrectly positioned as "complete" server-based solutions. As the Internet is a server-based environment, beware of any solution that does not fully adhere to this model and still executes ANY processing (SQL generation, calculations, sorting, correlation of result sets, formatting, etc.) on the client.

188

5.4   Access to All Popular Data Sources

Whether organizations choose to deploy their Web-enabled decision support solution within UNIX or Windows NT environments, it is essential to have complete flexibility in mapping to backend data sources. This includes access to data warehouses, data marts, and corporate, departmental and personal databases.

5.5   Single Solution for Web and Client/Server Users

In all probability organizations will want to deploy both client/server and Web-enabled decision support solutions. With a single decision support tool that is architected to provide robust support for both environments, an organization can cross-leverage its client/server and Web investments – reusing and redeploying assets for both environments – saving time and money in the process.

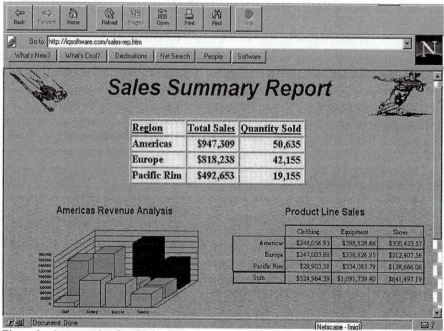

Figure 1 - An example of multiple objects on a complex OLAP page as seen from a standard Web browser.

6. Additional Characteristics

The OVUM report judges the following to be important considerations when considering OLAP tools and Web support

6.1 Functionality

Functionality includes - selection, rotation, drill-down and export are the most important. However, Information Advantage, for example, allows you to see the latest message delivered by an agent to your own portfolio - a useful feature for mobile users

6.2 Design

Does the tool help you design a Web page or do you need to use an authoring/design tool and embed the relevant commands? Ideally you will convert existing pages into Web pages

6.3 Complex functions

Can you extend the commands that can be embedded in the HTML - or are you restricted to the functionality provided by the vendor? For example, can you enhance your Web pages using VRML to display multidimensional data? Some vendors provide toolkits that enable developers to extend the functionality available over the Web

6.4 Packaging

Packaging - some vendors are offering a Web gateway as an intrinsic part of the OLAP engine, others are making it available as an optional extra.

7. The Architecture for Dissemination

To address the need for broader dissemination of corporate information, there are vendors who have delivered complete Web reporting solutions for disseminating corporate database information over intranets. The correct product can be installed on either UNIX and Windows NT servers, and provides everything a company needs to disseminate database information on an intranet. The correct product consists of both client and server components:

7.1 Building Blocks or Objects

The vendor should provide end-user query and reporting tools for designing and building reports -- from simple ad hoc queries to sophisticated reports. A single report can be built containing multiple queries, even against different data sources, allowing users to deploy sophisticated reports that integrate and consolidate diverse information – without requiring any programming or scripting. Once defined, reports can be saved and reused as "building blocks" for designing additional reports, productivity gains in building and maintaining an organization's suite of Web-enabled reports.

7.2 Three Tier Architechture

The vendor should provide three-tier decision support server architecture enables users to deploy reports for the Web to be executed on a regularly scheduled or on-demand basis. The correct product should have administrative features include complete status information for all reports, comprehensive task monitoring, and tracking and error handling to simplify and reduce system support requirements, making a Web solution easy to setup and even easier to manage. In addition, the correct product supports multiple UNIX and NT application servers, allowing scalability from dozens to hundreds or even thousands of users.

7.3 Internet Ready

By taking advantage of the existing Internet backbone, the correct product makes it possible for companies to give their end users the ability to access database reports that have been published to their intranet on a scheduled basis via standard Internet browsers (e.g., weekly/monthly/quarterly sales reports). In addition, users can request up-to-the-second database information by initiating "on-demand" queries and reports which are dynamically executed against the corporate databases (e.g., latest inventory report).

The correct product is a total Web-enabled database reporting solution that enables initial intranet reporting solutions to be deployed in a matter of days – all without programming or scripting.

8. Critical: Immediate Return on Investment

If an organization already has an intranet and databases, the fundamentals required to begin deploying Web-enabled decision support solutions are already in place. With the correct product an organization can deploy these solutions against its backend data sources and enjoy immediate business impact by leveraging the full benefits of its data warehouse or data mart investment.

The correct product offers compelling reasons to begin deploying Web-enabled decision support solutions today including:

8.1 Radical Reduction in the Cost

The Internet offers a cost-effective platform for information distribution. For example, instead of printing and distributing hundreds or thousands of reports every week, organizations can publish their database information on the Web and let users access it when they want. In many large organizations, the Web offers the potential for millions of dollars in cost savings every year in this area alone.

8.2 Low-cost of Deployment and Training

Adding users is as straightforward and inexpensive as equipping them with a standard Web browser. In addition, training costs are kept to a minimum because the browser delivers a standard interface for navigating and selecting information – consistent across all Web applications. Thus, anyone familiar with a browser can begin immediately leveraging the correct product for decision support functionality.

8.3 Low Startup Costs

An intranet and data sources are the key requirements to begin deploying Web-enabled decision support solutions. The correct product takes advantage of the existing infrastructure investment to allow an organization to build and deploy an intranet decision support system quickly and easily – usually in three days or less.

8.4 Lower IS Expenditures

Because the correct product is server-based, organizations can enjoy the benefits of a centrally managed and administered solution. When the Web reporting solution changes, only the server needs to be changed – not hundreds or thousands of clients – making it easier and less expensive to support these users. In addition, batch scheduling, processing and on-demand execution of reports enable organizations to automate their entire Web reporting operation – saving significant time and money in the process.

8.5 On-demand Access by Anyone – Anytime and Anywhere

Because The correct product leverages Internet standards, an organization can deploy platform independent solutions that enable anyone, anytime, anywhere to access the information the company wants them to have. Whether a user wants to view last month's sales report or request the latest inventory figures for on-demand execution, whether the user is at the office, at home or on the road, with The correct product each user has immediate access to corporate database information – anytime, anywhere – through a standard Web browser.

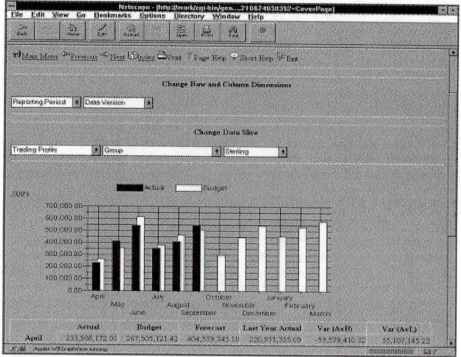

Figure 2 An example of a fully functional OLAP report published on the Web with all
graphics performed by Jave applets.

9. The Internet for Web-Enabled Decision Support

The Internet is accelerating the deployment and wider usage of decision support
solutions, especially in data warehouse environments. As the Internet now provides
the common platform for cross-organizational and inter-enterprise communication, it
has resulted in new paradigms for data access and dissemination of information on
corporate and global scales.

9.1 Reduced Costs

By eliminating the need to deploy client/server infrastructures across the enterprise,
the Internet has minimized ongoing maintenance and costs of decision support tools
by shifting towards server-based (thin-client) architecture. While Web-enabled
decision support is still evolving, as is the Internet itself, today the technology for
implementing Web reporting solutions is mature and available.

9.2 Future Directions

The correct product provides a viable solution for cost-effective deployment of
intranet decision support. With the correct product organizations can utilize a
complete Web reporting solution today that will allow their users to begin using the

intranet for dissemination of information. With a strategy for incorporating future Web technology and standards including Java and ActiveX components, the correct product delivers immediate return on investment while ensuring that the organization stays at the forefront of Web-enabled decision support technology.

10. Access to server based applications via Net

The major problem with the WWW is that all the links are static. It reminds us of the early EIS systems, where if South was split into SW and SE, the page had to be changed and hotspots moved/created, a high maintenance operation. Imagine then the number of changes that would be needed on a large Web site. In addition, there is very little in the way of development tools for managing large numbers of Web OLAP documents.

10.1 Dynamic

Some OLAP products have eliminated many of these issues by its dynamic nature. It is capable of producing the correct interface look and feel in lots of different client platforms from the same stored object.

10.2 Open

The ideal product supports a very diverse set of client server operating systems and interfaces. It can exploit all models of client server architectures from a standalone system to full three tier client server using application partitioning for high scalability. One of the ideal models supported is where simply the presentation layer is run on the client, but the application is run on the host accessing a data and object server on the same or different machine.

Consider an OLAP product running in an X-Windows environment (figure 2). X-Windows workstations receive the messages from the OLAP application server as to what windows and objects to display. Messages are received back as to what interaction has taken place and the OLAP product responds by generating new data for a table, or navigating to a new page and dispatching the appropriate messages to the X window workstation to display the appropriate image to the user.

10.3 Develop Once, deploy many

Imagine instead of generating and sending X-Window commands, generating and sending HTML documents. All HTML browsers would be able to interact with an ideal OLAP product's applications running on the server. This is far in advance of any Web gateway so far demonstrated by most vendors of relational or multi dimensional database. It provides an integrated application development environment on the server, dynamic generation of data, tables, charts and most importantly hypertext links, dependent upon user interaction. It provides a central object store that could easily hold Java code objects that can be attached to any generated page and

194

executed on the client. If local processing and storage of data is required, as users increase their level of functionality, then by downloading the client OLAP environment, any portion of the application can be executed locally, perhaps working with local data, rather than on the server, making use of the local windowing environment automatically.

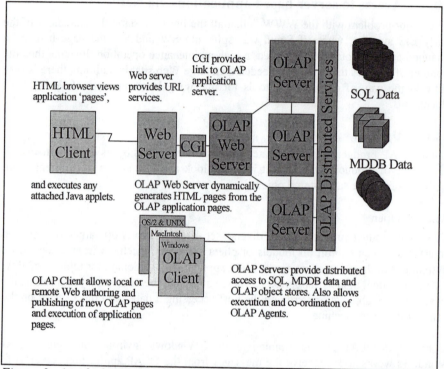

Figure 3. An ideal Web Server architecture. The OLAP Web application server provides multi threaded execution of application pages, dynamically generating HTML documents for viewing by the user through standard Web browsers. The OLAP Web server may also call upon any existing OLAP services available to it for object store access, multidimensional (MDDBs) or SQL data retrieval. Application pages may be built using a standard OLAP client and published to an object store accessible to the OLAP Web server where it is dynamically processed into HTML whenever called by a user.

There is much excitement by this new approach to Web based Data Warehouse applications and it is believed that it has a far superior solution to enable these types of applications than most OLAP vendors in the market.

References

Entire work is an adaptation of:

"Automating Information Dissemination Across the Extended Enterprise on the World Wide Web" A White paper by IQ Software, available at
http://www.iqsc.com/products/products.htm

with references to:

"Ovum Evaluates: OLAP" An Ovum report by Eric Woods, Elizabeth Kyral and Philip Carnelley, December 1996 available at
http://www.ovum.com/evaluate/olap/olap000.html

And includes portions of

"GENTIA on the Web" A White Paper from Planning Sciences Inc., available at
http://www.gentia.com/gen_gws1.htm

About the Speaker:

Vincent Boudville is a Director of Consulting Services at Infosis Software (HK) Limited, a solutions provider in the Data Warehousing and OLAP fields.

Born To Be Parallel

Why Parallel Origins Gives Data Warehouses Enduring Performance

Carrie Ballinger, NCR Parallel Systems, El Segundo
Ron Fryer, NCR Solutions Marketing, Denver

1.   Preface

Twenty Questions to Ask About Parallel Databases

1. Are some query operations not parallelized?
2. Is parallelism always invoked for every query?
3. How many times does a query undergo optimization?
4. Does the amount of parallelism vary between queries, within queries?
5. Exactly how are the units of parallelism coordinated?
6. How does the data partitioning offered ensure a balanced workload?
7. What effect does growth have on this partitioning?
8. What techniques ensure multiple users can successfully execute?
9. Under what conditions must data or messages traverse the interconnect?
10. Are there any techniques to conserve interconnect bandwidth?
11. How is locking maintained across multiple units of parallelism?
12. Does the optimizer know how many units of parallelism will be used?
13. Does the optimizer cost joins differently in an SMP and MPP configuration?
14. What happens to other units when one unit of parallelism aborts a query?
15. Is the optimizer sensitive to the data partitioning scheme in use?
16. Do the units of parallelism recognize and cooperate with each other?
17. Is the degree of parallelism reduced when the system gets busy?
18. How is transaction logging parallelized across nodes?
19. Are multiple code bases (parallel and non-parallel) being maintained?
20. What are the single points of control and potential bottlenecks within the system?

2.   Introduction

Parallel processing has become both fashionable and necessary as data warehouse demand continues to expand to higher volumes, greater numbers of users and more applications. Parallelism is everywhere. It has been added underneath, layered on top, and re-engineered into almost all existing data base management systems, and in the process has left some in the user community confused about what it means to be a parallel database. Teradata is a product consciously designed from the base up to be a parallel machine for decision support.

This paper reveals some of the techniques architected into this database that have allowed parallelism in its fullest form to blossom. Being born for parallelism is the single most important fact in data warehousing today, and we would like you to understand why.

The following sections are included in this paper:
1.   Query Parallelism
2.   Data Placement for Parallel Performance
3.   Intelligent Use of the Interconnect
4.   The Parallel-Aware Optimizer
5.   Synchronization of Parallel Activity

3.   Query Parallelism

What is Query Parallelism?

Executing a single SQL statement in parallel means breaking the request into smaller components, all components being worked on at the same time, with one single answer delivered. Parallel execution can incorporate all or part of the operations within a query, and can significantly reduce the response time of an SQL statement, particularly if the query reads and analyzes a large amount of data.

With a "Just say no!" attitude toward single-threaded operations, designers should parallelize everything, from the entry of SQL statements to the smallest detail of their execution. A database's entire foundation should be constructed around the idea of giving each component in the system many sister-like counterparts. Not knowing where the future bottlenecks might spring up, developers should weed out all possible single points of control effectively eliminating the conditions that breed gridlock in a system.

Limitless interconnect pathways, optimizers, host channel connections, gateways, units of parallelism increase flexibility and control over performance that is crucial to large-scale decision support today. A basic unit of parallelism can be the VPROC. From system configuration time forward all queries, data loads, backups, index builds, in fact everything that happens in a data warehouse, is shared across those pre-defined number of VPROCs. The parallelism is total, predictable, and stable.

The Basic Unit of Parallelism

The basic unit of parallelism is referred to in this paper as a VPROC. In Teradata V1 these VPROCs were physical uni-processors known as "AMPs." With Teradata V2 they became "virtual AMPs" or "virtual processors" with many co-existing on a single node as a collection of UNIX processes.

3.1. Dimensions of Query Parallelism

While the VPROC is the fundamental unit of apportionment, and delivers basic query parallelism to all work in the system, there are two additional parallel dimensions which can be woven into a data warehouse specifically for query performance. These are referred to here as "Within-a-Step" parallelism, and "Multi-Step" parallelism. A description of all three dimensions of parallelism that can be applied to a query follows:

1. **Query Parallelism.** Query parallelism is enabled by hash-partitioning the data across all the VPROCs defined in the system (hash partitioning is discussed in the next section). A VPROC provides all the database services on a pre-defined allocation of data blocks. Before the database is loaded, the system must be configured to support a given number of these VPROCs, in the 5100M that is commonly 4 to 16 per node. All relational operations such as table scans, index scans, projections, selections, joins, aggregations, and sorts execute in parallel across all the VPROCs. Each operation is performed on a VPROC's data independently of the data associated with the other VPROCs.

2. **Within-a-Step Parallelism.** A second dimension of parallelism that will naturally unfold during query execution is an overlapping of selected database operations referred to here as within-a-step parallelism. The optimizer splits an SQL query into a small number of high level data base operations called "steps" and dispatches these distinct steps for execution to the VPROCs in the system. A step can be simple, such as "scan a table and return the result" or complex, such as "scan two tables with row qualifications, join the tables, redistribute the join result on specified columns, sum the redistributed rows and return the result". The complex step specifies multiple relational operations which are processed in parallel by pipelining. Pipelining is the ability to begin one task before its predecessor task has completed.

Pipelining of 4 operations within one SQL Step, performed on each VPROC

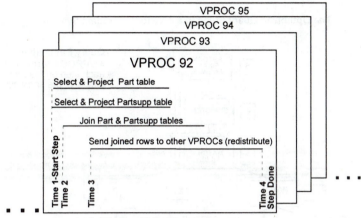

Inside One Unit of Parallelism

This dynamic execution technique, in which a second operation jumps off of a first one to perform portions of the step in parallel, is key to increasing the basic query parallelism. The relational-operator mix of a step should be carefully chosen to avoid stalls within the pipeline.

3. **Multi-Step Parallelism.** Multi-step parallelism, an added level of parallel activity, is enabled by executing multiple "steps" of a query simultaneously, across all units of parallelism in the system. One or more processes are invoked for each step on each VPROC to perform the actual data base operation. Multiple steps for the same query can be executing at the same time to the extent that they are not dependent on results of previous steps.

Below is an exact representation of how this 3-dimensional parallelism appears in a query's execution.

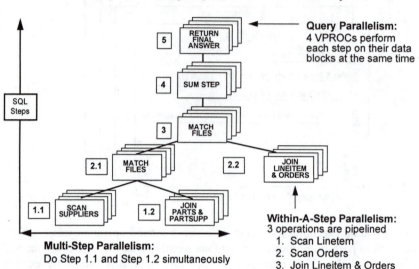

The above figure shows a system configured with four VPROCs, and a query that has been optimized into 7 steps. Step 2.2 demonstrates within-a-step parallelism (as does step 1.2), where two different tables (Lineitem and Order) are scanned and joined together (three operations), all three pipe-lined within one step. Step 1.1 and 1.2 (as well as 2.1 and 2.2) demonstrate multi-step parallelism, as two distinct steps are made to execute at the same time, within each VPROC.

3.2.   And Even More Parallel Possibilities

In addition to the three dimensions of parallelism shown above, An SQL extension called a Multi-Statement Request allows several distinct statements to be bundled together and sent to the optimizer as if they were one. These SQL statements will then be executed in parallel. When this feature is used, any sub-expressions that the different SQL statements have in common will executed once and the results shared among them. Known as "common sub-expression elimination," this means that if six select statements were bundled together and all contained the same subquery, that subquery would only be executed once. Even though these SQL statements are executed in an inter-dependent, overlapping fashion, each query in a multi-statement request will return its own distinct answer set.

This multi-faceted parallelism is not easy to choreograph unless it is planned for in the early stages of product evolution. An optimizer that generates three dimensions of parallelism for one query such as described here must be intimately familiar with all the parallel weapons in the arsenal and know how and when to use them. Only the most rudimentary brand of basic query parallelism is offered today by many database products. As an example of incomplete parallelism and its effects, consider the DBMSes which do not have insert parallelism. In addition to obvious problems at load time, these platforms will need to create all intermediate answer sets serially. This will quickly become a serious bottleneck.

To visualize unpredictable parallelism, consider DBMSes which delay query execution or reduce parallelism based on the order of the parse steps or the current system load. A user (or even a DBA) can never predict if a given query will utilize parallelism, as parallelism is based on the whims of the graphical user interface and current system workload. Since the insert part of insert/select statements is not parallelized by all vendors, this can be particularly troublesome for the many complex queries that require temporary tables between SQL statements.

3.3.   I'll Have My Parallelism Straight Up, Thanks

"Knowledge of Self" has been a valued trait throughout history, usually spoken of in terms of the human spirit. But this concept of self-awareness can also apply to database systems. For example, knowledge of the number and power of the parallel units, along with their predictability, are advantages which enable operational simplicity. A data warehouse should operate as a single, integrated, parallel unit, with all units intrinsically aware of the entire system. Most parallel databases often operate as discrete copies (called instances) of the data base software with a piece of coordinator software controlling all information flow between the instances.

Knowledge of self means that fewer internal questions need asking or answering. Persistent parallelism eliminates conversations instances of a DBMS must have with each other to figure out how to divide the work for parallelization of the first step, and then how to re-divide (if necessary) the work for the fewer units available in the next step.

Imagine a relay race in which the runners did not know ahead of time who or how many runners would be making up each team. A lot of hand signs, shoulder shrugging, and yelling might be needed to accomplish smooth and equally spaced hand-offs during the race, taking energy that could and should be directed at performance. Database systems communicate internally with messages, and the more unnatural and erratic the work being attempted, the more time and energy the system must spend in generating, sending and reading these messages.

3.4.   Parallel Systems with More than One User Don't Have to Die

Because parallel systems have the potential of giving a single user a high percentage of total system resources, they also have proven to be very vulnerable in controlling allocation of the same resources when they must be shared. This deficiency in sharing resources is similar to Bed & Breakfasts, which often run out of hot water in the morning when demand is high, compared to hotels built for mass accommodations, which never do.

This can be avoided by planting techniques deep in the product's base that allow throughput to be maximized while multiple dimensions of parallel activity are being made available for each user on the system. Many other products simply did not have that luxury because they have approached parallelization as transplant surgery, performed after product maturity.

In order to operate near the resource limits without exhausting any of them and without causing the system to thrash, requires effective work flow management by monitoring the utilization of critical resources (such as CPU, memory, interconnect). If any of these reach a threshold value it triggers the throttling of message delivery, allowing work already underway to complete. This internal watchfulness is automatic to the product and is not dependent on a staff of 7 x 24 DBAs. It does not prevent new or lower priority queries from executing or reduce their parallelism.

What is Thrashing?

In a virtual memory system, physical memory is filled with pages of active processes. If there are too many active processes needing access to too many pages for the available physical memory, paging between physical memory and disks takes place. This overhead, commonly referred to as thrashing, is non-productive work, and can reduce the overall system throughput.

The ability to throttle messages controls the amount and type of work performed in a system if a congested state is building up, since messages are the unit of work delivery. Information held in the message headers that come from the optimizer contain the user priority of the originating request, the amount of work that this message represents in a rough sense, and the spawn level of the message. Spawned messages are always given higher priority over new work in order to quickly complete work already in progress and free up resources. (See the final section on Synchronization of Parallel Activity for an explanation of spawning.) The message subsystem in conjunction with the interconnect software allows the throttling information to be passed upstream. This has the effect of controlling message generation at the origin, and cooling the demand immediately.

Scheduling resource usage combined with a system of task controls the flow of parallel activity when multiple users are on the system. A single VPROC may support hundreds of queued and up to 80 active tasks at any one time, from either the same request or many different requests, and it is the priority scheduler that recognizes order, importance, decides who's up next, and passes control of resources around appropriately.

4. Data Placement for Parallel Performance

When conceptualizing how we could optimally process data within an MPP system, it became clear that physical data partitioning could either help or hinder that parallel advantage. From an MPP perspective, many of the available partitioning choices were no longer useful. One of the most common problems encountered with these traditional data placement schemes was that while the data might be balanced across disks or nodes, this did not guarantee that the actual database work was going to be balanced. Equal processing effort across parallel units became a key criteria.

The balance-of-work issue can be solved by permanently assigning data rows to VPROCs and using an advanced hash algorithm to allocate data. This decision to marry data to the parallel units led to the selection of a single partitioning scheme, a scheme that enforces an even distribution of data no matter what the patterns of growth or access, while formalizing an equal sharing of the workload--hash partitioning.

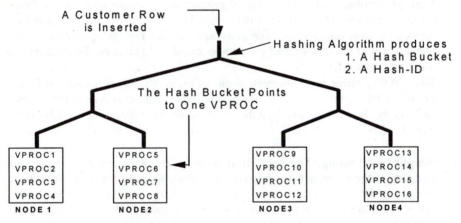

4.1. Hash Partitioning

Data entering the database is processed through a sophisticated hashing algorithm and automatically distributed across all VPROCs in the system. In addition to being a distribution technique, this hash approach also serves as an indexing strategy, which significantly reduces the amount of DBA work normally required to set up direct access. In order to define a database, the DBA simply chooses a column or set of columns as the primary index for each table. The value contained in these indexed columns is used to determine the VPROC which owns the data as well as a logical storage location within the VPROC's associated disk space, all without having to perform a separate Create Index operation.

To retrieve a row, the primary index value is again passed to the hash algorithm, which generates the two hash values, VPROC and Hash-ID. These values are used to immediately determine which VPROC owns the row and where the data is stored. There are several distinct advantages in decision support applications that flow from this use of hash partitioning.

- **No Key Sequence.** One dramatic side-effect of using the hash algorithm as an indexing mechanism is the absence of a user-defined order. Most database systems use some variant of balanced trees (BTrees) for indexing, which are constructed based on an alphabetic sequence specified by the user. As new data enters the system, and random entries are added the BTree indexes, these structures will gradually become unordered, requiring overflow techniques. Either the index quickly becomes more expensive to use, or the entire structure must be made unavailable for re-organization. Hash algorithms do not care about user-defined alphabetic order, they do not use secondary structures that require reorganization, and there is never a need to sort the data before loading or inserting.

- **Ease of Joining.** Hash partitioning of primary index values allows rows from different tables with high affinities to be placed on the same node. By designating the columns that constitute the join constraint between two tables as the primary index of both tables, associated rows-to-be-joined will reside on the same node. Since two rows can only be joined if they reside in the memory of one of the nodes, this co-location reduces the interconnect traffic that cross-node joins necessitate, improving query times, and freeing the interconnect for other work. (See the diagram on the following page.)

- **Simplicity of Set-up.** The only effort hashed data placement requires is the selection of the columns that comprise the primary index of the table. From that point on, the process of creating and maintaining partitions is completely automated. No files need to be allocated, sized or named. No DDL needs to be tediously created. No unload-reload activity is ever required.

Hash partitioning is the only approach which offers balanced processing and balanced data placement, while minimizing interconnect traffic and freeing the DBA from time-consuming reorganizations.

Setting up a join to avoid Interconnect overhead: Rows-to-be-Joined
are owned by the same VPROC

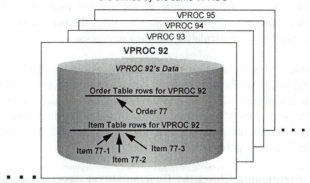

4.2.   Why Traditional Data Placement Schemes Conflict With MPP Goals

The traditional data placement choices listed below all fall short of parallel processing requirements because of their inability to provide a balanced workload, their inherent data accessibility weaknesses, and their tendency to flood the interconnect.

1. **"Data Set" Partitioning Guarantees Hot Spots.** The data base administrator, who must batch up data into data sets as it arrives into the system, has total control over where the data physically reside when using this primitive approach to data placement. It is possible to accomplish a balanced data load with data set partitioning, however, it is impossible to establish a balanced processing load. Because the DBA is manually assigning the data one load file at a time, a small subset of the files will contain the most recent data. Because the majority of processing in a data warehouse is comparing the most recent data to some earlier time period, the vast majority of users will be attempting to access the newest data sets at the same time.

    In MPP or clustered environments the DBMS has no way of telling if rows from two tables which are to be joined are located on the same processing node. Any join activity using this approach is likely to pass enormous amounts of data across the interconnect, reducing overall system throughput.

2. **Range Partitioning is an MPP Teeter-Totter.** Range partitioning appears to be a good fit when there is repetitive access based on the same constraint, because the DBA can partition the table into multiple collections of rows based on the those particular values. But range partitioning offers several difficult challenges for a parallel database and its DBA.

    First, business data is never politely balanced, so a thorough analysis of the data distribution must be undertaken to start setting up the partitions across nodes. Second, a method to locate commonly joined rows from different tables onto the same nodes to reduce interconnect traffic needs to be considered. Third, a method of balancing the data for each table across multiple nodes must be achieved. Fourth, since data demographics change over time, the partitioning scheme must be regularly revisited, recalculated, and data re-juggled.

Even assuming this tremendous data balancing effort is successful, processing may remain unbalanced. Most realistic range partitioning strategies are in some way a function of time. Even the seemingly random selection of item color for a retailer will vary greatly by season. Some of the processing nodes will always contain significantly more current data than others. As with data set partitioning, this will tend towards unbalanced processing.

3. **Random Partitioning Closes the Door on Direct Access.** Random, or round-robin partitioning is the assignment of data to data sets based on a random number calculation. Unlike the similar hash partition, a random partitioning mechanism is non-repeatable, meaning the DBMS never understands where a particular row for a table resides and so has no direct hook into a specific data row. While this technique will evenly spread the data across nodes, it also means rows will always require redistribution for a join or an aggregation, or even the final sort of an answer set.

4. **Schema Partitioning Can Be Abusive to the Interconnect**. Schema partitioning is the assignment of data to specific physical processors or nodes and has proven useful when there is a need to restrict portions of the hardware to handling certain groups of tables, or schemas. While this is generally viewed as a means of increasing performance for specific tables, and can be applied in useful ways on an SMP-only database, it has not proven hugely successful in the MPP world. In most cases to join data from two schema-partitioned tables all rows have to be redistributed across the interconnect for each query. This data movement may significantly impact performance for the affected queries and the increased interconnect traffic may also impact overall system throughput. Further, node imbalances are aggravated if this option is used on anything but very small tables.

4.3.   Local Autonomy

Besides balanced processing another goal has to do with ownership of or responsibility for the individual data rows. Without dividing up or parallelizing data integrity responsibility, activities such as locking have to be handled in one central place, or in a unnatural hand-off fashion, which could consume large amounts of CPU and interconnect resources and create a bottleneck. Parallel responsibility for data, alongside of parallel processing, emerged together as simple twin births that followed the hash partitioning decision.

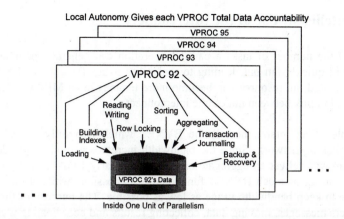

Inside One Unit of Parallelism

With most systems, any process can take temporary control of an object but some central process must control locking access to ensure data integrity. But the problem with the central locking mechanism is two-fold. First, the locking strategy itself will become a bottleneck unless locking can be completely suspended. Second, a task which wishes to use a row must retrieve a lock. When it is done, it must pass control, usually in the form of the row itself, to the next process wishing access. While this is quite feasible in an SMP environment where shared memory pointers are available, it will quickly saturate any interconnect on the market.

An extreme example of this is one reason a shared disk approach will never be able to offer high-end scalability. Systems which rely on shared-disk will always use some dynamic algorithm to determine which instance of the database accesses which data rows. The accessing instance may or may not be the same as the instance which owns, and therefore controls the locks, for the row. Bottlenecks will develop on all but the most lightly used systems.

Some specialized warehouse products attempt to avoid this problem by not using locks. In such a system, any number of data base processes could be attempting to update, insert, read, or delete one row simultaneously, and data or system integrity breaks down. Where there is no data accountability, Process A could update Row X, then Process B, using an old copy of Row X, could make a different change causing A's work would be lost.

Local autonomy within a DBMS defines precisely who owns a particular object (row or index). Each row is owned by exactly one VPROC, and this VPROC is the only one which can create, read, update, or lock that data. All transaction logging is under the local control of the VPROC. A local lock manager functions independently in each VPROC and maintains its own set of locks. Because of this both logging and locking are parallelized, control of data is consistent, and interconnect traffic can be reduced.

5.   Intelligent Use of the Interconnect

Because of the number of tasks a parallel operation can generate, poor use of any resource will quickly fan out, leading to scalability issues for a parallel database. If taken for granted, no resource can become more tenuous in an MPP system than the communication link between nodes, the interconnect.

An example of an interconnect is the BYNET which is a fully scaleable folded Banyan switching network. Since the bandwidth increases as nodes are added, a 24 node system will deliver an aggregate bandwidth of nearly 1 GB/second. One should attempts to utilize as much BYNET functionality as possible, while at the same time taking care to keep bandwidth usage as low as possible. The purpose of the BYNET is to delivers messages, moving data, collecting results and coordinating work among VPROCs in the system.

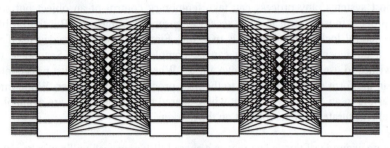

**The redundant BYNET for a 64-Node Teradata configuration. Each node
has two BYNET paths to each other node in the system.**

Just as telecommuting frees up traffic lanes by keeping employees off congested roads, interconnect traffic can be minimized by encouraging stay-at-home, same-node activity where possible. VPROC-based object ownership keeps activities such as locking local to the node. Hash partitioning that supports co-location of to-be-joined rows reduces data transporting for a join. All aggregations are ground down to the smallest possible set of sub-totals at the local (the VPROC) level first. And even when BYNET activity is required, use of dynamic BYNET groups keeps the number of VPROCs that must exchange messages down to the bare minimum. BYNET-driven semaphores (described in the final section) provide a short-cut method for coordinating parallel query processing across the interconnect. A query optimizer can use the known cost of sending a table's rows across the BYNET and factor this expense into the final join plan that it constructs.

Considering all these techniques, probably the most important bandwidth preservation method is point-to-point communication.

5.1. Point-to-Point Communication

The BYNET point-to-point communication is very similar to a standard phone call over the public telephone network. These monocast circuits connect one sender node to one receiver node. Generally known as a non-collision architecture, this approach ensures that the total volume of data the interconnect has to handle is minimized. One should, for example, always try to use the cheaper point-to-point messaging, except in cases where all VPROCs in the system require the same information, such as the duplication of the rows of a table, or the sending of a dispatcher message for an all-AMP operation such as applying a table-level lock.

5.2. Packet-Based Protocols

As discussed above, many parallel DBMSes are built using available components for SMP systems. Some manufacture parallelism by creating separate copies of the DBMS, and communication using available protocols, such as TCP/IP, become necessary. Other products use TCP/IP for all communications between instances.

The problem with this approach is that general purpose transports such as TCP/IP service many needs, and have never been fine-tuned for parallel query processing. The messages are encased in packets, with headers, messages, and footers. If a message is too large for the protocol, it will be broken up into multiple packets. One of the reasons LANs never carry close to their theoretical limits is that large amounts of interconnect bandwidth available for messages is consumed by packet overhead.

The interconnect is more than a postman delivering mail; it is also a group coordinator. For example, a BYNET back channel could be used to perform what amounts to a 2-phase commit on each message transmitted. A packet-switched network would be required to perform a minimum of 3 separate serial transmissions to accomplish the same goal. Because the BYNET was designed specifically for parallel query activity, it is more lightweight and efficient than the packet networks.

5.3. Bandwidth Conservation

Because the interconnect is often an after-thought when MPP architecture evolves from an SMP base, it has become an easily abused resource. Like a socially-active teen-ager given his first credit card, parallel DBMSes can quickly over-extend an unfamiliar resource. It is generally not one single shortcoming or product bug that floods the interconnect, but a poor data partitioning scheme, a multitude of excessive messages and unnecessary data shipping.

In an emulation of SMP processing, some systems will use a process called package shipping in an attempt to re-balance the workload at various checkpoints throughout an individual query's life. With this approach, the system is monitored at various points throughout a query's life in a search for nodes which are not currently as busy as others. In order to re-balance the workload, packages (each consisting of a set of instructions and their associated data) are passed from the busier nodes to the less-busy nodes. This short-sighted approach will generate extremely high interconnect usage for a very temporary gain, as the next evaluation point in any query will cause the entire process to be re-evaluated.

6.   Parallel-Aware Optimizer

The optimizer is the intricate piece of database software that functions similar to a travel agent, booking the most efficient travel path through the many joins, selections and aggregations that may be required by a single query. If a candidate wants to make speeches in 10 cities across the U.S. and has only 3 days to cover all the campaign stops, the travel agent must be highly sensitive to time, sequence of stops, and distance traveled when putting together the itinerary. The same sensitivity is required by a query optimizer.

> Total number of different join sequences an optimizer may have to choose from...
>   for a 4-table join -- 24
>   for a 6-table join -- 720
>   for an 8-table join -- 40,320
>   for a 10-table join -- 3,628,800

6.1.   Recycled Query Optimizers

Two factors determine how well an optimizer will do its job: First, the quality and depth of environmental knowledge that is available as input; and second, the sophistication and accuracy of the costing routines that allow an efficient plan to be produced. Optimizers created for single-server database are ill-equipped if asked to do double-duty in a parallelized version of the same database. Extensive code changes or optimizer re-writes will be required because the cost of most operations and choices that are available with parallelism will be different. Imagine on a road trip that you have to choose between a four-lane highway that is 10 miles long or a one-lane road that is 6 miles. If you do not see and understand the highway's parallel abilities you might choose the route that is fewer miles but which will take longer to drive.

DBAs that spend significant time in complex MPP data placement tuning exercises, in the hopes of ensuring future query performance by complex placement of the data, may only see a benefit for very simple queries. No matter how the data has been cut up, classified and ordered, if the optimizer has not been trained to look for and interpret data partitioning changes, then none of this work can influence the final query plan.

In evaluating the quickest way to perform a 6-table join an optimizer needs to know about how long each operation that makes up the query will take, so it can decide which two tables to join first, at what point to build the aggregation, and whether to apply selection criteria before, after or during a join. An optimizer that is costing operations as if they were going to be done in a single-threaded fashion will make inappropriate decisions. Even if statistics have been collected on database tables, that information may not be useful if the optimizer has no knowledge of parallel capabilities. A inefficient optimizer will cost high volume decision support queries hours, not seconds, of time.

Multiple Optimizations. Some parallel implementations require optimization to be performed not just once, but a second time for one query: first by the base product non-parallel optimizer, and then by a second-level optimizer that makes decisions about the parallel activity. This approach suffers from lack of integration and the inflexibility of top-down decisions. The non-parallel optimizer receives the SQL first, not expecting any parallel behavior to be available, and builds a plan that might be reasonable for a single-server database. This single-server plan is passed to the second level optimizer who attempts to add parallelism, but without having the capability of influencing the original plan's formulation. It will be difficult to take full advantage of parallel potential under these conditions.

Double or Nothing. A further problem with databases that have evolved parallel operations is that vendors will commonly support two different software code bases: one base for the original product which may be widely installed, and a different set of code for the new parallel version. Not only does this add to the development cost and overhead, but one base or the other at any point in time may lag in features and functionality, and the customer will be forced to make a choice between the two.

6.2. Parallel Knowledge

An optimizer should be grounded in the knowledge that every query will be executing on a massively parallel processing system. It knows the number of VPROCs per node configured in the system and understands that the amount of parallelism is the same for all operations. It has row count information and knows how many of a table's rows each parallel unit will be managing so I/O can be costed more effectively, and considers the impact of the type and number of CPUs on the node. The optimizer calculates a VPROC to CPU ratio, that compares the number of parallel units on a node against the available CPU power. It uses this information to build the most efficient query plan.

Using the VPROC-to-CPU Ratio. One result of this awareness is that CPU-intensive activities, when there is a choice, will tend to be chosen less frequently when the optimizer senses that proportionally less CPU power is available compared to number of parallel units. Consider a product join, which is a many-to-many activity like a square dance in which the DBMS tries to join every row of one table to every row of a second table. This type of activity, which tends to be high on comparisons usually requires a larger proportion of CPU resources than other join choices. The optimizer should choose a product join less frequently in a configuration that has less powerful or fewer CPUs feeding into the VPROC-to-CPU ratio.

In another example, the optimizer uses its knowledge of the number of VPROCs in order to decide whether or not to duplicate one table's rows as one alternative in preparing for a join. Table duplication will happen less frequently in a system with hundreds of VPROCs compared to a system with tens of VPROCs, because duplication is a broadcast activity from all nodes in the system to all other nodes in the system. This type of broadcast, while it does engage the BYNET, is frequently CPU-intensive, as all VPROCs in the configuration are involved in a more extensive amount of sending and receiving effort compared to other join choices. The optimizer weighs the cost in CPU resources for the duplication activity, and knows that this cost will be relatively more expensive as the number of VPROCs increase.

And finally, hashed partitioning dovetails smoothly with the predictable number of parallel units. The even spread of data keeps the optimizer's estimates in tune with reality.

In simple queries at low volume a parallel-aware optimizer may not greatly out-distance the less intelligent models. Like a multiple choice test with only 1 choice listed for each question, when few decisions are required, the level of skill behind the making of the decision is less important. Today's powerful hardware can easily hide a multitude of software sins at the low end, but no amount of hardware can hide software failures as data volume and environmental complexity increase. With a changing, dynamic MPP application running against a large and growing volume of data the intelligence and thoroughness of the optimizer will make or break the application.

7. Synchronization of Parallel Activity

When the master plan includes a clear well-defined vision, the master builder can blueprint efficient and tightly fit connections between all the components that evolve into the superstructure. Whether it is the chapters in a Pulitzer-prize winning novel or the instrumental voices of a classical symphony, creating harmony and counter-point among contributing parts is a formula for success.

Some of the architectural directions and techniques that both promote and take advantage of a tight integration of file system, messaging sub-system, locking mechanisms and optimizer are discussed below.

7.1. Sharing and Teamwork During Query Execution

A key winner from and contributor to this singular synchronization is query processing itself. When replying to SQL requests, database requests are broken down into independent steps, as explained in the first section. The steps are dispatched across the BYNET from one of the Parsing Engines, one step (or several steps in the case of multi-step parallelism) at a time, to VPROCs in the system. Only after the step is completed by all participating VPROCS will the next step (or steps) be dispatched, ensuring that all parallel units are working on the same piece of work at the same time.

Because they move to the same rhythm, VPROCs can spawn some of their work to other VPROCs, cooperating to complete the work of one step between them. Spawned tasks initiate "sender" tasks at the VPROC of origin, and "receiver tasks" at the second VPROC, where the spawned work will be done. Because of the system awareness that distinct units of parallelism are working together, the system can assign a higher execution priority to receiver tasks than sender tasks. This technique ensures that work already started gets finished faster than new work. Some types of journalling activity, the insertion of unique secondary index entries, fallback processing and the final positioning of rows in the Fastload utility all take advantage of spawning capability.

Spawned work executes at a higher priority, ensuring ongoing work gets completed before new work is started.

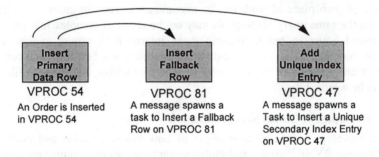

Insert Primary Data Row	Insert Fallback Row	Add Unique Index Entry
VPROC 54	VPROC 81	VPROC 47
An Order is Inserted in VPROC 54	A message spawns a task to Insert a Fallback Row on VPROC 81	A message spawns a Task to Insert a Unique Secondary Index Entry on VPROC 47

7.2. Building on the Cooperation

Building on top of this natural teamwork are some new features such as synchronized scans, an approach to increasing overall system throughput. Traditionally, database systems have tried many ways to maximize the value of one piece of work. One example is the caching of disk data blocks to avoid re-reading them. The effectiveness of this caching for large table scans can be improved through the use of a feature called "synchronized scans". "Synchronized scans" permits new table scans to begin at the current point of an already running scan of the same table resulting in the avoidance of IO for the subsequent scans. Since these scans may not progress at the same rate, any task is free to initiate the next data read. The benefit of this feature increases as active users are added to the system.

Synchronized Table Scanning in parallel across all VPROCs

Inside One Unit of Parallelism

The value of each piece of work can be maximized by reusing intermediate answer sets within the same query. The spools may be the result of complex join processing that required hours to build. Reusing these intermediate results avoids redoing expensive work such as scans, row re-distributions and joins. Self-joins and correlated subqueries are just two of the examples of where re-usable intermediate files have proven to be worthwhile.

7.3. Examples of Global Synchronization

Two techniques provide a good example of how this integration and cooperation work: Dynamic BYNET groups and global semaphores. Both minimize message flow within the database software by offering simpler alternatives to intense message-passing when parallel units require coordination. And even more significantly, these "features of few words" both show a healthy reliance on the BYNET, demonstrating a melding of database and interconnect intelligence that has proven to be greater than the sum of its parts.

Dynamic BYNET Groups. The Dynamic BYNET Group is simply an on-the-spot association of the VPROCS that will be working on one specific query step. It is possible for many of these BYNET groups to exist at any point in time. When a query is optimized and the first step is ready to be dispatched, a message will be automatically sent across the BYNET, but directed only to the VPROCs that are actually needed in doing that step's work. This may be all the VPROCs in the system, or it may be a subset, or just one. When a VPROC receives this step message, that event causes the VPROC to be automatically enrolled in the BYNET group, without the database software having to initiate a separate communication.

One Day in the Life of a Success Semaphore

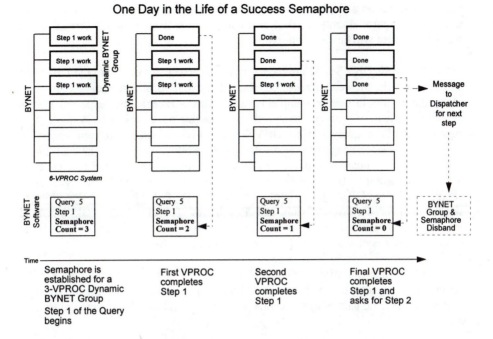

Semaphore is established for a 3-VPROC Dynamic BYNET Group Step 1 of the Query begins

First VPROC completes Step 1

Second VPROC completes Step 1

Final VPROC completes Step 1 and asks for Step 2

Semaphores. Associated with the dynamic BYNET group are "success" and "failure" semaphores, which have monitoring and signaling functions. Each success semaphore contains a " count" that reflects the status of that BYNET group's activity. Semaphores are parallel infrastructure objects that are globally available because they live within the BYNET software. If you think of the BYNET as a continuously moving train, BYNET software is the easy-to-get-to train station that sits between the interconnect and the more distant database software. The semaphore's job is to signal when the first VPROC in the group completes the optimizer step being worked on, and when the last VPROC in the group completes the same step. The success semaphore's count is reduced by 1 when a VPROC reports in, and will register zero when the last VPROC completes.

When the final VPROC completes its work, it sees that the semaphore is registering zero, and it knows it is the last one done. Because it is the last participant to complete this step, this VPROC sends a message to the dispatcher to send out the next optimized step for that query. This is the only actual message sent to the dispatcher concerning this step, whether the dynamic BYNET group is composed of 3 or 300 VPROCs.

MPP Abort Processing. Global Abort processing, an unfortunate shortcoming in many MPP systems, can be supported by semaphores. Failure semaphores signal to related tasks within the same dynamic BYNET group to abort a given step should one VPROC in the group experience a serious error condition, thus freeing up system-wide resources immediately. In a decision support workload, it is possible for hours of time to be spent on a single step of a query. If one VPROC experiences a fatal error and the other parallel units are deaf to it and continue their work, the throughput of the entire system will be compromised.

Most other MPP DBMSes do not have recovery mechanisms built into the DBMS. If an instance fails, the vendor relies on external software to initiate recovery. In some cases, this results in queries completing all segments except those expected from a failed component, only to have to start from the beginning. Consider an example. You submit a 20 hour query against DBMS "PE." Five minutes into your query, an instance of the underlying DBMS code fails, but the others are intact. The coordinator waits until the 20 hours are up, then realizes it did not get the expected answers from the failed instance. Because of the platform's lack of self-knowledge, other components of the DBMS have simply assumed that the failed instance had nothing to say to them for the last 19 hours and 55 minutes. The coordinator asks the final instance for its results, and it responds that it was down for 60 seconds over 19 hours ago, so the user is now told - 20 hours later - to resubmit their query.

With global synchronization, with the ability to recognize and orchestrate the parallel activity that is going on, with no single points of control, it becomes increasingly straightforward and natural to streamline performance and handle growing volumes of users.

8. Conclusion

Watching some of the world's best athletes perform in the Summer Olympics, it is hard not be impressed by how often quality is accompanied by a sense of effortlessness. In this paper we have illuminated some of the processes and underpinnings contributing to Teradata's effortless nature: Automated data placement, multi-dimensional query parallelism, database/interconnect synergy, and a High-IQ optimizer. When a product is born to be parallel, then most wasted energy and unnatural efforts can be eliminated, resulting in a product that is focused, integrated and enduring.

About the Speaker

Albert Leung began his IT career by joining NCR Hong Kong in the 70's as systems analyst. Since then he has worked in both technical area as well as sales area. He also advanced to take up sales management role with other computer vendors including ICL, Unisys and Philips Electronics in Toronto Canada. In the last 8 years, Albert participated in development and implementation of the first A T & T data warehouse in Canada. Then he move on to supporting data warehouse systems for NCR Canada's key customers including major banks and large data warehouse projects. He specializes in large database design, installation and tuning. He has tremendous experience in Teradata, Oracle with parallel query, Data Modeling, Powerbuilder, and various front-end query tools. Before transferring to the Greater China Area, Albert was the Senior Consultant of the Scalable Data Warehouse - Centre Of Expertise in NCR Canada where he was responsible for SDW pre-sales and post sales support. Albert graduated from the Hong Kong Baptist College majoring in Business Management.

Data Mining in the age of Object/Relational Database Management Systems

Tony Banham, Director of Technical Services, Informix

Abstract:

This paper sets out to explore the impact which the migration to ORDBMSs will have on the capabilities of Data Mining and Data Visualisation. Until now, Data Mining (DM) tools have run as clients to an alphanumeric data source. The migration to ORDBMSs gives the opportunity of adding DM functions directly to the database server, and applying DM to non-alphanumeric data. New models produced by the DM can also be added as native data types to the ORDBMS.

Data Mining: Data mining is used to identify hidden patterns and relationships in data using advanced algorithms and statistical techniques. These patterns are uncovered by building a model consisting of independent variables (such as income, marital status, etc.) that can be used to predict a dependent variable (such as credit risk). Data Mining applications promise very high return on investment and are an important source of competitive advantage.

Object/Relational Database Management Systems: ORDBMSs are relational databases which have been extended to allow user-definable data types and methods to be added to the relational model at peer-level to alphanumeric data and functions. Based on the SQL3 draft standard, they encompass the best of the traditional RDBMS ease-of-use model with the ability to handle intelligently and efficiently data types with extremely complex structures.

1.   Introduction

This paper sets out to explore the impact which the migration to ORDBMSs will have on the capabilities of Data Mining and Data Visualisation. Until now, Data Mining (DM) tools have run as clients to an alphanumeric data source. The migration to ORDBMSs gives the opportunity of adding DM functions directly to the database server, and applying DM to non-alphanumeric data. New models produced by the DM can also be added as native data types to the ORDBMS.

2.   The Universal Warehouse

Initially, vendors selling data warehouse concepts did so on the idea that corporations would benefit from having a single repository for all their information, and that analyses of these enterprise-wide data repositories would therefore give the best possible support for information-based decisions. However, in actual fact data warehouses up till now have been implicitly limited to storing only alphanumeric data.

Studies have consistently shown that only 15-20% of a typical corporation's data is currently stored in alphanumeric form. The remaining 70-85% consists of spreadsheets, word processor files, paper documents, maps, photographs, videos etc., and also non-alphanumeric data types consistent with an organisations business. These might range from seismic charts for petrochemical exploration, to Magnetic Resonance Imagery for healthcare.

An ORDBMS has the advantage of allowing the storage and intelligent manipulation of all these non-alphanumeric data types. A data warehouse based on an ORDBMS therefore, has the capability of truly holding *all* a corporation's data. This is significant as, for example with the seismic data referred to above, sometimes for decision making purposes the non-alphanumeric data which an organisation possesses can be the most valuable.

The data warehouse is the repository of data available for DM. Data Mining tools now have the potential of exploiting data warehouses based on ORDBMSs, so-called 'Universal Warehouses'. There are three key areas where DM will benefit from tight integration with ORDBMS technology:

- Access to non-alphanumeric data types within the Data Warehouse
- Moving complex DM algorithms into the ORDBMS engine as methods
- Storing DM-produced data types within the ORDBMS

Informix has produced an ORDBMS, the Informix Universal Server (IUS), which allows the extensibility of the database functionality through a technology known as DataBlades. DataBlades are collections of new data type definitions, together with new methods associated with them. DataBlades allow both DM algorithms and models to be stored intelligently within the database, and they also allow the storage of rich source data which can be utilised by Data Mining tools during knowledge searches. The IUS database and its DataBlades (Objects) will be used as the architecture behind the discussions in the remainder of this document.

3. Access to Non-alphanumeric Data Types within the Data Warehouse

As new data types proliferate and ORDBMSs support direct storage and manipulation of those types within the database, customers will want to leverage information contained in data of those types in order to make more effective decisions. Combining data mining on these types with correlated alphanumeric types is likely to be especially rewarding. Existing data types, thanks to ORDBMS technology, can also be mined in new ways.

3.1. Mining new types — Examples

Earth Remote Sensing data, previously held on magnetic tapes, is now being stored in ORDBMSs as combination latitude/longitude/time/amplitude data types. This allows data mining algorithms to detect changes, over time, in earth resource utilisation. In combination with data mining of correlated data, such as demographic studies in areas of deforestation, useful knowledge could be gained. Data Mining techniques are vital in this field, as in some projects up to one terabyte of data per day is being added to the database. Other methods of turning this raw data into useful information are insufficient.

For a hospital using medical imaging systems, data mining algorithms could be written to detect repeated patterns in x-rays, or generic changes in patterns of x-rays of individual patients with shared complaints. Similar Data Mining could be performed on other industrial images such as seismic charts, military reconnaissance photographs, and weather patterns.

As an ORDBMS natively understands the content of images, non-codified data is also available to Data Mining Tools. Miscellaneous information *about* images no longer needs coded by hand during data entry, thus a red shirt is simply photographed and stored as an image and the mining algorithm can decide to ask for new attributes (such as colour or texture or size or collar or buttons, etc.) as functions on the image without all these new attributes being coded by a data entry operator.

In an ORDBMS, time series can be defined as a native data type. For DM in a financial environment, this will give performance previously undreamed of when, for example, comparing five-day moving averages with the thirty-day moving averages of correlated share prices. Financial institutions might also be interested in finding patterns within large text objects, for instance, a company's name together with the words 'risk' or 'trouble' or 'problem'.

3.2. Mining old types in new ways — Examples

To illustrate how a ORDBMS can add new functionality to data mining on existing data sets, imagine an employee table containing the name, age, street address, and photograph of each employee:

```
create table Emp
        (name = varchar,
        age = int,
        address1 = char(30),
        address2 = char(30),
        picture = blob);
```

Use of this table is restricted to conventional queries, but if we were to add SQL3-based Objects to extend the functionality of handling name, address, and picture as follows:

```
create table Emp
        (name = Scottish_name,
        age = int,
        address = point,
        picture = image);
```

Then Data Mining tools would be able to invent more sophisticated queries such as :

```
select name
from Emp
where name < 'b'
and age > 50
and contains(address, circle ('107,47',5))
and beard (picture) > .7
order by ascending name;
```

This query finds all employees whose name begins with an 'a', whose age is above 50, who live within a five-mile circle surrounding the co-ordinate "107,47", and have significant beards. The original data is unchanged; in fact we already have the capability of taking a street address and zip code and convert it automatically to a latitude/longitude co-ordinate, and we have the capability to index existing images so that pattern recognition within the image is possible.

This query, though simple and straight forward to the average reader, is impossible in a traditional relational DBMS. First, in many countries other than the United States, names do *not* sort in ASCII order. Scotland is one such country because the following names are all members of the Tavish clan and all collate together:

- McTavish
- MacTavish
- M'Tavish

As a result, one cannot use the *varchar* data type found in SQL-89 because it supports a '<' operator which collates in ASCII order, and thereby generate an incorrect answer for many Scottish name queries. In addition, one cannot perform any single character substitution algorithm, such as supported in SQL-92, because {a, c,'} are only "silent" if preceded by an 'M'. Instead, to perform the above query, one requires a new data type, Scottish_name, with a type-specific notion of '<'.

Moreover, when the user requests the result of the query in ascending order, the system must generate the answer in Scottish_name order. Hence, sorting must be done using the user-defined notion of '<'.

In addition, the third clause contains a user-defined function (*contains*) and a non-standard data type (*circle*) while the fourth clause contains a user-defined pattern recognition function (*beard*) that looks at an image and determines whether the person in the image has a beard. The user-defined functions (*beard* and *contains*) must be writeable in SQL, a stored procedure language, or in a third generation language, such as C or Java. Since it is impossible to write the *beard* function in a stored procedure language, an object-relational DBMS must support coding functions in all three kinds of languages noted above.

IUS permits users to define such new types for the data that they store in the database. By providing the appropriate methods along with these types, users can ensure that attributes of these new types participate in DM models.

4.   Moving complex DM algorithms into the ORDBMS engine as methods

The core value of an ORDBMS for DM will be to execute the DM algorithms within the server as functions. There are several advantages of executing the DM model where the data resides:

- no need to cut and thrust the data into a proprietary storage manager, thus saving loading time
- interactive mining of live data, not a cut of a terabyte that is days or weeks old
- savings on infrastructure costs

As only one DBMS is used, there is no need to create integration between a DM storage manager and the ORDBMS, no need to load the DM's storage manager from the data in the ORDBMS, and no extra technical skills are required to manage the DM's proprietary storage manager.

These advantages mean that the data being used for DM is more up-to-date — in fact it is the live data. Performance will also be much higher for two reasons. Firstly, there is no need to send large data volumes over a network, the data stays on the server. Secondly, the ORDBMS in question is a fully-parallel modern database and can parallelise operations against non-alphanumeric data just as efficiently as alphanumeric data.

5.   Storing DM-produced Data Types Within the ORDBMS

Knowledge discovery is a multi-step, iterative process of collecting and transforming data, searching for patterns, interpreting and evaluating results, and further refining the discovery process. As a by-product of the discovery process, many different data types are generated through both the analysis and the reporting and logging of results.

By formulating the data components and functions of the knowledge discovery process as Objects, the ORDBMS can manage varied mining types and results, yielding a high level of flexibility and convenience. This means that other, user-preferred data access and visualisation tools — configured as other Objects — can also be integrated easily into the knowledge discovery process.

Data mining is rather non-scientific — typically it is trying to prove a suspicion instead of taking empirical facts and analysing the possible cause and effect relationships — and it is therefore iterative. The repetitive process of building a model, running it, and refining it needs a good management environment. In the case of an ORDBMS the server is the obvious place to store the attributes of a model, the conditions of running the model and the circumstances of the result sets.

There are several major schools of thought on DM technologies. Concepts such as neural nets, machine learning, inferred rules, tree search and so forth each have their own strengths and weaknesses. Experience shows that knowledge engineers want more algorithms to 'cross check' one answer and they want the one answer to be 'actionable'. The advice from an Neural Network (NN) may be pretty obscure and abstract if taken literally, for example : "Most televisions sell for $592 on sale and $555 on retail". But the final advice from the analyst using the NN will be quite removed : "Stop retail sales of small televisions and don't put cheap televisions on sale". The route taken by the analyst from the NN's findings to the advice may not be intuitively obvious, so the customer might prefer to cross-check the NN's result from an inferred rule system or some other DM algorithm. As many different algorithms can be added to an ORDBMS, this is perfectly feasible. The parallelism afforded by a modern ORDBMS such as IUS can be exploited by DM tools to rapidly construct and refine many models.

6.   Integration of Data Mining tools with the ORDBMS

Integrating Data Mining tools with the ORDBMS in the form of data mining Objects will unify the technologies of data mining with data warehousing, giving database analysts and end-users an accessible and highly leveraged knowledge discovery environment. By making the separate components of data mining — data, functions and procedures — into individual Objects, customers can develop and execute complex data mining applications completely within the Server. The blend of high-performance relational database technology with Object technology creates an integrated information management solution unparalleled in the database industry. Integration of DM tools with the database engine capitalises on the advantages of an ORDBMS at three key stages of the knowledge discovery process:

Development. Data mining engines require that data be presented in specific formats to achieve the utmost performance and accuracy. The transformational techniques such as sampling, conditioning, format conversion, pivoting and encoding are as important to successful knowledge discovery as the data mining tools. By incorporating these techniques and the data mining engines as Objects, knowledge discovery can be executed under the control of ORDBMS, maximising performance by executing within the database, and minimising storage requirements generated by copying data into intermediate files.

Analysis. Administrative control of the knowledge discovery model is given to ORDBMS, which can store the parameters that are input to the data mining tools and maintain statistics that are output by them in relational tables. In this way, detailed information resulting from the execution of the discovery process can be recorded for later analyses and comparison. For example, SQL statements can be used to compare the results of two different neural net models, or to compare the accuracy of different methods of analysis (neural net and decision tree).

Deployment. As the data mining process is administered via the ORDBMS, and because the ORDBMS maintains information on previous trials and data mining models, it becomes possible to select a model and apply it to an appropriate data set. For example, if a model has been developed that has been used to determine the fraudulent use of credit cards, and has been successfully used in a number of similar trials, it is possible to execute the model as an SQL statement on a new data collection with a minimum of set-up, since the process has previously been established and defined.

7.   Market Segmentation

The use of complex (non-alphanumeric) data types by Data Mining tools is still immature, as is the movement of DM processing from the client to the server. However, some clear markets for this technology are already emerging :

- Consumer product/service marketing (includes many banking applications)
- Fraud detection (credit card, cellular phone)
- Financial forecasting
- Error detection

New markets for DM will emerge as more and more large sources of data come on line. Examples include click-stream analysis from World Wide Web applications, specialised demographics from various mail order catalogues and special interest groups, scientific applications such as DNA sequencing, and foot traffic in retail stores. The key to success will be anticipating the availability of information-rich data sources. Many of these data sources will include non-traditional types which DM tools will leverage through user-defined methods.

Using Data Mining technology on top of ORDBMSs, complex relationships and patterns can be determined independent of preconceived notions, providing powerful capabilities for generating prediction models, explaining associations in the data, or generating optimal business outcomes. These techniques can be used to solve complex business problems across many industries.

8.   Conclusion

Running sophisticated knowledge discovery functions as Objects within an ORDBMS (in this case, DataBlade modules in the Informix-Universal Server) allows DM tools to accomplish what many knowledge discovery and data mining vendors have only dreamed of in the past: instead of moving huge amounts of data to the knowledge discovery and data mining algorithms, the Universal Server moves the algorithms to the data. The high degree of parallelism afforded by the Universal Server during query evaluation facilitates very efficient knowledge discovery. In the Universal Server, users can define new data types and methods for manipulating them. The Universal Server stores and efficiently manipulates objects that are significantly more complex than the typical numbers, text, and dates stored by most relational database management systems. Users can also define functions for manipulating both built-in types and user-defined types. Since the Universal Server treats these types and functions as built-in types and functions, DM tools are able to utilise these new, complex data types and functions when constructing models.

In conclusion :

* An ORDBMS is the enabling technology for running DM as close to the data as is feasible
* DataBlades are a perfect vehicle for running DM models against the data where it resides
* Data Mining is value add to a data warehouse

Existing DM tools have been a powerful, successful technology for niche business segments (retail customer analysis, financial risk management, etc.). However, the ORDBMS approach to DM outlined here will expose this technology to everyone with a data warehouse. This all leads to the conclusion that a logical progression of both decision support and business applications is to introduce DM and visualisation as integral features of the database itself.

"Integrating data mining functions with the database management system will allow users to develop some very exciting applications, increasing the utility of the corporate database. For example, in the telecommunications industry not only could data mining perform customer churn analysis within the decision support environment, but fraud detection could be deployed as part of the transaction system." Herb Edelstein, President of Two Crows

About the Speaker:

Director of Technical Services for Informix's Greater China region, Tony Banham has worked for Informix since the inception of the Asia/Pacific operation seven years ago. A graduate in Computer Science with many years experience in high-tech user environments with organisations such as Shell and the European Space Agency, Tony worked for both Database Consultants Europe and Oracle before joining Informix. His current responsibilities include managing all technical issues in the region, and co-ordinating with other Informix operations internationally.

Tony Banham
Director of Technical Services
Informix Software (HK) Ltd.
2801 Central Plaza
18 Harbour Road
Wanchai
Hong Kong

Email: tbanham@informix.com
http://www.informix.com

"Aligning IT with a Consumer-Oriented Business Model"

James Alderton
Marketing Director, Asia Pacific, Computer Systems Group, NCR

Synopsis:

Organizations today must be able to respond quickly and creatively to changes in the marketplace. Flexibility mandates maneuverability; purposeful movement to a position of advantage.

Data warehousing enables organizations to gain a clear understanding of customers and provides an improved ability to detect changes in the internal or external environment. By analyzing a new condition for its potential business impact and selecting an appropriate response with speed, organizations can create and sustain a competitive advantage.

In his presentation, Mr. Alderton looks at the business impact of data warehousing and finds answers to three simple questions of interest:

- How should a data warehouse be implemented to be perfectly aligned with the corporate strategy of a global company?

- How can data warehousing enable an organization to have a closer, more flexible and more differentiated relationship with its customers?

- What is the potential business impact of data warehousing?

In his presentation, Mr. Alderton will review case studies from NCR's leading data warehousing customers to highlight the key success factors in implementing an enterprise data warehouse and the business impact of these projects.

About the Speaker:

James Alderton is the Marketing Director for NCR's Computer Systems Group in the Asia Pacific region, responsible for the marketing of NCR's enterprise computing technology and solutions. He is a frequent speaker at seminars and conferences on Data Warehousing and Client/Server computing environments. Mr. Alderton has been in the Information Technology industry for 20 years and has held executive sales and marketing positions with Honeywell Information Systems, International Computers Limited, and Sequent Computer Systems before joining NCR in 1993.

12 Steps of Creating a Successful Data Warehouse

Ringo Chan W. K., Director of Presales Technical Support
Oracle Systems Hong Kong Limited

Abstract:

To compete in today's fast-paced, highly competitive business environment, we cannot afford to waste time searching through mountains of data, looking for valuable nuggets of information to make business-critical decisions. Even if you have access to your day-to-day operational data, it is not enough. To track trends, analyze performance, and make better business decisions, we need a Data Warehouse. However, when developing a Data Warehouse, the challenge lies in extracting the data from the source databases, integrating that data into the target Data Warehouse, and managing the meta data. With the meta data in place, we can extract data from operational and other systems, scrub or otherwise repair it, and then summarize, sort, and organize it before loading it into your Data Warehouse. Though we can rely on ETT (Extraction, Transformation and Transportation) tools for helping us to extract, transform and load data from operational databases into a Data Warehouse, the design of a data warehouse still rely on experienced Data Warehouse architect, to build a successful data warehouse. This paper will be using a Building Estate OLTP database as an example to illustrate the concepts and how to build a successful Data Warehouse. It is used to check and forecast the rental rate and sell amount in Hong Kong.

Introduction

Since a data warehouse is not a product, it is an architecture. It has to be built. A data warehouse project requires business skills, analysis skills, modeling skills, database design and administration skills, and even more critically, considerable political, interpersonal and project management skills. There are not yet, nor likely to be, any complete off the shelf solutions.

The Building Estate OLTP database project will illustrate the concepts and methods in building a successful Data Warehouse which used to check and forecast the rental rate and sell amount in Hong Kong.

Figure 1. Building Estate

We keep emphasis on Data Warehouse rather than Decision Support System because sometimes Decision Support can be based on an existing operational database. Users can continue to use their operational databases and use appropriate development tools to produce decision support information to their users. However, there will be a performance impact on existing OLTP environment when running the Decision Support queries.

228

Therefore, we should have a separate Data Warehouse to provide decision support functionality into a separate environment from the operational, transaction system. A Data Warehouse can be viewed as a Decision Support database that is maintained separately from an organization's operational databases. Actual definition of a Data Warehouse as per Bill Inmon's definition is "a subject-oriented, integrated, time variant, non volatile collection of data that is used primarily to aid organizational decision making". This definition is so important that I would like to elaborate on each point.

Subject Oriented: The classical operational systems are centered around the applications of the company, whereas, a data warehouse is centered more around the common subject areas.

Integrated: This is the most important aspect of a data warehouse. The data warehouse gets information from various other functional systems in the organizations.

These systems might be storing the same information in different ways, i.e., Sex of a client may be stored as Yes or No, 0 or 1, M or F, etc. in different systems. Whereas, when this information has to be stored in the data warehouse, a common schema needs to be identified. Therefore, inconsistencies of the various operational systems are undone and data is entered in an integrated way. The same concept needs to be applied to column names, index names, and attributes, etc.

Data Warehouse is Integrated

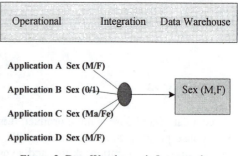

Figure 2. Data Warehouse is Integrated

Non Volatile: Unlike the operational system the data in the data warehouse is not modified. However, in real life, I have seen so many data warehouses which have a business need to change the data in the data warehouse.

Time-Variant: This definitely is a key distinguisher between an operational and data warehouse systems. The data in the warehouse is typically stored for longer duration than the operational systems. A data warehouse keeps current values for any columns at different point in time, whereas, in an operational system generally a single current value is stored. Queries on the warehouse data are mostly for a time range.

Following steps guide you step by step to design a Warehouse database and to build a powerful, manageable and cost-effective Data Warehouse.

Step 1: Define the Questions and Understand the Problem Domain

The first step in building the Data Warehouse is to understand the semantics or meaning of the information involved. In operational systems, data is held within functional divides. In a Data Warehouse context, the focus of interest is not the function, but the subject of the function, for example the number of sales. Those subjects, and the properties needed to describe them, need to be defined. We need to define and identify the subject areas about which data is to be held. That is why a Data Warehouse is subject oriented — the data is organized around subjects.

As we want to build a successful Building Estate Data Warehouse which used to check and forecast the rental rate and sell amount in Hong Kong, we need to define our goal. Our goal is to provide timely, accurate and pertinent Building/Estate sales information to the senior management so that they can make timely decision and to allocate different resources to different region. Top management commitment for building a Data Warehouse is a critical success factor. The right approach for building a data warehouse is a spiral approach. We need to deliver the Data Warehouse quickly. The first delivery cannot more than six months. We can then incrementally add the new functionality to the Data Warehouse. Assumed that following questions is being defined, the end-users will pose for a Building Estate Data Warehouse.

- List the daily sales activities in HK Island for the month of April
- List all sales for with sales amount > 4M for domestics medium size tenement
- Compare the sales of Whampoo Estate and Kornhill for particular period
- Find out top 3 area that have the most number of unit sold
- What is the cumulative total of the unit sold?

Figure 3. Questions will be posed for a Building Estate Data Warehouse

The ability to answer these questions is the goal of the Data Warehouse design. Data Warehouse presents the data in a format that is consistent and much clearer for end users to understand.

Once we understand the Problem Domain, we also need to capture the following information for doing analysis:

- How often the user needs the data and how often this query will be executed?
- How long will the system allow for staleness of data? This is an important consideration, since the warehouse requires periodic updates, and some processes will not require live data. For example, will the sales analysis query yield sufficient trend analysis if the data is one week old?
- What are the primary ways the user will want to drill down or up on this data? These are called Data Dimensions in warehousing terms. For example, sales analysis might be shown per week, drill up to by month, drill up to financial quarter, finally drill up to financial year.

- What is acceptable to the user for the query response? Can the process be automated to produce results every day, week or month or must the process be run in real-time?

Step 2: To Identify Appropriate Hardware or Software for Building the Data Warehouse

Choosing the underlying RDBMS to support a Data Warehouse is no easy task. There are many issues to consider and many subtle differences in the implementation of technology. The impact of those issues and in particular implementation differences is magnified by the amount of data a Warehouse will typically store, as well as style of processing it. Following criteria are the decision factors for choosing an appropriate RDBMS:

- RDBMS vendor background and support, including support packages, training and consultancy services support;
- managing large amounts of data and managing large amounts of data well;
- correctly supporting subject area partitioning and multiple levels of granularity;
- allowing the Data Warehouse schema to change as it evolves without denying or restricting access to data;
- providing tools and partnering industry leading tools vendors to deliver sophisticated data extract management capabilities;
- providing a high-speed bulk data loader that can assist with data transformations and derivations and subject area partitioning at load times;
- allowing data to be aggregated in many ways;
- allowing data to be readily purged and archived to multiple levels of storage media;
- allowing index creation to occur in parallel and by offering index compression, index-only processing and multiple indexing and data access techniques;
- providing a CASE tool for Data Model management and by partnering with industry leading tools vendors to deliver true meta data management;
- executing DSS queries, including user written analysis routines in parallel;
- managing data storage dynamically and allowing the physical placement of data to be controlled;
- offering intelligent and efficient lock management;
- enforcing data integrity constraints within the RDBMS;
- providing the tools necessary to monitor and administer the Data Warehouse

Some structural limits in the storage area, and identify operational issues that need to be examined in Data Warehouse environments. It is important to remember that interaction among multiple limits and operational factors often play a bigger role than each issue or limit in isolation. For example, while a 10GB size for a table may be supportable, it may not be appropriate given a specific set of performance and availability requirements. The key to successful Data Warehouse Implementation lies in meticulous planning and analysis of all the underlying structural and operational issues.

In considering structural limits related to storage issues, we found that in several cases, structural limits from the RDBMS side are not very relevant. These limits are either practically infinite or far exceed limits imposed by other system components like current hardware and/or operating system capabilities. A few limits, however, do necessitate careful planning for Data Warehouse environments. Here are some examples of the structural limits related to storage:

Number of datafiles: The limit on maximum number of datafiles per database is one of the limits necessitating some planning in Data Warehouse environments. Administrators need to pay attention to file addition and sizing decisions, to stay within this limit. For example, if the maximum number of datafiles per database per database is 1022, then we need to avoid straying to either extreme — too many very small files or too few very large files — within the 1022 limit. Dynamic resizing of datafiles, available from some RDBMS, will help in some cases by avoiding the need to add small files.

Size of a datafile: Today, most of the hardware platform can support 32KB database block size, datafiles can be as large as 128GB, raising the limit on database size to around 128TB.

Number of tablespaces: The effective limit will be based on the number of datafiles limit.

Number of columns per table: User needs to check the limit of the columns support per table.

Availability of adequate hardware resources to meet throughput, response time and availability requirements is also a major consideration for implementing Data Warehouse. We need to choose a RDBMS which has the best scalability track record in the open system world with proven capabilities on SMP, clustered and massively parallel systems. However, even the best architected system can fail to deliver if hardware resources are inadequate. We need to pay attention to all the hardware components, including:

- Processing power: no. of nodes, processors per node
- I/O: no. of disk drives, total disk capacity
- Memory: server, client
- Client/Server link: speed, bandwidth

to avoid situations where a single subsystem becomes the bottleneck. The initial choice of hardware configuration is typically based on rules-of-thumb estimates and calculations, often using data provided by hardware vendors or system integrators. In Data Warehousing environments, however, this estimation must be followed by extensive testing and benchmarks, preferably using production-level loads, to validate the capability of the configuration to meet current and near-future requirements. While incremental resource addition is a good strategy, it must be used in planned stages, primarily to support system growth — not to correct a resource-starved situation. The best way to attack a resource shortage is to avoid it altogether through careful planning.

Today there is currently a religious war about the best way to implement an OLAP model. Some of vendors believe that the best way to provide OLAP functionality is to place data in specialized, multidimensional databases. They called this Multidimensional OLAP (MOLAP), but some of them want to physically represent multidimensional cubes on disk or in memory namely Relational OLAP (ROLAP). This approach, they say, provides the best performance for the least cost with the least administrative overhead. OLAP tools that provide multidimensional storage are often referred to as MOLAP tools, while those that access data stored in relational databases are called relational OLAP or ROLAP tools.

Figure 4 layout the Typical MOLAP and ROLAP architecture. It is hard to say which one is better.

For MOLAP, a multidimensional database (MDDB) stores data in a series of array structures. It is indexed to provide optimal access time to any element. These structures can be envisaged as multidimensional cubes. For ROLAP, although we know that relational databases are not optimised for multidimensional analysis, they do have advantages over MDDBs in other areas. In particular, they scale to large data sets and include support for replication, rollback and recovery.

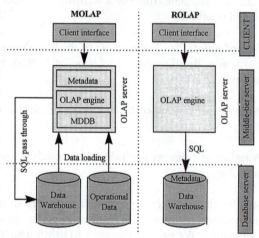

Figure 4. Typical MOLAP & ROLAP architecture

There are many different types of Analytical Applications in the world and many different types of user requirements. Actually, no single tool or approach can meet all user requirements. Therefore, we must assess which of the requirements are most important to us and then evaluate prospective tools in light of those requirements. Figure 5 shows the ROLAP and MOLAP Positioning.

ROLAP and MOLAP Positioning

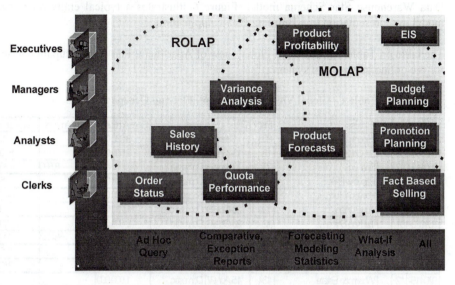

Figure 5. ROLAP and MOLAP Positioning

Step 3: To use Normalized Logic to add some Additional Entities

To start modeling data for a Data Warehouse system, we should review an existing Entity Relationship diagram of the relational database. The normalized data model documents data relationships. We understand data warehouse usually involves consolidation of multiple systems. Often, these systems have disparate ways of representing information. It is necessary to map the information needed to all the systems which feed the warehouse.

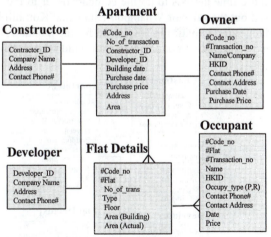

Figure 6. An example of Building Estate OLTP E-R Diagram

234

To simplify the case, the example is assumed to be taken from same RDBMS sources. Then we can focus on how to transform existing OLTP Entity Relationship diagram to Data Warehouse Star Schema model. Figure 6 illustrates a typical entity-relational model in representation of a Building Estate application.

The table on Table 1 illustrates a global view of Apartment, Flat and Occupant dataset for the online information system.

Table 1 - Global View of Apartment, Flat and Occupant Tables

Code	...	Address	Flat	Date	Type	SalesAmount	RentalAmount	Area sq.m
940101-101	...	Tseung Kwan O.	808	1-Jan-94	Domestic	3,000,000		25
950613-200	...	Lai Chi Kok.	12	13-Jun-95	Others	2,500,000		630
960112-092	...	Sha Tin.	23	12-Jan-96	Domestic		8,500	35
960412-223	...	Fairview Park..	34	12-Apr-96	Domestic	4,234,000		125
960415-300	...	Kowloon Tung...	13	15-Apr-96	Shops	8,000,000		400
961020-112	...	Tsuen Wan...	124	20-Oct-96	Commercial	11,230,000		810
961030-101	...	Tai Koo Shing...	12	20-Oct-96	Domestic	2,000,000		400
961212-020	...	Mid Level...	1	12-Dec-96	Shops		55,000	300
970101-011	...	Central...	12	1-Jan-97	Domestic	3,000,000		100
970331-012	...	Happy Valley...	145	31-Mar-97	Domestic	10,000,000		210
970415-112	...	Whampoo Estate	134	15-Apr-97	Domestic	1,500,000		300
...	...	......	...	......	....	....		......

We need to consider the entities we might add to address the user queries collected in Step 1. For example, time is sometimes omitted as an entity in relational database, because its contents are implied by standard calendar-year periods. However, we need to use time periods to do the comparison or to trace out some events, for example to find out the sales of Whampoo Estate and Kornhill for particular period, or to list the daily sales activities in HK Island for the month of April. Those events have start and end dates that do not coincide with standard periods such as month, quarter and year.

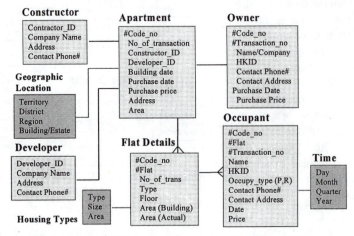

Figure 7. Additional Entities that Supports Building Estate DW System

Figure 7 shows additional entities — Housing Type, Geographic Location and Time Period.

These new entities will help to examine the performance of the sales in specific territory or region and in particular Building or Estate.

Data warehouse design is an iterative process. You may decide for performance reasons to combine two tables, or to avoid a join. Then you see that you really cannot do this, because the one-to-many relationship will be too difficult to manage in this way.

Step 4: To Identify Dimensions

The primary-key and foreign-key relationships in a database reveal strong associations between tables. These associations are likely to become dimensions in building a Data Warehouse Star Schema.

A star schema is a natural data representation for many data warehousing applications. The star schema derives its name from the fact that the diagram of a star schema resembles a star, with points radiating from a center. The center of the star consists of one or more fact tables, and the points of the star are the lookup tables. In the language of star schemas, measures are the centers of stars, which are also called fact tables; dimensions are the radiating star points. In many cases, dimensions have fewer rows than measures. Dimensions might have hundreds or thousands of rows, while fact tables have millions.

In our example, the central fact table is Sales. That is the details of Rental/Purchase Price of each unit. Most queries are interested in information about Sales. For example, list all sales with sales amount greater than 4 million for domestic medium size tenement, and daily sales activities, etc. The points of the Star are detail tables. If query needs to find the owner of apartment, these can be retrieved from the peripheral tables. Since these tables are often accessed less frequently, the most commonly used queries will not have to access them and will avoid the join overhead.

As mentioned, Data Warehouse is subject-oriented, we need to understand the purpose of the data warehouse. From the problem domain, we need to decide whether the Data Warehouse supports only specific reports or ad hoc queries. We understand ad hoc queries for dynamic decision support frequently involve time dimension. They also usually involve drill down and drill up. Decision makers are usually looking for trends. If there is a trend which is merits special attention, they will drill down to get more detail. In this scenario, we need to include those drill down capabilities in our Data Warehouse system by allow them to drill down into detail transaction. However, if the Data Warehouse is only for support specific reports, we can even take out some unnecessary tables. We can see that a system which supports drill-down ad hoc queries is designed very differently from one which only supports particular reports.

We can use a database object called a Dimension to create indices to data and give a unique name to each dimension in a database. Into these Dimensions we will enter the actual indices to the data. These indices will become Dimension members.

In our example, as we concentrate on Sales and support particular reports, we will eliminate those unnecessary entities as shown in Figure 8.

So we can concentrate on entities including Apartment, Time, Flat Details, Occupant, Housing Types and Geographic Location for designing the Data Warehouse Star schema. In this example, we only choose three dimensions: Geographic Location, Housing Types and Time. We will base on the Apartment, Flat Details and Occupant to build the Fact table.

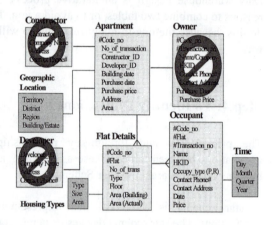

Figure 8. To eliminate unnecessary entities

As we have chosen to index the Sales Data in three ways by creating a Housing Type, Geography and Time dimensions, in the Housing Type Dimension we enter the Type, Size and Area Code; in the Geography Dimension we enter the Territory, District and Region Code and in the Time Dimension we enter the Date. Now we can store Sales data at logical locations which represent the intersection of each of the members of these three dimensions.

Some Multidimensional OLAP system will internally keep an indexing table that contains all the possible combinations of these dimensions.

The physical location where the data is actually stored exists on a Sales Variable memory page. The Dimensions we designate for the Sales Variable will serve as indices, or logical layout, of the Sales data that is physically located on a sales memory page. The internal MOLAP indexing table will take the indices we select and translate them into the physical data locations to retrieve the Sales data. Therefore, we can choose the Sales data we want to see by manipulating the Housing Types, Geography and Time indices.

Step 5: To Create Hierarchies

After we have decided the dimensions, we can review the dimensions and create hierarchies that organize them.

A hierarchy is a data model object that defines parent-child relationships among the levels in a dimension.

Hierarchies define how data is to be rolled up and how data is summarized from lower levels to higher levels. The levels Year, Quarter, Month and Day in the Time dimension are an example of a common hierarchy. Each dimension value at the Day level has a parent at the Month level, each Month level has a parent at the Quarter level, and each dimension value at the Quarter level has a parent at the Year level. For example, we can base on the content of column DATE in Occupant table to design the Time Hierarchy as shown on Figure 9.

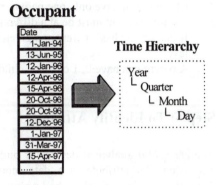

Figure 9. Derivation of Time Dimension

While it is not required, Dimension members will typically be organized into Hierarchies. Hierarchies are used for two things: drilling down and summarizing up data. Hierarchies are the most misunderstood Multidimensional Database design concept. For simplicity, I will first discuss the case where there is only one hierarchy per Dimension then move on to more complicated schema involving multiple hierarchies.

In a simple hierarchy, various types of Dimension members, or indices, will exist. The key to understanding hierarchy design is to clearly understand the relationships between these Dimension members. We will use the family metaphor to describe these relationships.

To begin with, we will group Dimension members by level. The members of a given level must be siblings of each other. That is to say, they are peers in that they represent the same level of aggregation. In order to reduce the size of the index table, lookup time and potentially the number of physical memory pages, it is very important to try to use as few dimensions per variable as possible. This can usually be done by integrating data into a hierarchy level, into a separate hierarchy, or using an attribute as discussed in the following sections.

The next step in understanding a hierarchy design is to determine the relationship between levels. We can lay down five rules that should be followed in hierarchy design.

1. There is only one member who is only a parent, not a child; this is the top member.
2. Children can have only one parent.
3. A child's parent must be at a different level from the child.
4. If our sibling has a parent at a given level, we also have to have our parent at that level.
5. A parent can have 0, 1 or many children.

Step 6: To Identify Attributes

Another useful analytical device for building a Data Warehouse is an attribute of a dimension. An attribute is a data model object that describes characteristics of dimension values other than the level of summarization. Whereas levels are grouping based on levels of summarization, attributes represent logical grouping that allow users to select data by characteristics. An attribute can apply to any level or to multiple levels in a dimension. As shown in Figure 10, Class (S,M,L) are attributes of Housing Type dimension.

Housing Type dimension lookup table

Type	Size	Area sq. m	Class
Domestic	A	10-39.9	S
	B	40-49.9	S
		50-69.9	M
	C	70-99.9	M
	D	100-129.9	M
		130-159.9	L
	E	160-199.9	L
		Over 200	L
Industrial		10-129.9	S
		130-299.9	M
		Over 300	L
Shops & Commercial		10-49.9	S
		50-129.9	M
Others/Misc			

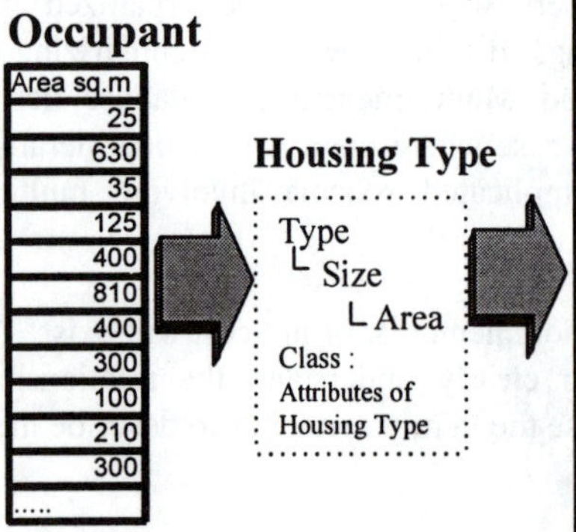

Occupant

Area sq.m
25
630
35
125
400
810
400
300
100
210
300
.....

Housing Type

Type
  L Size
    L Area

Class :
Attributes of
Housing Type

Attributes

Figure 10. Attributes in a Housing Type dimension lookup table

Step 7: To Create the Fact Tables and Determine an Appropriate Granularity

A fact table is a data warehouse table that contains actual data values or facts. Fact tables also contain the relational keys that uniquely identify each row of data in the table. Accordingly, there are two types of columns in a fact table: fact columns and key columns. A fact column contains actual fact data of a particular type. A key column lists keys that are represented the fact table; together, all key columns form a composite key that is the primary key of the table.

Sales Fact Table

Time
Location
Type
Area
Occupant Name
Purchase Price
Rent
.....

Figure 11.
Sales Fact Table

The entities left over after we identify dimensions are fact tables. We need to identify measures. Columns that are not foreign keys in these tables will probably be measures in a Data Warehouse. In Figure 11, we can see that Purchase and Rent of a particular flat are the key measures.

Once the fact tables and dimensions are defined, our next step is to determine the appropriate granularity for the data in the Data Warehouse. Granularity refers to the level of detail held in the units of data in the Warehouse and it is common to see true detail data existing alongside lightly or highly summarized data. Since the volumes of data that a Data Warehouse must typically administer and the style of processing it must support, there will always be multiple levels of granularity in the data stored in a Warehouse. The level of granularity has significant impact on the type of question that can be answered by the Warehouse and is therefore the single most important design aspect of a Data Warehouse. At this point, we know why our users have requested a particular level of information within a dimension. We need to estimate the resource requirements to provide the requested level of granularity, and based on the costs decide whether we can support this level of granularity or not.

Step 8: To Create a Data Warehouse Model

Once we have a list of all facts, dimensions and the desired level of granularity, you are ready to create the star schema. The relationship between the facts and the dimensions are defined by keys. The next step is to define the relationships between the fact and dimension tables using keys.

A primary key is one or more columns which make the row within a table unique. The primary key of the fact table comprised of several fields is called a composite or concatenated key, each of which is the primary key of a dimensional table. It is a good idea to use system-generated keys for linking the facts and the dimensions. This will prevent the necessity of a mass update to the fact table, in case of business key changes.

Based on above steps, we can then create a Building Estate Data Warehouse model. Figure 12 shows the differences between Building Estate OLTP database model verse a Data Warehouse model. There is no straight formula of how to transform an OLTP environment to a Data Warehouse OLAP environment. It really depends on the problem domain that specified by the end-user. However, the process of translating the data from the OLTP and loading the target star schema requires mapping between the schemas. The mapping may require aggregations or other transforms.

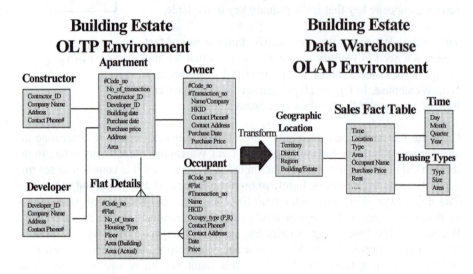

Figure 12. Transform from OLTP to Data Warehouse OLAP environment

Step 9: To Fine Tune a Data Warehouse Model

Creating a data warehouse is very iterative. It is an art. We must always monitor it and tune it as requirements and data changes. Tuning should be performed on a module-by-module basis during development and as one of the last steps before initial implementation. Additional tuning should take place at each phase of a rollout, whenever conditions and/or requirements change, whenever application performance changes, and on a regular basis after deployment. A small amount of "well-baby" tuning on a regular basis will help to head off the ill-effects of unexpected crisis-inspired tuning.

We need to think about how to aggregate the data efficiently so that we can deliver the acceptable performance. An aggregation is a method that creates redundant data at an attribute level above the most atomic level. The aggregate table stores redundant data in that the same values available in the aggregate level fact table can be calculated by summarizing data from the atomic level fact table. The primary reason for storing aggregate level data is to improve query performance. The trade-off is that creating and maintaining aggregate tables requires more resources in the batch jobs and increases the overall size of the warehouse.

In a Data Warehouse multidimensional system, data can be aggregated along any dimension independent of other dimensions. This rule is also true for the creation of aggregation tables. For example, if the lowest level of data exists at the store, item, day level, an aggregate table can be created by presummarizing along one dimension, such as at the region, item, day level, or along multiple dimensions, such as at the region, department, week level. Data should be created at a level which is frequently used for analysis. The structure of the table should mimic the structure of the atomic table, except for the substitution of higher level attributes. By utilizing summary tables, the designer shifts processing time from the user query to the batch job. Warehouses often will contain more aggregate tables than are actually used. The technique of presummarizing data is not effective unless it actually lessens the processing time for user queries, which is to say, unless users will actually query the summary table.

In determining the optimum design for our data warehouse, performance should be a primary consideration. An inefficient warehouse design can result in such slow response time that users might find certain types of requests to be completely impractical. This will limit the usefulness of the system. Although the factors of maintainability and storage requirements must also be considered, query performance should be a top priority.

As shown in Figure 13, depending on the normalization of the lookup tables, we can create a Snowflake schema rather than a Star schema for the Data Warehouse. The important difference in the snowflake schema, as compared to the star schemas, is in the structure of the lookup tables. Each lookup table in a snowflake schema contains only the level that is the primary key in the table and the immediate parent of the level, along with any attributes that apply to the primary key. No higher-level parentage beyond the immediate parent is provided in any lookup table. However, because of the extra joins required to access summary-level data, snowflake schemas are sometimes less efficient in terms of query performance at runtime. That becomes a trade-off in choosing the type of schema to use. We need to decide whether we want to have normalized lookup tables or to have a higher query performance Data Warehouse.

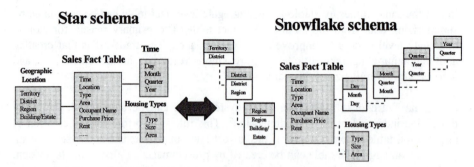

Figure 13. Star schema versus Snowflake schema

The main principles related to the design of an optimized data warehouse are:

- Avoid runtime aggregation of data in cases where large numbers of records must be processed. In other words, we can create summary level fact tables instead of requiring runtime aggregation.
- Joins should involve the smallest number of tables, which should contain the least number of records, as possible for a given query.
- Create ID codes for keys as ID codes are more efficient for searches than text-based keys.
- It is useful to build arrays in the Data Warehouse environment because the number of blocks in the array is usually known. If it is required to store the seven days' sales figures in a particular row then it could be implemented by storing it in seven columns of the same row. This approach does save data and index space substantially, but requires additional amount of processing to be done while querying.
- Since the data in the data warehouse does not change very often, it is reasonable to add redundant data fields to speed up the query. As a rule of thumb, it should not be required to join more than 3-5 tables to answer most of the queries.
- If is useful to create small tables on the side which will record various very popular details. This is done to speed up the event based queries.
- Group data by stability, i.e., propensity to change.
- Data Partitioning is also required for performance and manageability. In a data warehouse application large vertical tables may need to be split horizontally, for ease of backup and recovery. Data Partitioning can be achieved in several ways. The first step is to separate obvious potential bottlenecks, such as dividing data from indexes to spread the I/O load. The I/O can be further spread by using mechanisms such as striping to spread data across multiple spindles. Data can also be partitioned at the application level, by dividing it out vertically into separate tables, or horizontally into sub-tables. The later can be achieved for example by partitioning by date or by key range. It is worth noting that for performance purposes partitioning can be achieved virtually with the use of the Parallel Query, which divides the data out amongst multiple processes as the

query is running. However actual data partitioning may still be required to avoid I/O contention, as multiple parallel processes try to query data on the same disk.

Step 10: To Propagate the Data into the Warehouse Storage

One of the most time consuming aspects of building a Data Warehouse environment is the design of the interface between the Warehouse and its source systems. We need to design an appropriate mechanism that will extract data from source systems prior to loading the Warehouse. Because the data in a Data Warehouse is derived from a wide variety of systems, the processes that extract data from those systems are crucial to the accuracy, consistency and timeliness of the Data Warehouse.

Before propagating those data from the source systems to the Data Warehouse, we need to estimate the size of the Data Warehouse, in order to create a Data Warehouse which is large enough to accommodate all the data as well as cater for its future growth.

Here is the rule of thumb of estimating the size of Data Warehouse:

- Estimate the size of one row in the fact table.
- For each dimension, check the granularity you want and estimate the number of members in the finest level.
- Multiply the numbers for each dimension and multiply the result with the fact table row size.
- We need to find out the Density Factor by deciding sparsity (most rows missing) and density (most row filled) of the fact table and estimate the reduction in size. For example, a retail company has 5000 different products and owned 300 stores, each stores will only sell 2500 products. The Density Factor is 0.5.
- We also need to find out the number of summary tables. If we have few summary tables, the total size of the star tables is three times the size of the fact table. If we have many summary tables, the total size of the star tables is five times the size of the fact table.

This is an iterative process usually. Each time there is a change in the design we will need to go through above calculation steps again.

Once we have gone through the sizing calculations, we can validate our assumptions by doing the following:

- Extract sample files
- Load data into the Data Warehouse
- Compute exact expected row lengths
- Add overhead for indexing, rollback and temp tablespaces, file system staging area for flat files

A Data Warehouse environment places several key demands on its extract mechanism:

- The extracts must be efficient enough to allow the Data Warehouse load and maintenance time windows to be met.
- The extract mechanism must be able to access a variety of database and file management systems.
- The extract process must be able to perform field transformations, to reconcile inconsistencies in naming conventions and data types that exist in the source systems. For example, the process must be able to recognise that a numeric field CUSTOMER_NUMBER in one system is the same as an alphanumeric field CUSTOMER_KEY in another.
- The extract process must be able to consistently encode data. For example, the field GENDER may be indicated by the characters "M" and "F" in one system and the digits "0" and "1" in another. As the data is prepared for loading into the Warehouse, a consistent structure for GENDER must be applied.
- The extract process must be able to perform unit of measure transformations (that is to say, reconcile inconsistencies in the units of measurement that may exist in the source systems).
- The extract process must be able to identify those pieces of data in the source systems that have changed since the last extract, in order that they may be selected for inclusion into the Data Warehouse.

We may need to schedule a regular batch job to refresh our Data Warehouse from our data sources. Depending on the data volumes and system load, this job may take several hours so the refresh process is typically done at night. We need to plan our Data Warehouse refresh so that under normal circumstances it can be accomplished within the batch window. Another consideration in our planning process should include the estimate of the data volume that will be refreshed. We need to develop a strategy for purging the data beyond the specified retention period.

Step 11: To Build a Data Warehouse Application

A wide range of end user data access and analysis tools are available for developing decision support applications. All tools which conform to open systems standards, and can generate queries can be integrated into the Data Warehouse architecture. Most tools include the ability to schedule queries, and some the ability to govern the amount of resources that will be used.

Multidimensional tools provide flexible trend analysis and predictive modelling capability against summary data. Relational tools are best suited to analysing detailed information which is held at the lowest level of granularity. They are used in decision support applications in which a great degree of flexibility is required over the way queries are framed. They are typically used to provide data mining, ad hoc querying and drill down capability in application.

We need to decide an appropriate tool for end-users to access the data held in the warehouse, including: ad hoc querying and reporting, drill-down and pivot, and full analysis such as modelling, forecasting, what-if analysis, etc. The majority of users need a straightforward, intuitive tool that allows them to easily access the data to make common business decisions. A separate set of analytical tools, users need to do more sophisticated, lengthy analysis in support of business strategies. Therefore, the tool should enables users to query the warehouse, graph results, create reports, perform drill and pivot analysis. Ease of use, Performance and Flexibility are three major criteria for choosing the end-user tools. As an example shown in Figure 14, it illustrated the graphical result of trend analysis of Building Estate Data Warehouse.

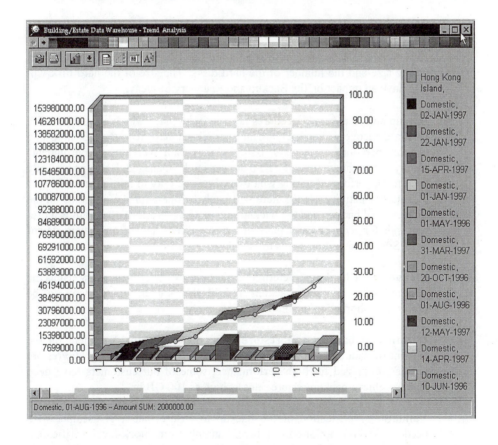

Typically, a single tool meets the decision support requirements in the proof of concept phase. As the data warehouse grows and usage increases, the requirements for new types of decision support arise. This leads to additional tools being introduced into the architecture. At this time, the need for more automated query management increases.

Step 12: Administration of the Data Warehouse

The following points need to be considered for the data warehouse administration:

1.   Security Management

- Group based security to ease the specification and maintenance of Warehouse access rights;
- Automatic data encryption across local area and wide area networks

2.   Backup and Recovery

- How large the data warehouse is going to be. This will have a direct impact on the size and the number of the hard disks. The size of the hard disk will also have an impact on the Backup and Recovery Strategy.

- Backup and Recovery procedures need to be in place which can support full database recovery, hot backups and partial database recovery. Backup and restore operations are a major issue in large Data Warehouse environments simply due to the volume of data that needs to be managed. Backups typically need to be performed during windows of low activity to minimize the impact on database activity. Hence there will likely be operational constraints on the frequency of backup and the backup rate required. Restore operation is a pre-requisite for recovery and therefore, has a direct impact on system down-time. Specific attention needs to be paid in terms of:

  Frequency of backups: determines the time to perform recovery using the backup. More frequent backups reduce the amount of recovery to be performed, shortening the duration of recovery.

  Duration of backup and restore operations: directly dependent on the amount of data and the backup/restore rate. Using advanced backup/restore utilities optimized for high performance, some of our customers have been able to achieve backup/restore rates as high as 100 GB/hr.

  Validation: verification of the backup to ensure that it is useable when needed. Several options exist here, ranging from block-level verification performed as part of the backup operation, to periodic restore and recovery using the backup on a different system.

3. Highest Availability

- The availability requirements need to be worked out. This will help in determining whether there is a need for a redundant hardware to speed up the backup and recovery time. This would provide for a very high availability at the cost of the redundant resources.

4. Data Management

- If the updates to primary keys are very frequent then the time window to rebuilt the indexes needs to be identified. This may also lead to fragmentation in the underlying table.
- The extract programs require substantial resources and therefore proper attention should be given to this phase of the Data Warehouse development.
- Due to the volume of data to be loaded every day, it is very important to design an extremely efficient load strategy. Some utility like Direct Path parallel loader is highly recommended for this purpose. All the pre-processing should be done by the extraction programs. The output of the extraction program should be one or more flat files which could be loaded directly into the data warehouse without any modifications.
- If the data is stored along various dimensions, it is very important to create flat files for each combination of the various dimensions and load them using direct path parallel loader.
- It should not be presumed that a single index on the large tables will suffice all the queries. Due to the amount of data present in a Data Warehouse, indexes are absolutely must, and any query not being able to use the index will take a long time to run. Therefore, secondary indexes are generally required.
- The batch jobs are a good candidate for using the indexes. It is absolutely crucial for batch jobs to have proper indexes defined to be able to execute them in the available batch window.

5. Data Ageing

- Data Ageing needs to be worked out. The application design needs to take account of the data life expectancy. We need to know how long will data have to live in the database. We may be able to reduce the amount of data held by summarising and aggregating older data. For example you may be able to aggregate data into monthly and weekly summaries at the end of each month, and then remove the raw data itself. We also need to establish how long you want to hold data before removing it completely from the database. There may be a requirement to archive old data to tape or even to another database. In larger data warehouse, the data volumes involved is significant. The problem is that when data archiving begins it can impose a regular heavy load on the system. If this is not planned for in the design and implementation, it can have a detrimental effect on performance.

Summary

Building data warehouse is an art, however we tried to create several basic steps for creating a successful data warehouse. Interview end-users to understand the problem domain and the questions they need to ask. Examine the normalized logical view of existing OLTP databases or external sources to see what additional entities might support analytical queries. Focus on the problem domain to eliminate unnecessary entities. After deciding the dimensions, we can then determine hierarchies to organize them; decide which attributes end-users need to analyze. The entities left over after we identify dimensions are fact tables. Then we need to identify measures for the fact tables. After that, we need to fine tune the data warehouse model to think about how to aggregate the data efficiently so that we can deliver the acceptable performance.

Finally, we need to build a Data Warehouse application. We need to choose data-query tools wisely. Data-query tools are end-users' window to the data warehouse. Of course, it is closely related to our Data Warehouse design as well. We need to spend time evaluating user and IT requirements and to select a tool that best suits our needs.

References

[1]   Oracle Magazine - March/April 1996
[2]   Michael Schrader and Bonnie K. O'Neil "Data Warehouse and Physical Database Design"
[3]   Kraft, Jon. "Designing the Data Warehouse on Relational Databases", ECO 1995
[4]   Oracle Express Relational Access Manager installation guide.
[5]   Meta Group Inc. Data Warehousing 1996 : Part 2 - File 487
[6]   Ovum Evaluates: OLAP
[7]   Deepak Gupta, "Designing a Data Warehouse Application: Tips and Techniques"
[8]   E. Neal Benshimol, "Peformance Tuning Tips & Techniques for Express Server"
[9]   Oracle White Paper - Oracle7 The Distributed Data Warehouse
[10]   Oracle Data Mart Suite Cookbook

About the Author:

Ringo Chan W. K.
BCS, ACS, HKCS, MBA, B.App.Sci (Comp. Sci), CNE, ECNE, CNI
Director of Presales Technical Support, Oracle Systems Hong Kong Limited
Email : RCHAN@hk.oracle.com

Ringo, Wai Keung Chan received his Bachelor of Computer Science degree from RMIT University, Australia and an MBA from Southern University, USA. He has more than 15 years experience in IT industry focusing on Relational Database Management Systems, client/server development, Object Oriented design, networking and application development. He is currently the Director of Presales Technical Support of Oracle Systems Hong Kong Limited. His active involvement in several DataWarehousing projects enables him to become an expert in that area. He has achieved CNE, ECNE, CNI. He is members of HKCS, BCS, and ACS.

Using the Web to Transform Data into Knowledge

C.S.Lo, SAS Institute Ltd.

Abstract:

The widespread popularity of Web technology has created a new information technology model in which thin clients enable the widespread distribution of information using standard protocols. This paper focuses on how enterprise decision support systems and the information technology industry are impacted by this paradigm shift.

Introduction

Enterprise decision support systems are typically designed to provide access to data regardless of location or format and allow analysis and transformation of the data into meaningful information that can be delivered to a wide variety of user interfaces. In many cases, enterprise decision support systems act as the primary user interface to a data warehouse. Web enablement offers the potential to increase users increase functionality or decrease client support cost within many decision support environments.

Because decision support systems are diverse, numerous Web methods must be considered. Many overlaps and costs and benefits differ for each. The list of factors that impact the choice of Web methods often includes GUI requirements, response time, the costs of development, deployment and maintenance, and the complexity of the underlying decision support applications.

The following diagram demonstrates many of the most popular methods that use local clients within a decision support system environment (DSS). Also note that many decision support systems provide traditional client/server methods that do not involve Web technology.

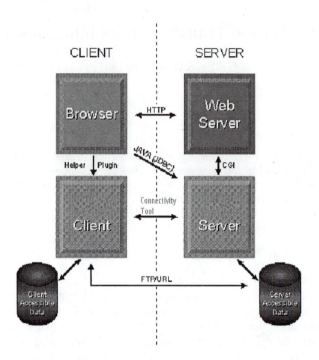

Expanding Decision Support Through the Web

Traditional Approaches to Information Delivery Enterprise decision support systems have evolved over the years to become some of the most innovative and comprehensive software systems available on the market. To be effective at the enterprise level, a decision support system is required to process data from a wide variety of data structures on a wide variety of platforms.

The enterprise decision support system should be multitiered and allow any platform to act as a data server, an application server, or a client. The bi-directional delivery of information from any supported platform to any other platform requires the use of sophisticated peer-to-peer communication protocols.

The enterprise decision support system should also take advantage of a multi-vendor architecture in order to manage data repositories that exist on many diverse platforms. Using a multi-vendor architecture allows the decision support system to provide identical functionality on different hardware platforms including Intel, SUN, HP, IBM, Digital, and Apple.

Complete and open read/write access to both internal and external third-party proprietary databases, including Oracle, Sybase, Informix, and DB2, frees application developers to use the most appropriate data structures for their decision support system. Decision support system vendors have traditionally relied on multiple database engines to deliver that freedom, and allow information from disparate and proprietary information sources to be blended into a generalized resource.

The Web Paradigm

The explosive growth of the Web has changed user expectations concerning the delivery of information to a client. The traditional decision support approach allowed any client to communicate as a peer to any available data server. The Web introduces a new model in which the client is less functional and relies upon the data or application servers for services traditionally executed on the client.

This new Web-enabled scenario allows either a two- or three-tiered communication process. With two tiers, the data/application server communicates directly with the client. With three tiers, the traditional approach to information delivery, the client communicates with a data server and/or an application server.

In the Web-enabled world, the client is effectively reduced to a viewer of information surfaced by the servers and is popularly known as a 'thin client'. A true thin client is not capable of program execution unless the executables are downloaded to the client.

Task Partitioning

The concept of a true thin client raises the issue of task partitioning. Partitioning a task between clients and servers is an effective way to distribute the computing resources required to complete the necessary components of the task. The most flexible decision support systems allow applications developers to control task partitioning (selective partitioning). By allowing the applications developer complete discretion over the partitioning of the task, decision support systems can achieve optimal performance regardless of hardware configurations.

The Web's thin client philosophy constrains the ability of application developers to effectively partition applications. This is due to the limited functionality on the client side. In the Web environment, nearly all functionality is delivered from the server side of the application while the client performs very simple display and querying functions. This model is often referred to as enforced partitioning.

The Irresistible Thin Client

The most appealing aspect of Web technology to information technologists is the thin client. The thin client allows application developers to eliminate the notion of software distribution at the client level, to eliminate the notion of maintaining software on remote clients, and to eliminate the notion of maintaining most software and hardware configurations for remote clients. This reduces the cost of application deployment and is driving the development of intranets throughout the world in companies of all sizes.

How does the thin client do all of these things? Thin clients, by definition, have the minimal hardware and software requirements necessary to function as a communication front-end for a Web enabled application. Hardware requirements are as simple as a network or modem connection to a server and a 386 Intel chip running Windows.

Even simpler requirements are surfacing in the marketplace as lightweight operating systems find their way to microchips that can be embedded in devices like telephones, cable set top boxes, and personal digital assistants. The primary software required is a Web browser such as Netscape's Navigator, Microsoft's Internet Explorer, NCSA's Mosaic, or others that allow HTTP (HyperText Transport Protocol) communications between the thin client and the remote server.

The newly defined 'Internet Appliance', a combination of minimal hardware and software configurations, takes the concept of thin clients to the extreme. An Internet Appliance will be prepackaged as a single product that totally relies on network communications to reach applications on servers. Oracle Corporation and others have proposed Internet Appliances as the next generation of PCs for Web enabled applications. Although this type of device is very appealing because of small footprint and low up-front cost, an organization's average network bandwidth will have to increase by an order of magnitude before widespread use is possible for most decision support applications.

Despite modest hardware and software requirements, the thin client is quite capable of delivering considerable quantities of information using standard protocols. The primary limitation of a thin client is its inability to perform even simple tasks without requesting services from the server. Local data validation, context sensitive menus, online pop-up help windows, locally controlled drill-down menus, and other functions that traditionally execute on the client are executed on the server in a thin client environment.

The Java language is now being used to overcome some of these limitations. Java allows the creation of applets, which are automatically downloaded and executed on the local client. Applets can significantly increase the interaction between the client application and user, and allow tasks to be executed on the client.

Java and other languages that deliver locally available executables are, however, still dependent on network bandwidth to deliver the executables. Depending on the scope and capability of the applets, large numbers of executables may need to be downloaded in order to accomplish the task. Executables are only resident during execution and are removed from the local disk after the completion of the task. As the demand for larger applets grows, significant download time could be incurred and memory and disk space on the thin client may become a limiting factor.

Downloading all required executables on demand is very attractive from a deployment perspective because the footprint of an application on the client remains small and manageable for large scale deployment. Alternatively, keeping commonly used applets resident on the client can significantly reduce download time, although this practice runs counter to a purely thin client model.

Java applets are interpreted on the client by the Java Virtual Machine, which is usually embedded in the Java-enabled browser. Speed of execution once the download is complete is not an issue with the small applets that are in use today. Large applets or groups of applets linked to perform a task will run slower than single purpose compact applets. Including a just-in-time compiler in the browser could increase applet execution speed as applets become larger.

The Future

The Fully Functional Intelligent Client

The qualities of thin clients mentioned in the previous section are regularly highlighted in the media, and direct comparisons of thin and fat clients abound. In reality, a wide range of client configurations exist between the extremes of thin and fat clients. At one end of the spectrum is the ultimate thin client; a hand-held portable device with a chip set capable of supporting a bare-bones operating system allowing the client to perform single function tasks. At the opposite end of the spectrum is the fully featured fat client built upon the service environment of a high powered workstation. The fat client has many system resources at its disposal and is able to fulfill the complex needs of the most sophisticated decision support systems.

In between the extremes of thin and fat clients lies a continuum of client configurations. Thin clients that address more and more sophisticated types of, applications and fat clients trimmed to deliver more focused functionality fall somewhere in the middle. The 'intelligent client' appears at the point in the continuum where the client is capable of providing the local functionality required by a decision support system. Intelligent clients can take advantage of system services for printing and 1/0, can take advantage of the hardware for graphics display and redisplay, and can take advantage of the surrounding network to retrieve and transform additional data on behalf of the client application.

What are the advantages of the intelligent client when compared with the thin client?

First is the wide range of localized functionality available with an intelligent client. For instance, drilling down through a successive series of steps within a data structure is very rapid with an intelligent client because the metabase upon which the drill downs are based are processed locally. The client does not encounter network delays that would be encountered when instructions and data are passed to and from the server for processing. Decreasing application response times can elevate productivity levels for power users.

A related advantage is the ability to partition application task requirements efficiently between the client and the server. The intelligent client allows the developer to determine which tasks would be most effectively executed on the client. By assigning frequently executing tasks to client-resident applications, the need to download and/or compile code across the network is reduced.

The most compelling reason for the use of an intelligent client in a decision support system is the need for sophisticated user interfaces. Ease of use is often the primary factor for considering a Web based solution, however, the current limitations with HTML and the Java class libraries make the implementation of complex front ends very difficult. The intelligent client offers the opportunity to deliver highly graphical, highly interactive user interfaces that provide point-and-click navigation through complex data models and reporting structures. Exploring complex Data Mining trends, subsetting dimensions in an OLAP environment, or drilling though successive graphics in an Executive Information System requires easy-to-use, highly visual interfaces. Clearly, the full-featured screen control language typically available in a decision support system has many advantages over the rudimentary offerings of Java and HTML.

New Standards for Enterprise Decision Support Systems

Decision support systems must meet new standards if they are to remain viable in a Web-enabled environment. The thin client model appears irresistible to information consumers and will probably be incorporated into most decision support architectures. Fortunately, there are several open protocols and techniques currently available that allow decision support systems to take advantage of thin clients.

The most common techniques are based on the Common Gateway Interface (CGI). CGI allows a thin client to request the services of a decision support system via the Web server. After receiving a request for information via CGI, output from the decision support system is simply returned to the browser in HTML format.

Similar methods of transferring information from decision support systems to thin clients include Microsoft's Open DataBase Connectivity (ODBC) protocol and the Java DataBase Connectivity (JDBC) protocol defined by Javasoft. Support of these two prominent delivery mechanisms is a key factor in the acceptance of a decision support system in a Web-enabled environment.

With thin clients, the ability to transparently access multiple data types are placed entirely upon the server. As a result, an enterprise decision support system must provide direct access to transactional data stored in a wide variety of popular database management systems as well as providing data storage optimized for decision support functions. JDBC and ODBC can often be utilized to reach such data, however, more direct access is often more efficient. A Web-enabled decision support system that uses multiple data engines to achieve data transparency to the client is widely regarded as best of breed from a data warehouse perspective.

Additional Web-based techniques should be considered when the intelligent client model is appropriate. There are numerous applications on the market today that require the use of significant client resources and would benefit from application segmentation. These applications fit well with the intelligent client model and can be implemented in a Web environment using selected components of a decision support system as helper and plug-in applications. Helper and plug-in applications allow the distribution of some processing to the client, yet the browser remains the primary user interface. Intelligent clients can also benefit from the data access and back-end communications protocols described above.

Conclusion

Web and thin client technologies are already impacting the way decision support systems are used. Due to the reduction in client costs, thin clients provide an attractive way to deliver information to consumers at the low end of the technology spectrum. Although there are many techniques that allow thin clients to download and execute applications, network bandwidth will ultimately determine the usefulness of the thin client in a decision support system context. In order for the Internet Appliance to become the ultimate thin client, a significant increase in network bandwidth will be necessary.

Although intelligent clients offer the best method for the delivery of sophisticated user interfaces, given the present limitations of network bandwidth, decision support systems must support both thin and intelligent clients to cover the wide range of user expectations. As technology matures and more services can be delivered using thin clients, decision support systems will evolve and reserve the use of intelligent clients for the more complex and sophisticated applications.

An intelligent business workbench for

the insurance industry:

Using data mining to improve decision making and performance

Grant J. Keats and S. Grace Loo
gkeats@voyager.co.nz, g.loo@auckland.ac.nz
Tamaki MSIS, The University of Auckland
Private Bag 92019
Auckland, New Zealand
Fax +64 9 3737566

Abstract:

Insurance is a data intensive industry. There are enormous volumes of transaction data stored by New Zealand insurers in various distributed, heterogenous databases. To gain competitive advantage many insurers are now trying to extract additional meaning, patterns and relationships from the data which they already hold and to use this extracted knowledge to improve decision making and performance. There have been many tools proposed to assist with this decision making over the last thirty years. These traditional methods of analysis are not viable given the size and dimensionality of modern databases. Recently the fields of data warehousing, knowledge discovery and data mining have emerged as potential techniques for addressing these problems. This paper outlines an intelligent business workbench specifically designed for the insurance industry. We have chosen to concentrate on three potential uses. Our work to date has resulted in a proposed data model and system architecture for the insurance industry. Preliminary data analysis has been performed using a rule induction tool to generate potentially interesting rules to investigate. Examples of these are presented in this paper.

1. Introduction

Knowledge discovery in databases, including the step of data mining, is the combination of machine learning, statistics, visualisation and database technologies. It has been proposed for automatically discovering patterns and relationships from data [FAY96]. The insurance industry, amongst others, has built up enormous quantities of transaction oriented data over the last thirty or so years and many companies are now looking to utilise this largely untapped store of potential information and knowledge. A commonly encountered situation is the need for a choice between multiple, often conflicting and uncertain options. Many tools have been proposed to assist in the decision making process over the last four decades ranging from the Management Information Systems (MIS) of the sixties and the Decision Support Systems (DSS) of the seventies and eighties to the Executive Information Systems (EIS) of the eighties and nineties and more recently On Line Analytical Processing systems (OLAP). The most recent developments have seen data mining becoming prominent. In this paper we propose a data model and architecture for an intelligent business workbench which incorporates data mining technology and which is intended specifically for the insurance industry.

As discussed in [SIM96] a single data mining technique on its own is often insufficient for extracting useful knowledge. By combining multiple techniques enhanced results may be achievable. In many companies independent databases and applications have been created in the various functional areas; for example there are claim, premium, policy and client databases and these may contain redundant and/or conflicting data. Furthermore they contain data at a low level whereas decision makers generally think in terms of higher level and aggregated concepts.

Our definition of the proposed workbench[1] is a loosely coupled, tightly integrated group of modules which can be modified or replaced independently, for example when faster or more powerful algorithms are developed. The data mining components of the workbench are intended to be integrated and used in conjunction with other tools such as managed SQL query environments, OLAP tools for multi-dimensional and drill-down analysis, and with graphical tools.

Our position is that when organisations are given more data, provided it is relevant, together with better analysis tools and methods, then better decisions will follow. We define better decisions to mean that in the long-run profit are raised by either increasing income, reducing costs or both. The benefits accruing may be classified as short term/long term and as tangible/intangible.

The rest of the paper is organised as follows. Section 1.1 discusses how we believe the workbench could improve performance and decision making. Section 2 examines the insurance industry, the representation of knowledge which we infer from the stored data, and the potential insurance uses for data mining. Although our focus is primarily exploratory we also look at some technical issues of data mining in this section. Section 3 then outlines a conceptual data model for an insurance company and discusses the types of rules which would be valuable to discover or to validate. Section 4 proposes an architecture and reviews some of the workbench's modules. Section 5 presents some examples of discovered rules. Section 6 evaluates the work done so far and summarises the future work needed. Section 7 presents our conclusions.

1.1 Performance Improvement and Decision Making

The use of the workbench will improve an insurer's performance by two aspects. The first will be to improve both workgroup and company workflows as data mining will

---

[1] The architecture is described in detail in Section 4.

enhance our ability to analyse the process data. The second will be through obtaining better outcomes[2] from the company's decision making.

In the insurance industry choices are constantly being made between alternatives and this decision making is often not rational or optimal due to a number of factors including [KLE95]:

1. Time and cost constraints which inhibit a comprehensive search.
2. Lack of information on problem formulation, alternatives and consequences.
3. Human imperfections in perceiving and handling large volumes of information.
4. Differing resources and power bases amongst the decision participants.

Our workbench addresses points one, two and three. We have examined the recent literature and have built on the ideas put forward in the following tools[3]: IMACS [BRA93], KNOWLEDGE MINER [SHE94], RECON [SIM96], KEFIR [PIA96]. These architectures were studied closely and we have expanded on the areas we felt were most promising. The next section introduces the insurance industry and some potential uses of data mining for enhancing its performance.

2. The Application of Data Mining Techniques for Enhancing Performance in the Insurance Industry

It is worthwhile at this juncture to examine the insurance industry, its characteristics and its decision situations. In this particular paper we concentrate on the pre-data mining stage of transforming of data to a suitable format, examine one data mining technique namely decision trees for classification rule creation and briefly mention the post-data mining work which is still needed. Section 2.1 is a general overview of the industry and in it we suggest several generic objectives. Section 2.2 examines the types of data and information encountered in an insurance environment. Section 2.3 discusses data transformation and the creation of reusable data sets. Section 2.4 proposes a number of potential uses of data mining in insurance companies, three of which we expand upon. Section 2.5 introduces the rule structure we use for representing knowledge about risk.

2.1 Insurance Industry Objectives

Any proposed solution should at a minimum have features which address some, or ideally all, of the following objectives:

---

[2] Other short term benefits include speeding up the decision making process and increasing customer satisfaction. These should lead to higher profit in the long term and a larger customer base.

[3] The interested reader should refer to the original papers for additional information.

- To be able to understand better and predict customer behaviour, such as likely customer reaction to promotions and the changing insurance needs over a client's lifetime.
- To improve the ability to evaluate and reduce risk.

- To assist in maximising return on investment.
- To provide the capability to lower direct marketing costs.
- To provide the capability to quickly develop new products.
- To move easily to an electronic delivery path to reduce costs.
- To reduce the reporting cycle; this may be especially important where demutualisation has occurred and new legislative requirements have arisen.
- To meet regulatory requirements at lowest cost.
- To reduce the time lag between the lodging of a claim and its payment. The primary goal is to find the optimal claim settlement, as over generous or lenient claims handling will lower profits while an overly hard stance may lead to increased appeals, possible litigation and investigation by industry regulators.

In addition we propose that data mining can assist in answering more specific insurance questions such as these:
- What patterns can be found to detect fraudulent claims?
- Are there relationships detectable between attributes, or combination of attributes, which impact on the likelihood of a claim? Specifically we are looking for those relationships which are not widely considered obvious.
- What are the customer profiles that characterise high-risk policy applicants?
- Which customers are more likely to respond to a policy promotion?
- What are the profiles of high profit customers who are likely to leave for another insurer?
- What are the key factors that impact customer satisfaction?
- What macro-economic factors will affect investment returns?
- In what order, and at what ages, are people likely to purpose specific products?
- What portfolio splits are the most likely to produce the most stable/highest/lowest returns over various time frames?

Although an insurance company will have detailed historical information about topics such as claims it may still have trouble in isolating likely indicators of fraud or high risk. Existing large relational database systems do not currently include the production of patterns amongst the standard or proprietary SQL capabilities. This is an opportunity for automatic, system-led discovery to provide more value than the current manual, user-led techniques. The above questions depend heavily on the judgement of people and they can be performed manually, though not without a great deal of effort. We have chosen three areas to explore in Section 3 where we believe data mining can improve significantly these manually intensive procedures. The next section will focus on data relevant to the insurance industry.

2.2 Insurance Data and Information

A company's raw data contains within it information about its products, its customers and its markets. The value of this data lies in what can be extracted, abstracted and inferred from it. An interesting point to note is that although profit is the main objective, customer service is often seen as the differentiating factor between insurers. This is ironic given that many insurance databases were designed with a product rather than customer focus. The majority of existing data is currently stored in relational databases. As mentioned it is often distributed across heterogeneous functional databases. The data needs to be extracted from these operational databases and transferred to a data warehouse where the focus can now be changed to emphasise the customers. The data from the data warehouse may then need to further transformed to a form appropriate for each data mining algorithm or module.

Another consideration is that in a relational database environment it is difficult to process SQL queries like "Select all claims likely to be fraudulent". In recent years a number of techniques have emerged for processing of vague/approximate queries. These include the fuzzy set approach, the metric approach and the rough set approach [LOO96, MOT90, PAW91, ZAD89]. The application of rough sets-based data mining methodology has shown potential in the analysis of medical data when investigating the relationships between two, user-defined groups of attributes and decision attributes [TSU96]. The rough set approach has also been shown to provide a theoretical basis for the solution of many problems within knowledge discovery [MOL96]. Exploration of these techniques will take place at a later stage of the project. The next section discusses the conversion of insurance data into a suitable format for data mining.

2.3 Creation of Reuseable Intermediate Data

For individual tasks we will require different subsets of our data warehouse and the various data mining algorithms may require different input formats To maximise reuse we produce intermediate datasets which can be stored in the data warehouse and retrieved and further transformed if and when needed.

Each insurance policy names an insured entity or entities and the level of cover provided. Various attributes of these entities and additional details relevant to the contract have been captured. Beginning with the policy database our first step was to consolidate the multiple transactions found for many policies. This includes policy condition amendments and sum insured increases/decreases for example. The individual steps needed to transform the data were as follows:

- General data cleaning: e.g. converting birth dates to an age (at a specific date).
- Calculation and inclusion of derived fields e.g. number of policies held by a client.
- Decision on how to handle missing or suspect values. For the purposes of our initial investigation we simply ignored any records with one or more missing values.

- Other factors which need additional consideration, but are outside the scope of this paper, include the period of exposure to the risk and the fact that only a small number of records may have claims against them. Appropriate handling of the statistical aspects is very important, and this will be included in an upcoming paper.

The next section presents a summary of potential uses for data mining in insurance.

2.4 Data Mining Techniques for Insurance

We summarise some potential uses of data mining techniques in an insurance context in Table 1 below. Within the limits of this paper[4] we can not discuss all of these. The categories shown are not meant to represent all possibilities, they are merely intended as an initial guiding framework. In Section 5 we present our work with examples from the prediction, clustering and sequence analysis categories.

Table 1. Suggested data mining applications

Technique	Potential uses for the Insurance industry
Classification/Prediction	• Build models of characteristics which identify highly profitable clients and/or clients likely to let policies lapse. • Build profiles for clients showing suggested cover and/or appropriate portfolios.
Clustering	• Group database into clusters, which can then be overlaid with demographics and use for targeted marketing. From this we may try to identify under-insured people and possibilities for cross-selling. • Identify high and low risk groups, and adjust rates accordingly.
Association/Sequence Analysis	• Identify products which are commonly brought together. • Identify the sequences followed by stocks and bonds. • Identify the sequence in which products are brought in the course of a person's lifetime. • Analyse the workflow processes and detect the patterns of efficient workgroup practises.
Deviation Detection	• Detect patterns which identify fraudulent claims. • Detect unusual return on investments patterns.

---

[4] Further information will be available in later papers or interested readers can contact the authors.

2.4 Risk

Insurance is a business which deals predominantly with risk. To assist in evaluating risk there are a number of techniques for building prediction and classification models. These include neural networks, genetic algorithms and fuzzy logic. In an insurance context we often need to make risk estimation decisions based on historical and geographic information [GOO96]. The geographic information may be naturally represented using a Geographic Information System (GIS) and in the future this is an additional module which could be included in the workbench.

Regardless of the data mining method used it would be desirable to have a common representational structure for the extracted knowledge. Our approach follows the lead of others, for example EXPLORA [KLO96] and RECON [SIM96] in choosing to generate rules of the type:

IF Occupation [Air-traffic controller] AND Age [30-40] AND Smoker [Yes] THEN Risk [High]
These rules could then be saved and manipulated via a deductive database.

3.   Conceptual Modelling and Task Discussion

It should be noted that we are concentrating on knowledge discovery in this paper, which we propose deals with the generation of understandable knowledge and not on the machine learning aspects which deal with improving the performance of an agent. The data mining tasks which we discuss in Sections 3.3, 3.4 and 3.5 should be read with this in mind, as we are not claiming completeness or efficiency as our main objectives at this stage.

There are generic data mining tools[5] available, for example Darwin and Clementine. Other tools have been slightly customised with an insurance flavour and are available from vendors such as Information Discovery and IBM. It is hard to ascertain the extent of the use of these tools in the New Zealand market due to the competitive nature of the insurance business. Some degree of secrecy often surrounds leading edge developments and as a result commercially sensitive business analysis are not usually published.

The data which we want to combine and investigate is from the client, policy, premium and claim areas. This data is initially transaction oriented and a number of processes may be needed to convert it to an appropriate format for analysis. As stated

---

[5] Darwin - www.thinking.com, 12 Apr 97;
  Clementine - www.islco.uk, 10 Apr 97;
  IBM issc2.boulder.ibm.com/insur/insur1.htm, 5 Apr 97;
  Information Discovery - www.datamining.com, 25 Mar 97.

our approach is to extract and build rule based models. To achieve reuse we will build templates and construct meta-data as the models develop.

The low level structures used to describe the data in the databases are very different from the concepts a decision maker thinks in terms of. If possible the proposed conceptual model should encode some or all of the domain knowledge we hold. This may be by indicating the importance of various attributes and the relationships between attributes. Another example of domain knowledge is currently believed rules.

Working with datasets from a large New Zealand insurer we have been performing some preliminary analysis and investigation. In this paper we have concentrated on three specific applications, one in marketing, one in workflow analysis and one in premium setting. For the mining undertaken we restricted ourselves to dealing with a trial subset. This was extracted from the insurer's Oracle database, stored in a temporary database and provided to Sipina in the required format, flat file in our case. As discussed in Section 2.3 various dependent variables can be selected based on the intermediate datasets and hypotheses can be generated or tested. The rules which are generated can be denoted as exact, strong or probabilistic. The probablistic rules can be represented by certainty factors (CF) and this point is expanded upon in the next section.

3.1 Constructing Rules from Decision Trees

For the purposes of classification type problems we could have used one or more of the following data mining techniques: neural networks, decison trees, nearest neighbour or case based reasoning. Our choice was to use the Sipina-Windows tool which automatically generates rules from a decision tree. More details on Sipina-Windows are given in Section 3.2. Potentially a very large number of rules could be generated and as we are only concerned with interesting rules we need paprameters to reduce the number of rules to be considered. One approach is to only investigate the rules with the highest CFs. An alternative approach is to investigate those where the CF exceeds a certain threshold. A second parameter which we considered was the number of examples supporting a classification rule. Rules with a low number of supporting examples were ignored at this early stage as they may represent overfitting based on an inappropriately small sample size. As already stated our belief in the rules can be expressed by certainty factors. The certainty factor represents the degree of prior evidence which has been obtained. Potential methods for expressing certainty factors include Baynesian probabilty, Dempster-Shafer, the frequency pproach and a statistical approach. Interested readers should refer to [SIL96] for a comparison. Our simple approach has been to calculate certainty factors as ratios: for example XY/X.
XY = number of clients with matching attributes who have policy of certain type
X = number of clients with matching attributes

3.2   Sipina-Windows Application

Sipina is both the name of an induction learning method [ZIG85] and of the software which we used (Sipina-Windows). Sipina-Windows produces lattice graphs, and trees are a particular case of a lattice. The software documentation claims that the Sipina method is more general than ID3 and C4.5 although we have not attempted to substantiate this claim.   The lattice graph can be automatically translated into production rules and these are then stored in an internal knowledge based system (KBS). Sipina-Windows can merge KBSs and can also detect and resolve problems such as redundancy and contradiction within a set of rules. Sipina-Windows allows the preferred discretisation method to be chosen. The methods available for selection are:

- Chi-merge (Kerber 1993)
- MDLPC (Fayyad and Irani 1993)
- Fusinter (Zighed et al. 1995)
- Contrast method (Van de Merckt 1993)

We have used the default only so far, i.e. the Fusinter method.

3.3   Direct Marketing using Prediction/Classification

This predictive task involves analysing portions of the database with rules generated from sample sets. There is an obvious trade-off based on the fact that the training has been done on a sample and we expect that larger samples should lead to lower estimation errors and variance but will require additional time for transformation and training. Our first exercise was to build a dataset of clients and their various attributes (referred to as independent or exogenous variables), which could then be combined with various endogenous (or dependent) variables and used to build prediction and classification models. We attempt to find a rule z which classifies an individual w into the set of classes defined by the values able to taken by the dependent variable. All instances of w are drawn from a population Ω and can be described by a set of characteristics $X(w) = (X_1(w), ..,X_P(w))$. Our method is to select a sample Ω_1 where the state of the attributes for the chosen sample is known.

The ability of trees to be responsive to local phenomena is sometimes offset by a tendency towards overfitting. The pruning of the trees is handled in our case by inspecting and testing the rules generated. This is obviously not desirable once the trees exceed a certain size. A final decision on the models incorporated can be deferred to a later stage in the project. Our specific focus so far has been on identifying characteristics of clients who hold disability policies with the aim of performing a targeted mailed campaign to clients who do not currently have this type of insurance but have similar characteristics to clients who do. We then compare the results to the response rates of previous campaigns. We have selected twenty attributes initially and have been discretising continuous variables and performing other necessary transformations. The list of attributes includes obvious ones such as income, age, sex, marital status and occupation but the full list cannot be displayed due to confidentially requirements. In the future this process could be repeated to predict which clients are likely to purchase retirement products.

3.4 Workflow Analysis

Our next step was to analyse the workflow processes with the intention of identifying duplicated effort and potential areas of savings. There are many historical instances of processes, eg. claims handling, which can analysed. The specific attributes which we are looking at are:

- Processing and idle time.
- Who executed the process; for example employee, role or unit.
- What activities were performed.
- Which customer, policy or other entity was affected.
- Parallel, or sequential processes running.
- Metrics such as quality and cost.

One possibly interesting outcome will be the identification of bottlenecks in the workflow processes. This is potentially a rewarding area but much of the data is dispersed and not held in a suitable format. A large amount of data aggregating and summarising work is currently being pursued within the project for this purpose.

3.5 Claim Analysis and Premium Tuning

The third area we are investigating involves factors which may be predictors of potential claimants, in this case concentrating on the life insurance sector. Our purpose in doing so is to enhance, rather than replace, the actuaries making premium setting decisions. Premiums are generally based on a small number of factors. These are often affected by occupation, by existing medical conditions, and by age and by various other parameters. The two extremes for premium setting would be to charge the same premium for everyone or to charge individual premiums for each person. Our aim is to allow the fine-tuning of premiums by identifying and considering more factors which possibly affect the risk. Our work so far has involved cleansing and consolidating data and trying to identify relevant and irrelevant attributes. It should be noted that only a small percentage of the clients and policies have claims against them. Using the fact the a claim has been made as the dependent variable we construct a decision tree and from it a number of rules. Once we have generated a number of potential rules these will be validated against currently believed knowledge and possibly refined further. The other uses mentioned in Table 1 are currently being investigated by the authors and will be reported on in a later paper.

266

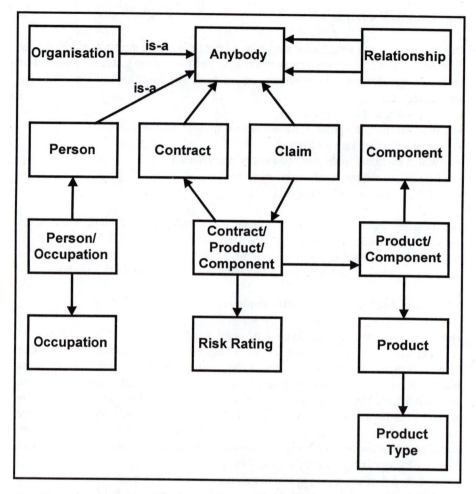

Figure 2 - Data model for an insurance company with policy and client emphasis

This is a general data model and is not meant to represent the structure of the data warehouse.

The choice of a data mining tool and method depends on the volume and type of the data and on the goals. For our insurance tasks we would like users other than information technology professionals to be able to use the workbench. This means that we would like to hide, as much as possible, the algorithm and database specifics. We centralise the different actions which a user needs to carry out during a knowledge discovery session; that is data selection, extraction, manipulation and result visualisation.

These requirements have driven the conceptual development of an architecture which is outlined in the next section.

4. Proposed Architecture

The kernel of our proposed workbench architecture is a data warehouse. This is used for consolidating data from various internal sources. It is also used for capturing external data such as industry averages.

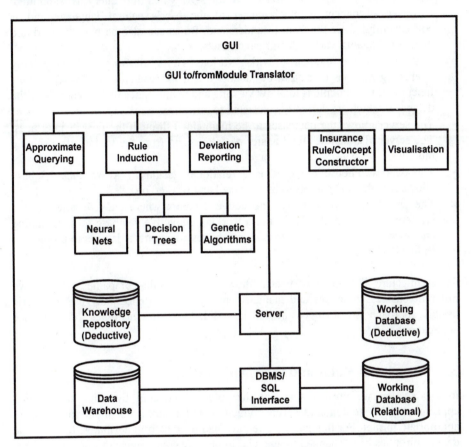

Figure 3. Workbench architecture

Components of the Proposed Architecture:

- The interface is consistent across the tools. Each of the modules will be able to be invoked in a similar way and will present its relevant services to the user.
- We have been working with the rule induction tool Sipina. A number of machine learning algorithms are also available in MLC++ [KOH96]. Additionally there are a number of other methods such as decision trees, neural networks or genetic algorithms which can be used for building models.

- The deviation reporting module is useful for continuous data mining where data is received in an ongoing stream. This would be for fraud detection, identifying process bottlenecks and the analysis of financial trading data for example.
- The rule/concept constructor is used to build and maintain concepts such as "high risk". These concepts are translated to SQL when the query is submitted. However a concept is much closer to the user's natural language and is consequently easier for them to understand. Rules can also be hypothesised and then tested against various historical datasets.
- The visualisation module provides various views allowing both potentially interesting portions of data to be identified and for results to be displayed. One function of this module is to allow viewing and maintenance of the schemas of the databases which are currently connected to.
- The server allows the databases to be maintained through the DBMS interfaces. The server also handles the transfer of data to and from the various data mining modules.
- The data warehouse proposed is a relational database[6]. A working database allows samples and subsets to be extracted and worked on.
- The knowledge repository is a deductive database where the rule-base and the concepts are stored. Again we use a working deductive database for maintaining and testing potential rules. The rules can be tested against a data set to provide an estimate of certainty.

An architecture like the workbench allows us to handle companies which have different business practices and management styles. We deliberately use a generic design approach so that the model is valid for different types of insurance applications.

5. Discovered Rules and their Application

In this section we present some of the rules[7] discovered by using the Sipina[8] application. This tool includes rule induction and it needs its input to be in an appropriate format. For this purpose we have had to transform attributes, for example date of birth has been changed to age, and to classify continuous attributes into either discrete values or categories. A dependent variable is chosen and training sets with examples covering the possible outcomes are then analysed by Sipina. The resulting rules can then be tested on other datasets and the rules can be then stored for further manipulation such as subsuming specialised rules with more general ones. Sipina also

---

[6] We have been using Oracle 7.3 but any suitable database could be used. At this stage most New Zealand insurers are using relational databases but we have kept the architecture flexible so that object

or object/relational databases could be used. Additional DBMS interfaces could be added as required. This also allows us to handle legacy network databases if necessary.

[7] We are bound by confidentially requirements so we only show here some of the simplest rules. Further examples are given in the appendix.

[8] The freeware version we are using is available from ftp://eric.univ-lyon2.fr/pub/sipina.

provides a visual representation of the rules in a decision tree like structure. We have changed some of the rule clauses below in order not to reveal commercially sensitive information and our intention is to provide the general format of these rules. The format of these rules is not exactly as seen from the Sipina output. We have changed them slightly for easier readability and have ignored the number of cases supporting and contradicting the rule as this is not relevant at this stage. The rules are grouped by subject area and a brief discussion is given for each.

5.1   Rules Generated from Marketing Analysis

Rule 5.1.1   IF Occupation-Code in [A..C]
                   AND Income > [X]
                   AND Has-Policy-Type [Z]
                   THEN Likely-To-Buy = Yes with CF .15

This rule is useful for cross-selling purposes. The customers have been clustered into occupational classes. A mailout could be done to customers who match the occupation and income conditions and who have a policy of type which is identified as complimentary to the target one. The aim is to improve the response rate from the mailout. Note that the certainty factors (CF) shown here are fictitious and do not have specific relevance for the insurance industry.

Rule 5.1.2   IF Income < [Y]
                   THEN Likely-To-Buy = No with CF .85

This rule allows us to work from another angle. In this case we eliminate customers who we reasonably sure would not reply. The remaining customers could then be filtered further if required.

Rule 5.1.3   IF Occupation-Code in [A, B, D]
                   AND Age in [20-45]
                   AND Married = [Yes]
                   THEN Likely-To-Buy = Yes with CF .065

Again this rule examines factors which may be potential predictors of whether or not a customer will response to mailout based on previous campaigns. These rules are currently being tested against other historical data.

5.2   Rules for Workflow

Our first cut for analysing the workflow within the claims department was to use summary statistics such as the mean to split instances of claims handling into the categories extremely slow, slow, average, fast and extremely fast. The aim is to identify factors which are potential bottlenecks. As has been mentioned claims is the critical function of an insurer as the majority of expenses arise here.

Rule 5.2.1   IF No-Times-Handled > 8
                    THEN Payout-Speed = extremely slow with CF .95

This is a fairly obvious rule indicating that if a claim is handled multiple times then the speed with which it is handled will be very slow.

Rule 5.2.2   IF Received-In-Dept [X]
                    THEN Payout-Speed NOT (extremely slow OR extremely fast) with CF .75

This is an potentially interesting rule indicating that if a claim is received in a certain department then the speed with which it is handled is not often at either extreme.

5.3 Rules for Premium Setting

To enable accurate premium setting we need external sources of demographic information such as number of people in the general population dying, or being injured from various causes.

Rule 5.3.1   IF Height in [X..Y]
                              AND Weight < [T] or > [Z]
                    THEN Decline

This rule has identified abnormal height/weight ratios from previous cases which have led to high levels of claims. This rule is valuable because the cost of turning away potentially profitable business may outweigh the cost of an occasional claim. An insurer needs to be as accurate as possible to maximise profit. We can also look at specific datasets and derive a decision tree which could be represented as rules to classify claimants and non-claimants.

Rule 5.3.2   IF Occupation-Class = [A] OR [C]
                              AND Level-of-Cover > [X]
                              AND Policy-Years-Held < [Y]
                              and Claim-Made = [Yes]
                    THEN Payout = Large with CF .32

This rule may help to identify customers with a high probability of claiming in the current period of analysis. Appropriate steps to reduce the risk may then be taken.

The rule induction tool, Sipina, has proven to be very useful for this phase. Some of the rules have been critically evaluated by our industry contacts and they have raised no great doubts over their possible validity. We should note however that a large number of rules have been generated and these require substantial further investigation. A deductive database will allow us to easily store, manipulate and retrieve these rules. This will also assist in the speed with which a company can respond to changing information and may provide significant advantage. These rules represent the vital information and knowledge which an insurance company may gain from using the workbench. The next section identifies the work which we are currently pursuing.

6. Work in Progress

The early results of our data analysis have been encouraging. This research project has now started to proceed onto subsequent steps. The following activities are currently being undertaken:

- Continuing data consolidation and investigation using rule induction.
- Evaluation of tools such as Darwin and Clementine which are generic, integrated tools under Piatetsky-Shapiro's classification [PIA96] and which may be an appropriate base for the workbench.
- Testing of algorithms such as those available in MLC++ [KOH96].
- Ongoing detailed investigation into insurance practices and data.
- We use Boehm's spiral model for software development for refinement of our conceptual model and architecture.
- Additional work is needed in interface design for investigating and reporting on automatic continuous data mining and deviation reporting.

We are continuing to use the datasets provided by our contacts at a large local insurer. At this stage we are using small datasets and in the next phase we will move to larger datasets in order to continue testing our hypothesis that the techniques of data mining will provide enhanced performance and decision making for insurance companies.

7. Conclusion

Initial results have been encouraging and indicate that data mining technology is effectively enhanced by integrating the various techniques as defined in our workbench, allowing higher quality rule-based models to be developed. An area for further investigation is the inclusion of the rough set approach into our workbench in an easy to use manner. This will be reported on in the near future.

For this paper we have concentrated specifically on the insurance domain. However the basic architecture of our workbench can be easily generalised for other financial industries and this will be discussed in another paper. Our workbench is modular in structure and is easily modified and extended when required. Thus our workbench will continue to add value as the amount of quality domain knowledge increases and is available in a form which can be used in a timely and accurate manner.

272

Acknowledgment

The authors would like to acknowledge the assistance they received in terms of supplied datasets and access to expert insurance opinion on the generated rules. The company involved has asked to remain anonymous at this time.

Appendix - further examples of generated rules

        IF Income > [X]
                AND Children = [No]
                AND Mortgage = [No]
        THEN Likely-To-Buy = Yes with CF .10

This is a similar rule to the 5.1.1. At some point the generated rules will be merged to eliminate possible redundancies. However the purpose here is to investigate the size of the population which needs to be mailed to and to balance this will the certainty factors.

        IF Request-For-Addn-Details = [Yes]
        THEN NOT (fast OR extremely fast) with CF .95

This is another rule indicating that if all details are not initially provided then the handling speed will suffer. This may lead to investigation to determine if additional training is required for the person/s assisting in completing the claim documentation.

        IF Received-From-Agent in [Smith, Jones]
        THEN incomplete with CF .35

This rule may indentify agents who are not providing quality paperwork.

        IF Height in [X..Y]
                AND Weight in [T..Z] or in [A..B]
        THEN Medical-Needed = Yes

This rule is similar to the one above and indicates people whose height/weight ratios are slightly abnormal and where medical opinion should be sought.

        IF Age > [X]
                AND Policy-Type-Requested in [Endowment, Whole of Life,
                Bonus Endowment]
                AND Smoker-Status = [Yes]
                AND Self-Employed = [No]
                AND Premium-Loading > [1.4]
        THEN Risk = High

    IF Level-of-Cover in [X .. Y]
        AND Total Liabilities < [Z]
        AND Married = [Yes]
    THEN Risk = Medium

These two rules are very similar and allow risks to estimated.

REFERENCES:

Brachman, R; Selfridge, P; Terveen, L; Altman, B; Halper, F; Kirk, T; Lazar, A; McGuiness, D; Resnik, L; Borgida, A. 1993. 'Integrated support for data archaeology'. Presented at *AAAI workshop on Knowledge Discovery in Databases, Washington DC*

Fayyad, U. 1997. 'Editorial' in *Data mining and knowledge discovery, An International Journal* Volume 1, Issue 1.

Fayyad, U; Piatetsky-Shapiro, G; Smyth, P. 1996. 'From data mining to knowledge discovery: an overview'. From *Advances in Knowledge Discovery and Data Mining.* Fayyad et al. (Eds.) AAAI/MIT Press.

Goonatilake, S. 1996. 'Risk assessment using intelligent systems'. *Insurance Systems Bulletin* 11(10):2-3. April.

Klein, M R and Methie, L B. 1995. *Knowledge Based Decision Support Systems.* John Wiley and Sons .

Kloesgen, W. 1996. 'Explora: A multipattern and multistrategy discovery assistant'. From *Advances in Knowledge Discovery and Data Mining.* Fayyad et al. (Eds.) AAAI/MIT Press 1996.

Kohavi, R; John, G; Long, R; Manley, D; Pfleger, K. 1994. 'MLC++: A machine learning library in C++'. *Tools in AI 94.* Electronic version obtained from ftp://starry.stanford.edu:pub/ronnyk/intromlc.ps

Loo, S. L.; Dillon, T., Zeleznikow, J. and Lee, K. H. 1996. 'Enhancing query processing of information systems'. In Z. W. Ras and M. Michalewicz, (eds.) *LNAI(LNCS) 1079 Proc.9th Int. Symposium ISMIS'96 Foundations of Intelligent Systems, ISMIS'96*, Zakopane, Poland, June. Springer, pp. 386-397.

Mollestad, T. and Skowron, A. 1996. 'A rough set framework for data mining of propositional default rules'. In Z. W. Ras and M. Michalewicz, (eds.) *LNAI(LNCS) 1079 Proc.9th Int. Symposium ISMIS'96 Foundations of Intelligent Systems, ISMIS'96,* Zakopane, Poland, June. Springer, pp. 448-457.

Motro, A. 1990. 'Accommodating imprecision in database systems: Issues and solutions'. In *Bulletin of IEEE Computer Society, Data Engineering,* V13.4, December, pp. 29-34.

Piatetsky-Shapiro, G. 1996. 'Data mining and knowledge discovery in business databases'. *Foundation of Intelligent Systems, Lecture Notes in AI 1079, 9th international symposium proceedings of ISMIS.* June.

Piatetsky-Shapiro, G; Mattheus, CJ; McNeill, D. 1996. 'Selecting and reporting what is interesting'. From *Advances in Knowledge Discovery and Data Mining.* Fayyad et al. (Eds.) AAAI/MIT Press.

Pawlak, Z. 1991. *Rough Sets - Theoretical aspects of reasoning about data.* Kluwer Academic Publishers.

Shen, W; Mitbander, B; Ong, K; Zanilo, C. 1994. 'Using metaqueries to integrate inductive learning and deductive database technology'. From *Knowledge Discovery in Databases: Papers from the 1994 AAAI Workshop.* AAAI Tech. Rep WS-94-03, Menlo Park, California.

Silberschatz, A. and Tuzhilin, A. 1996. 'What makes patterns interesting in Knowledge Discovery Systemd'. *IEEE Transactions on Knowledge and Data Engineering,* Vol 8, Number 6, December, pp 970-975.

Simoudis, E; Livezey, B; Kerber, R. 1996. 'Integrating inductive and deductive reasoning for data mining'. From *Advances in Knowledge Discovery and Data Mining.* Fayyad et al. (Eds.) AAAI/MIT Press.

Tsumoto, S. and Ziarko, W. 1996. 'The application of rough sets-based data mining technique to differential diagnosis of meningoenchepahlitis'. In Z. W. Ras and M. Michalewicz, (eds*.) LNAI(LNCS) 1079 Proc.9th Int. Symposium ISMIS'96 Foundations of Intelligent Systems, ISMIS'96,* Zakopane, Poland, June. Springer, pp. 438-447.

Williams, GJ; Huang, Z. 1996. 'Knowledge discovery in databases for insurance risk assessment: A case study'. *Technical report TR-DM-96014.* CSIRO Division of Information Technology. March.

Zadeh, L. A. 1989. 'Knowledge representation in fuzzy logic'. In *IEEE Trans. on Knowledge and Data Engineering,* V1.1, March, pp. 89-99.

Discovering Missing Semantics from Existing Relational Databases

Shing-Han Li, Shi-Ming Huang, and Huei-Huang Chen
Database/Knowledge Base Research Group
Department of Computer Science and Engineering
Tatung Institute of Technology, 40 Chungshan N. Road, 3rd sec.,
Taipei, 104, Taiwan, R.O.C.
Tel: (886)2 5925252-3291 Fax: (886)2 5925252-2288
E-Mail: smhuang@cse.ttit.edu.tw

Abstract. Discovering and handling the missing semantic of an existing database is an important issue for information systems reengineering. Traditionally, the database schema is determined by a database administrator. The database administrator may not fully understand the user's view of the real world. Therefore, the data semantic may be missing during system analysis. During the database design phase, the semantic meanings may lost in the logical schema once the conceptual model is mapped into the logical model. This paper investigates a default automatic relational database schema translation system to map an existing relational database schema into an EER (Extended Entity Relationship) database schema. The translation mechanism uses the systematic approach by accompaning with the data mining technique. The knowledge discovery process can lead to suggested additions or alternations to the known structure of the database and thus can suggest modifications to the database schema for the database migration or conversion.

Keywords: Knowledge Discovery, Data Mining, Schema Translation, EER model, Data Dictionary System

1. Introduction

Database system reengineering is important for putting high software maintenance costs under control, recovering existing database system assets, and establishing a basis for future database system evaluation. It consists of three elements: schema translation, data conversion, and program translation [FON97]. The schema translation technique involves semantic re-construction and the mapping of the original schema into the new schema. The global database schema of heterogeneous database systems can be built by using such technique to capture the semantic meaning of each local database. The database conversion employs this technique to recover the semantic of original databases into new databases.

Recapturing semantics is a complicated and difficult work in the schema translation. Traditionally, a database administrator determines the database schema. The database administrator may not fully understand the user's view of the real world. Therefore, the data semantics may be in the system analysis phase. During the database design phase, the semantic meanings may be missing lost in the logical schema once the conceptual model is mapped into logical model. It is difficult to recapture it. Much research has been done to solve this problem [HUG96], [FON92], [PUT90], [CHI93], etc. Unfortunately, these works can not recapture the missing semantics automatically. They require extra information or knowledge from users to identify the missing semantics. Furthermore, only limited missing semantics can be recaptured through their works.

In recent years, data mining technique has been applied to this area. The techniques have increasingly been employed to enable knowledge to be discovered from the data held in the database. The knowledge discovery process can lead to suggested additions or alternations to the known structure of the database.

In this paper, the authors discuss a Default Automatic Relational Database Schema Translation System (DARDSTS) to recapture most of EER conceptual model semantics through an existing relational data dictionary system and databases. The related works for database schema translation are briefly described in the next section. Section 3 shows the entire process of the proposed database schema translation mechanism. Section 4 shows the system architecture. Section 5 displays the DARDSTS prototype system. Section 6 discusses the system evaluation. Finally, a summary is provided.

2. Database schema translation

A database system consists of three components: schemas, data and programs. Database reengineering starts with the schemas, which define the structures of data and their relationship in different models. Only after the schemas have been re-defined, can data and programs then be reengineered into a new database system, which makes use of the translated schemas [Fong, 1997]. Schema translation is the process of changing a schema expressed in one data model into an equivalent schema expressed in a different data model.

2.1. Direct translation
One can directly translate an original database schema or file structure to a new database schema. Certain semantics are lost once they are mapped from a conceptual schema (such as an entity-relationship model) to a logical schema (such as hierarchical, network, or relational model) during the original database design phase. Thus, such translation may cause loss of information because of its primitive method that cannot recover all the semantics of the original database.

2.2. Indirect translation
In much of the published literature on schema translation by direct translation, assumptions have generally been made on the semantics of the database. There is always the chance that the translated schema may not encapsulate the original designer's idea. This problem occurs because there are so many possible relational schemas that can be derived from a known conceptual schema and the translation analyst makes many very primitive assumptions.

3. The Database Schema Translation Mechanism

This section describes the knowledge discovery process (i.e. an indirect translation mechanism) to translate a relational database schema into an EER database schema as a kind of reverse engineering. The EER model carries richer semantics than a relational model. The translation mechanism uses the systematic approach by accompaning with the data mining technique to recapture most of EER conceptual model semantics through an existing relational data dictionary system and databases.

Using the data dictionary, a relational database model can directly reverse into a lower level semantic stage of EER model. For example, there is an employee database, which contains three tables.

EMPLOYEE(<u>Ssn</u>, Fname, Lname, Bdate, Address)
SECRETARY(*<u>Ssn</u>, TypingSpeed)
ENGINEER(*<u>Ssn</u>, year, Speciality)

The SECRETARY.Ssn is referring to the EMPLOYEE.Ssn and the ENGINEER.Ssn is referring to EMPLOYEE.Ssn. Fig. 1 shows the database schema, which can gain from the data dictionary system.

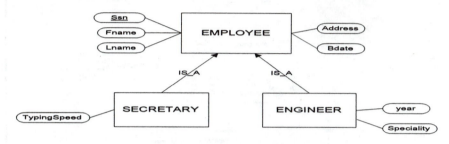

Fig. 1. The lower level semantic of an EER Model

The data mining technique can induce new knowledge from the data of the existing databases. For example, if the data which contains in the SECRETARY.Ssn and ENGINEER.Ssn is exclusive each other, then there is a disjoint relationship between SECRETARY and ENGINEER relations. The new knowledge is discovered. Figure 2 shows the higher level semantic of the EER diagram after the data mining.

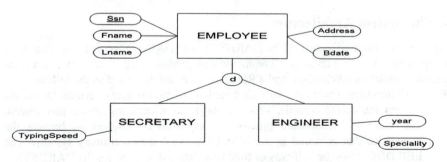

Fig. 2. The Higher Level Semantic of an EER Model

Since Fig. 2 contains more semantics than Fig. 1, it can be recognized as a better database schema.

278

There are 6 steps within the proposed database schema translation mechanism. Fig 3 shows the entire process. Each step represents different aspect to recapture the semantics of the database. The existing semantics of a relational database are retrieved from its data dictionary system. If any uncertainty or unsophisticated schematic is found, the data mining technique will be applied to discover more semantics from the real data. A reasonable result will be given as a default schema for the existing database after the data mining. The result only represents the situation of the current existing database. It stills is not the final database schema since some semantics has been missing. System designers must make the final decision for the database schema.

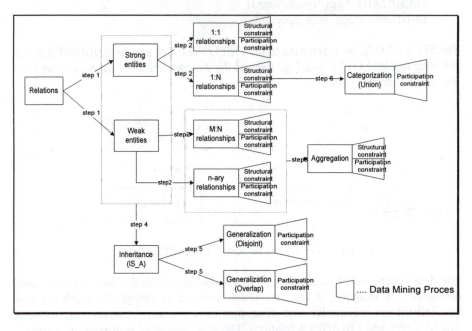

Fig. 3. The Entire Process of the Schema Translation Mechanism

4. The System Architecture

Fig. 4. shows the architecture of the DARDSTS. The DARDSTS consists of four main components: a user interface, a communication middle-ware, a relational database schema translation mechanism, and a RDBMS. They are described as the follows:

● User Interface: There are two main functions within the user interface. One is the schema translation console, which manage the schema translation mechanism. The other is the schema browser, which allows end-users to browse the knowledge that is stored in the EER DDS (EER data dictionary system). The EER DDS stores the half-way or final new database schema for the DARDSTS.

● Communication Middle-Ware: It is the communication channel between the client site and server site. ODBC (Open Database Connectivity) is an example.

● RDBMS: The existing database, which will be translated to the new EER database schema, is stored in the RDBMS. The EER data dictionary system is also stored here.

- Relational Database Schema Translation Mechanism: This component is the kernel of the whole system. The mechanism, which describes in section 3 is implemented here. There are three modules within this component: schema translation engine, data mining functions, and data dictionary functions. The schema translation engine controls the entire process steps of the schema translation. When the relational database schema translation mechanism receive the command from the schema translation console, it notifies the schema translation engine of the command. The schema translation engine is responsible for propagating messages between the data mining module and the data dictionary module. The engine, then, reconstructs the conceptual semantic and stores the results into EER data dictionary. The data dictionary functions analysis the existing data dictionary and EER data dictionary to discover the conceptual semantic. Sometimes the conceptual semantic are uncertainty, the schema translate engine needs to dispatch the data mining module to assist the processing. The data mining module mines the data from the existing database and return the results as a default solution to schema translation engine.

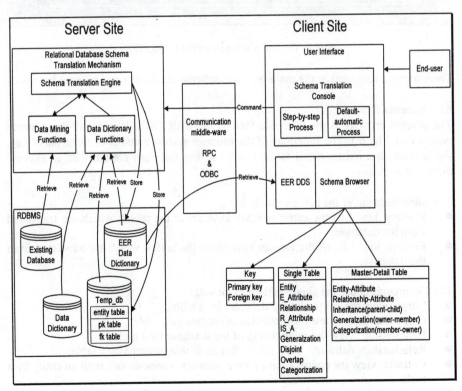

Fig. 4. The Architecture of the DARDSTS

5. The DARDSTS Prototype System

DARDSTS has been built on the client-server environment. The server site system is built on Microsoft Windows NT with Microsoft SQLServer RDBMS. The client site is built on MicroSoft Windows 95 with GUPTA SQLWindows. The communication middle ware is the ODBC. Fig. 5. shows the main window of the system user interface.

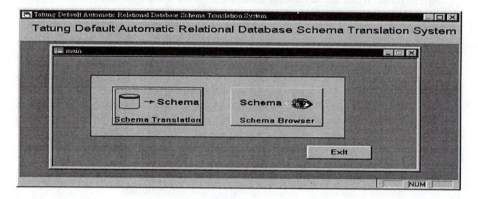

Fig. 5. The Main Window of the DARDSTS

There are two functions in the main window: schema translation and schema browser.

5.1. Schema Browser
The schema browser is the user interface of the EER DDS. It is a pull-down menu system (see Fig. 6.). The functions of the browser system consists of three parts: key, single table, and master-detail table. Users can use the push bottom icon to execute these commands.

The commands under the key part include:
- Primary_key: List the entire primary keys about the tables, which are translated from the database.
- Foreign_key: List all the foreign keys about the tables, which are translated from the database.

The Commands under the single table part include:
- Entity: view the entities of the database by a table.
- Entity_Attribute: view the attributes of entities by a table.
- Relationship: view the relationship of the database by a table.
- Relationship_Attribute: view the attributes of relationships by a table.
- Connect: view the connect information between a relationship with an entity by a table.
- Aggregation: view the aggregation relationship by a table.
- IS_A: view the IS_A relationship by a table.
- Generalization: view the generalization relationship by a table.

- Generalization_overlap: view the overlap relationship by a table.
- Generalization_disjoint: view the disjoint relationship by a table.
- Union: view the union member by a table.
- Unionowner: view the union owner by a table.

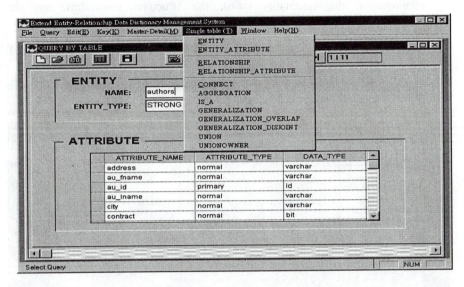

Fig. 6. The EER DDS Interface - Schema Browser

The Commands under the Master-Detail table part include:

- Entity-attribute: using a master-detail table to display the attributes and their owner entity.
- Relationship-attribute: using a master-detail table to display the attributes and their owner relationship.
- Overlap: using a master-detail table to display the member entities and their owner entity.
- Disjoint: using a master-detail table to display the member entities and their owner entity.
- Union: using a master-detail table to display the owner entities and their member entity.

5.2. Schema Translation

The schema translation function is a push button selection system (see Fig. 7.). Users can use the function to translate the existing relational database schema into EER DDS step-by-step or default automatic.

The commands of schema translation function are described as the following:

- Pre-step: This step will require users to install the EER data dictionary, called EER_DD, into the RDBMS. This step will, also, ask users to identify an existing database, which will be translated to an EER database schema. The step will, then, find the entire primary keys and foreign keys for each table of the identified database from the existing DDS.

- Step1: The first step is to identify the entity types (i.e. strong or weak entity) of a relation.
- Step2: This step is to recapture the semantics of relationships. In this step, the relationships, the cardinality ratios, the structural constraints, and the participation constraints will be discovered.

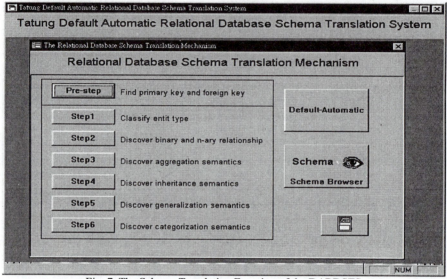

Fig. 7. The Schema Translation Function of the DARDSTS

- Step 3: This step is to discover the aggregation semantics. Because the aggregation semantics can not be demonstrated, a verification process is needed. The verification process will show the discovery result—aggregation semantics. Users are allowed to modify the result.
- Step4: This step is to discover the inheritance semantics.
- Step5: This step is to discover the generalization semantics (such as overlap and disjoint). A generalization relationship is derived from the "IS_A" relationships that are connected by a common owner entity. Such semantics need to be confirmed by the data mining method. Thus, a verification process will verify the semantics by the users.
- Step6: This step is to discovery the categorization semantics. categorization semantics may be composed of several 1:N relationships. A verification process will verify the semantics by the users.
- Default-Automatic: The default-automatic command is to translate the relational schema automatically. This command ignores the verification process and just uses the data mining methods to decide the semantics.
- Schema browser: The schema browser is used to show the results of each step. This function can help user to understand the result for every step. The function is the same as section 5.1

6. Case Study

To evaluate the system performance, a university relational database is chosen as a case study. The University database is popularly seen in much database research [ELM94; JOS92; THO95]. Fig. 8. shows the university relational database schema which is used in this case study.

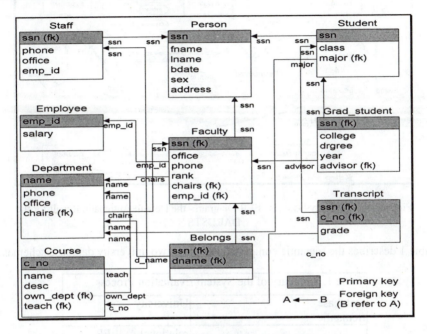

Fig. 8. A University Relational Database Schema

The relational database schema only presents the semantic of primary keys, foreign keys, tables, and attributes. After the default automatic database schema translation from DARDSTS, the result schema has shown more semantics than the original relational database schema. Fig. 9 shows the result EER database schema.

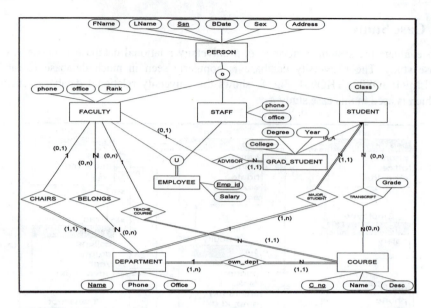

Fig. 9. The University Database EER Diagram - the Default Automatic Result for the
DARDSTS

Table 1 describes the semantic comparison of these two university database schemas.

Table 1. Summary of the System Evaluation Process		
Database Semantic	University	
	relational	EER
Primary key	✓	✓
Foreign key	✓	
Entity (strong)	✓	✓
Entity (weak)		
E_attribute	✓	✓
Relationship (normal)		✓
Relationship (identifying)		
R_attribute		✓
Cardinality_ratio	✓	✓
Structural constraint		✓
Participation constraint		✓
Aggregation		
Inheritance (IS_A)		✓
Generalization (disjoint)		
Generalization (overlap)		✓
Categorization (union)		✓

The results of this test have proved that the DARDSTS can default automatic recapture the missing semantics from the existing relational databases. The users do not require to answer any question, which other systems or research do.

7. Summary

This paper has demonstrated a new mechanism to translate the relational database schema into an extended entity relationship model. The mechanism can default automatically recapture most of EER conceptual model semantics (such as strong entities, weak entities, binary relationships, inheritance, generalization, aggregation, and categorization). The authors also implement this new mechanism into system, called DARDSTS. The prototype system is based on the client server architecture and can be executed with most RDBMSs. Finally, a case study is taken to evaluate the DARDSTS performance. After the default automatic database schema translation from DARDSTS, the result schema has shown more semantics than the original relational database schema. The results prove the success of this research.

ACKNOWLEDGEMENTS

The work presented in this paper has been supported by the Research Community, Tatung Institute of Technology, Taiwan, under Grant No. B84016 and the National Science Council, Taiwan, under Grant No. NSC 86-2213-E-036-005. We greatly appreciate their financial support and encouragement.

REFERENCES

[ANS88]   ANSI, (1988), "American National Standard Information Resource Dictionary System", ANSI X3H4 , American National Standard Institute, New York.

[BAT92]   Batini, C., & Ceri, S., & Navathe, S., (1992). "Conceptual Database Design: An Entity-Relationship Approach",. The Benjamin/Cummings Publishing Company, Inc. ISBN 0-8053-0244-1

[BEY91]   Beynon-Davies, P., (1991), "Expert Database System - A Gentle Introduction", McGraw-Hill Book Company, London, ISBN 0-07-707240-5.

[CHI93]   Chiang R.H.L., Barron T.M., Storey V.C. (1993), "Performance Evaluation of Reverse Engineering Relational Databases into Extended Entity-Relationship Models", Lecture Notes in Computer Science Entity-Relationship Approach— ER'93, December, 1993, pp352-363.

[ELM94]   Elmasri R.,& Navathe, S.,(1994). "Fundamentals of Database Systems"(2nd edition). The Benjamin/Cummings Publishing Company,Inc. ISBN 0-8053-1748-1

[FON92]   Fong, J., (1992), "Methodology for Schema Translation from Hierarchical or Network into Relational.", Information and Software Technology Vol 34, No 3, March 1992, pp159-174.

[FON97]   Fong, J. and Huang S.M., (1997), "Information Systems ReEngineering", Springer-Verleg Publishing Company, Inc. ISBN 981-3083-15-8

[HUA95]   Huang S.M., (1995), "An Information Resource Dictionary System for Expert System", Tatung Journal, Vol 25, Nov. 1995, pp281-291.

[HUA96]   Huang S.M.,& Li S.H.,& Fong J., (1996), "Translation Relational Database Model Into Extended Entity Relationship Model: A Reverse Engineering Approach", Tatung Journal, Vol 26, Nov. 1996, pp175-186.

[HUG96]   Hughes John G. et al., (1996), "SYNDAMMA Methodology Description", SYNDAMA ESPRIT III-9006 report.

[MIC94]   Microsoft SQLServer Transact-SQL Reference, Version 6.0, Published by Microsoft Corporation.

[MIC92]   Michalski R.S., Kerschberg L., Kaufman K.A., and Ribeiro J.S., (1992), "Mining for Knowledge in Databases: The INLEN Architecture, Initial Implementation and First Results", Journal of Intelligent Information Systems, 1,1992, pp85-113

[NAT95]   Nath A., (1995),"The guide to SQL Server (second edition). Published by Addison-Wesley publishing Company. ISBN 0-201-62631-4

[PUT90]   Put, F., (1990), "Schema Translation during Design and Integration of Database" Proceedings of 9th International Conference on Entity-Relationship Approach, pp399-421.

[ROD96]   Roddick J. F. & Craske N.G. & Richards T.J.,(1996), "Handling Discovered Structure in Database Systems", IEEE translations on knowledge and data engineering, Vol.8, No.2, April 1996, pp227-240.

[THO95]   Thomas Connolly, Carolyn Begg, Anne Strachan, (1995), "Database System A Practical Approach to Design, Implement, and Management", The Addison-Wesley Publishing Company, Inc. ISBN 0-201-42277-8.

[USA96]   Usama M. F.,Gregory p., Padhraic S., and Ramasamy U.,(1996), "Advances in Knowledge Discovery and Data Mining", AAAI press/The MIT press, ISBN 0-262-56097-6

Client/Server Web Database Design and Implementation: A CGI-SGML Approach

P. M. Tsang
Communications Technology
Open University of Hong Kong
ptsang@ouhk.edu.hk

C. K. Diu
Applied Computing
Open University of Hong Kong
ckdiu@ouhk.edu.hk

Sandy Y.Tse
School of Marketing and Info System
University of South Australia
9502314c@ntx.city.unisa.edu.au

Abstract. Databases are moving onto the Web to power the next generation of Internet applications. While the importance of having a database, be it for business, educational or even professional use, is well known [Wil97]. There are various practical issues of integrating the Web and the Database technologies, among which are the impeding conflicting objectives of cost, functions, quality and time of the development project. This paper discusses the experiences of designing a simple Common Gateway Interface (CGI) based Web Database Engine and using HTML as a middleware in a Web-Database Interface design. The engine was used in an online registration package in a 1000-delegate WWW conference. This paper should be of interest to academic and IT practitioners who want to implement a lightweight database engine for small to medium Web related projects such as online registration, magazine subscriptions, tutorial classes management and events scheduling [Diu96][Tsa96a][Tsa96b].

Keywords. SGML, Web Database, TFQC, Online Registration System, GUI

1.   Introduction

Change is a matter of life, but occurs even faster in the field of the Internet. From 1994-1995 the authors were involved in a major World Wide Web Conference in Australia (http://www.csu.edu.au/special/conference). The organisation of the conference spanned over 15 months from planning, running the conference in September 1995 and wrapping up a postmortem of the conference in October 1995. During the early phase of the conference planning, significant thought went into the implementation of an online registration system. In addition to the practical needs of an automatic or semi-automatic system to handle the online registration and the varying participant interests, there was also a publicity need for a dynamic system to demonstrate the transition from the First Web Generation to the beginning of the Second Web Generation.

In late 1994, after the 2nd International Web Conference in Chicago, writing static Web documents(pages) using HTML was quite well known, but developing dynamic Web pages or Web related systems was still in its infancy. The now well known knowledge of various configurations of Web servers[Min97][Aug97] and its associated language, Perl, were only known to a small community of the Open System /Unix professionals. Even many academics and computing practitioners had little understanding of what the CGI, HTTPD, SGML were about.

It was the thrust to develop a dynamic online registration database application in which the bulk of this paper result. While we are aware of the limitations and potential shortcomings of our system, the CGI scripts developed continue to be satisfactorily used in our Dynamic Web applications such as online survey, electronic address book, journal subscription system and Web Bulletin Board.

2.   Our Web/Database Requirements

2.1   Background

In a traditional international conference, a delegate usually completes a conference registration form (together with a check or credit card information) and sends it to the conference secretary by fax or by post. In mid 1994, the Web community introduced the innovative concept of online conference registration.

In July 1994, while chatting in our office in a remote town ,Wagga Wagga, in Australia, two of the authors developed the idea for the First Asia-Pacific Web Conference. In October 1994, endorsement from the International Web Conference Committee was received for the authors and their colleagues to run the First Asia-Pacific Web Conference in Australia in September 1995. In a Web conference event, a conference web page on the Internet is taken for granted. The design of the First Asia Pacific Web Conference home page consisted of a number of issues:

- structure of the page development
- graphic design
- html editing
- content management
- Perl script programming
- manpower allocation

The conference Web page consisted of some of the following features and functions (See Appendix A) :
- Conference logo
- e-mail contact of the conference organiser
- General information of the conference
- What-is-News of the conference (Press Release)
- Expression of interests (Made available a year before the conference)
- Online registration form (Made available four months before the conference)
- Conference programme
- Conference online proceedings
- Exhibition information
- Social events

While the design of the conference home page had been a labour intensive task, it provided many learning opportunities for both the authors and their students alike. The issue that is of relevance to our discussion in this paper is the Online Registration System that made use of Perl script and SGML concepts.

The importance of having online registration and expressions of interest dynamic pages can be easily understood given that a Web conference is supposed to showcase technology. There were some basic requirements for what the system should look like and what resources could be used:

2.2 The Basic Requirements

Since potential delegates were people from around the world, and the Internet links to Australia were of limited bandwidth, the following functional wish-list was outlined for the online system.

1. Accessibility both locally and internationally,
2. A user friendly graphical interface,
3. Dynamic in nature,
4. Centrally stored registration records,
5. Support sorting by country and by surnames,
5. Authorised organising members allowed access to the data from around the world,
6. The registration database invisible to the general public,
7. Capacity to handle up to 5000 potential delegates.

2.3 The Design Assumption

1. Turning on the world access parameter in the NCSA HTTPD configuration file enabled the inherent accessibility of the Conference Web Page for anyone on the Internet.
2. HTML was used as a middleware in providing the GUI to the database engine.
3. With a limited budget for implementing the online registration system, it was important to use software that could be obtained for little or no cost to the design team.
4. The input data described as records to be stored in SGML format to has allow easy registration retrieval.
5. With a very minimal conference budget, the Web design has to be based on the existing hardware, software and tools in order to develop a customised and generalised program for easy access.

Although the hosting university of the conference has an Oracle database, it was restricted to administrative use. Academics were not allowed to gain access to it for security reasons. But even if we could use the Oracle engine, the then rough Web/RDBMs Interface proved to demand a steep learning curve to most Web team members. The next candidate was the mini-SQL 1.1 shareware. Again this option was discarded as the set up and configuration proved to demand a high learning curve. The team ended up learning the Perl language for developing the system.

3. Architecture of a Simple CGI-SGML Database Engine

In a nutshell, the Hyper Text Markup Language (HTML) was used to develop the required GUI for the online registration systems (Expressions of Interest to start with and finally the Online Conference Delegate Registration). By using the GUI form and CGI script, input data were nicely and automatically formatted and stored in the SGML flatfile database. Another generic CGI script was written to translate the whole or a portion of the SGML- database file into the HTML format for viewing. To enable reuse of the CGI script, "template" and "fields" files were used. Details of the programming are illustrated in the "System Implementation Scheme". Figure 1 shows a conceptual architecture of the database engine and how it interacts with its environment.

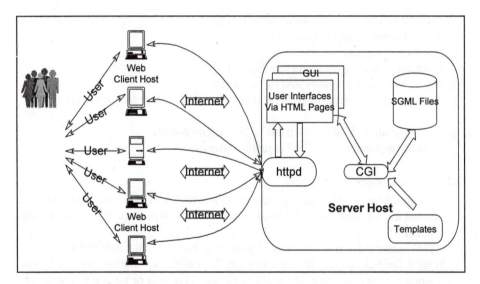

Figure 1: A Conceptual Architecture of the Database Engine

4. System Implementation Scheme

The system implementation and the development of CGI scripts are discussed in this section. A complete source code of the scripts will be made available upon request. Some of terminologies are explained first. These are followed by the programming structure with the functional description of each individual file.

4.1   Words on Terminologies

To enhance the descriptions in the next couple of sections, we would like to review some of the terminologies in closer details:

Universal Resource Locator (URL)

The easiest way to think of this term is to consider it as an address of a resource or a Web page on the Internet. It can take several formats such as the following:

http://www.apwww.com/
http://plbsun01.oi.hk/#top
http://plbsun01.oli.hk:8888/mt268/apr97/
http://plbsun01.oli.hk/cgi-bin/test.pl?data
ftp://plbsun01.oli.hk/pub/tools/
gopher://124.244.45.3/
wais://hostport/database
news:news.abc.com
mailto: editor@apwww.com

Hypertext Markup Language (HTML)

The Hypertext Markup Language (HTML) allows users to build hypertext documents that can be displayed by World-Wide Web clients. This is a highly popular Internet standard for developing Web pages.

Standard Generalized Markup Language (SGML)

The Standard Generalized Markup Language, SGML, is an international standard for electronic document exchange. SGML is a super-set of the HTML Internet standard. SGML has many features that make it rich and flexible enough to remain one of the premium standards for electronic document exchange in the next decades. The very idea behind SGML is "author once, use many". [Mar96]

Common Gateway Interface (CGI)

The Common Gateway Interface (CGI) specifications define the proper method for passing data to external programs from HTMl documents. It also defines how data returned from the external program should be formated in order to be viewed by a Web browser. The Web server and the CGI program work together to transform the first generation static Web technology into an interactive and dynamic frontier. Together they significantly enhance the Web's capabilities and pave the way for electronic commerce on the Information Superhighway. Dwright and Erwin [1996] do not exaggerate when they commented that "CGI, in one of its many forms, is what brings the World Wide Web to life".

5. Programming Structure of the APWeb95 CGI-SGML Database System

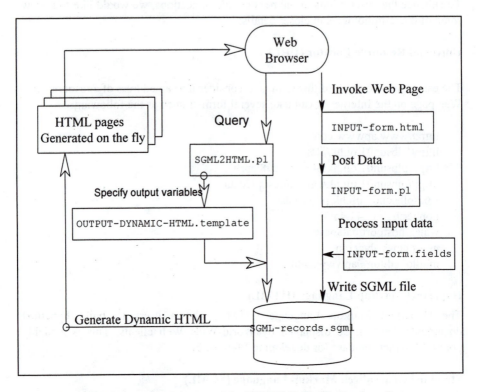

Figure 2. Programming Structure of the CGI-SGML Flatfile Database System

The programming structure consists of five files. Two of the files are generic CGI scripts written in Perl. For discussion purposes they are named as: INPUT-form.pl and SGML2HTML.pl. They are generic in the sense that they can be used by other projects with little or no change in the codes. The other three files comprise one graphical user interface web file called INPUT-form.html and two text template files, namely INPUT-formfields.template and OUTPUT-DYNAMIC-HTML.template.

5.1 Function of the files

INPUT-form.html
A Web fill-in form, as a GUI, was written in HTML to solicit input. This form used all of the four interactive input features of form design: radio, checkbox, single line a and multiple lines input. (See Appendix A for the web page presentation and Appendix B for HTML listing)

INPUT-form.pl

This CGI script was written in Perl to process the input data. It was invoked from the INPUT-form.html. See the boldfaced line in the html listing of INPUT-form.html (called st-regform.html in Appendix B) which has the following code:

**<FORM   ACTION=``cgi-bin/st/st-regform.pl''
METHOD=``POST''>**

The above statement tells the server where the CGI script is located and that input data will be acted upon by the script. It also specifies what data access method is used. A POST access method indicates that the browser sends data from a fill-in form to the Web Server.

The function of this script (together with the INPUT-formfields.template) is to translate the input data into SGML format and append it to a flat database file, SGML-records.sgml. It also sends an autoreply to the client, confirminh what he/she has entered in the fill-in form.

INPUT-formfields.template

This file contains all the input variables and is needed by INPUT-form.pl to produce a SGML file. Figure 3 shows a possible content of INPUT-formfields.template

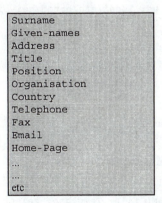

```
Surname
Given-names
Address
Title
Position
Organisation
Country
Telephone
Fax
Email
Home-Page
...
...
etc
```

Figure 3 shows a typical content of INPUT-formfields.template

SGML-records.sgml

This text file stores registration records in SGML format. Figure 4 illustrates how a SGML-records.sgml flatfile may look.

```
<record>
<message_id>85823020919446</message_id>
<datetime>Thursday, March 13, 1997 - 01:16:49 pm</datetime>
```

```
<Surname>Chan</Surname>
<Given-names>Amy</Given-names>
<Address>30 Good Shepherd Homantin HK</Address>
<Title>ms</Title>
<Position>COII</Position>
<Organisation>OLI</Organisation>
<Country>HK</Country>
<Telephone>12245</Telephone>
<Fax>909</Fax>
<Email>abc@abc.net</Email>
<Home-Page>http://www.csu.edu.au/special</Home-Page>
</record>
          .        .        .
          .        .        .
          .        .        .
```

Figure 4 shows a portion of the file SGML-records.sgml

SGML2HTML.pl

This script is used to convert the SGML database file into an HTML Web page using a template, OUTPUT-DYNAMIC-HTML.template, with some predefined variables. Figure 5 shows portion of the script.

```perl
#!/usr/local/bin/perl
#generic script to build an HTML page from SGML using a template
$filenames = "";
#location of sgmlfiles
$where_sgml = "/disk2/usr/local/etc/httpd/cgi-bin/8idw/sgml/";
#$where_temp ="/disk2/usr/local/etc/httpd/cgi-
bin/8idw/templates/";
@select_list = ();
@validate_list = ();
@groupby_list = ();
$list_field = "";
@list_keys = ();
@list_fields = ();
part of the entries omitted
$default_sort = "message_id";    #sort by message_id if no sort in
template
@sort_list = ($default_sort);
$list_option = 0;            #default to no list option
BEGIN
   #get parameters (SGML file, Template, select field - optional)

   ($filenames) = @ARGV;
   ($sgmlname, $templatename, $select) = split(/,/, $filenames);
   #build filenames
bulk of the file omitted here
                        $list_field = $list_in;}
                }
}
close (TEMPLATE);
}
```

Figure 5: A peek of the SGML2HTML.pl

OUTPUT-DYNAMIC-HTML.template

This sample template is used in querying the SGML flatfile database and specifies what and in what order the stored records (partly or wholly) should be written into the dynamically generated HTML file(s) for client viewing.

```
<sort>datetime,Name
</sort>
<header>
Content-type: text/html
<html>
<head>
<title> 8th International Database Workshop Online Database
</title>
</head>
<h1>
<font    color="#FF0000"><I>8th    International    Database    Workshop
online Registration Database
</I></h1>
</font><p>
</header>
<DL>
<body>
<foreach message_id>
<DT> <HR>
<DT><font color="#FF0000"><B>Surname: </B></font> $Surname
<DT><font color="#FF0000"><B>Given Names:</B></font>$Givennames
<DT><font color="#FF0000"><B>Title :</B></font>$Title
<DD><B>Organisation: </B>$Organisation
<DD><B>Postal Address: </B>$Address
<DD><B>Country:</B>$Country
<DD><B>Telephone:</B>$Telephone
<DD><B>Fax:</B>$Fax
<DD><B>E-mail: </B>$Email
<DD><B>Home Page: </B>$Homepage
</foreach message_id>
</body> <footer></DL><hr></body></blockquote></html></footer>
```

Figure 6: Structure of OUTPUT-DYNAMIC-HTML.template

6.   TFQC Analysis of the CGI-SGML Database

In this section, we briefly analyse the strength and weakness of the system from the perspective of time of delivery, functionality, quality of delivery and cost of development

The system was required to be up and running in less than a week's time and to provide those dynamic features as spelled out in the earlier section. With CGI, the working prototype was up in four days. While the intangible cost of development consists of four nights in designing and programming the CGI scripts by two of the authors, the tangible cost is negligible. In terms of functionality, it satisfied the basic requirements but could include additional features such as validating the inputs. As far as quality is concerned, areas for improvement exist but flexibility was introduced using the "author one use many" property of SGML. Use of a commercial strengthened database seemed to be an overkill and too expensive for such "one-off" application.

7.   Lessons Learned

Unlike years ago when there was a limited choice of CGI languages, a number of CGI programming languages are now available for one's computing platform as can be seen from Table 1. The choice of languages varies with experience, availability and organisation culture.

Language	Unix	Windows NT	VMS	Mac
Perl	✓	✓	✓	✓
C/C++	✓	✓	✓	✓
Visual Basic/VB Script	✗	✓	✗	✗
Java/Java Script	✗	✓	✗	✗
Tcl/Tk	✓	✓	✓	✗

Table 1: CGI languages and computer platforms

The CGI programming effort was well spent as we continue to find the scripts useful in our daily academic work. While a wish list of improvements may include record/file locking of the database and statistics reporting, the system worked fine and served our basic needs of a simple flexible Web/database.

Reasonable data accesses security are provided by standard Web Server password protection scheme such as requiring password and login or denying access by domain name.

8.   Summary

In this paper we described an implementation of a CGI-SGML flatfile database system which used the concept of reusability of SGML and CGI programming in Perl. While the system developed is of limited functions, nevertheless it provides a low cost option for users.

There are often impeding conflicting objectives [Time, Functionality, Quality and Cost, TFQC] of the software project development cycle: In most practical cases, no more than three can be achieved at any given time.

For mission critical Web database applications such as electronic banking services which may result in huge strains on the database engine and demand high performance over the Internet, one should definitely pay for high performance engine products such as Sybase, Oracle or Informix, which also provide user friendly development tools to provide easy Web/database integration.

ACKNOWLEDGMENTS

The authors wish to thank Mr. T. L. Fong for his constructive comments and suggestions while reviewing the draft of this paper. Appreciation should also go to Ms Sue Liu for polishing the final version of this paper. However the authors are to be blamed for any remaining overlooked areas or errors.

REFERENCES

[Aug97]   T. August. Demystifying Web-Enabled Database Applications, *IDUG Solutions Journal*. Issue 1, 1997. pp.29-33.

[Diu96]   C. K Diu. and T. S. Li. Development of a Large Class Size On-line Internet Management Tool in Open Learning Institute of Hong Kong in *Proceedings of the Asia-Pacific World Wide Web Conference & The Second Hong Kong Web Symposium 96*, Hong Kong & Beijing, August, 1996.

[Dwit95]   J. Dwight and M. Erwin *Using CGI* Que: Indianapolis. 1995.

[Mar96]   Marchal, B.(1996) An Introduction to SGML.
           http://www.brainlink.com/~ben/sgml/

[Min97]   D. Minium and B. Strom. DB2 and the Internet Architecture: Untangling the Web. *IDUG Solutions Journal*. Issue 1, 1997. pp.10-16.

[Tsa96a]   P. Tsang . "Designing Productive and Interactive Sites for the World Wide Web". Computing for the Social Sciences Seventh Annual Meeting: Assessing The Promise of Advanced Technology and Information Infrastructures. Minnesota, May 12-15. 1996.

[Tsa96b]   P. Tsang and S. Tse. Marketing on the Web: International Web Conference Experience, in *Proceedings of the Australian Telecommunications Users Group Conference*, ATUG, 1996, pp.221-225.
           http://www.softcom.com.au/atug96/

[Wil97]   J. Williams. Web Savvy Database. *SOFTWAREASIA Magazine*, Dec/Jan 97.

Appendix A.1: Asia-Pacific Web Conference '95 Home Page

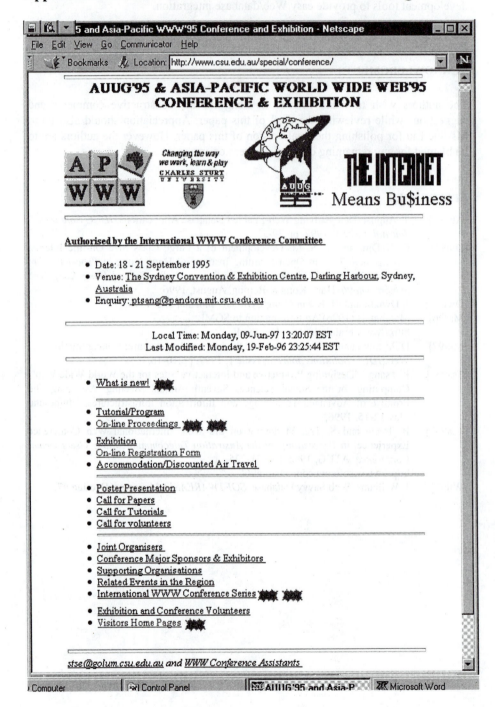

Appendix A.2: Asia-Pacific Web Conference '95 Online-registration Page

Registration Form - Netscape

File Edit View Go Communicator Help

Bookmarks Location: http://www.csu.edu.au/special/conference/test-dir/st-regform.html

AUUG'95 & ASIA-PACIFIC WORLD WIDE WEB'95 CONFERENCE & EXHIBITION

Changing the way
we work, learn & play
CHARLES STURT
UNIVERSITY

THE INTERNET
Means Bu$iness

AUUG'95 & Asia-Pacific World Wide Web Conference & Exhibition

17- 21 September 1995, Sydney Convention Centre, Darling Harbour, Sydney, Australia
url. http://www.csu.edu.au/special/conference/

Instructions:

1. You may complete the form on line or fax a completed form to the AUUG'95 and Asia-Pacific World-Wide Web Conference & Exhibition Secretariat, but your payment must follow within a week.

2. Please make the cheque payable to "AUUG 95 & APWWW 95".

3. There will be a surcharge of $100 for applications received after 13 August 1995.

4. Further Questions Contact.

        Australian Convention Management Services
        P O Box 468 Paddington NSW 2121
        Australia

        Tel: +61 2 332 4622
        Fax: +61 2 332 4066
        email:whfada_acms@intexconnect.com.au

SECTION A: PARTICIPANT PERSONAL DETAILS

```
Surname name:
First name:
Title:
Position:

Address:
Suburb:
State:
Postcode:
Country:

Organization:
Phone:
Fax:
E-mail:
Personal URL:
Organization URL:
Browser:  NCSA Mosaic

Do you manage a WWW server or service?  NO
```

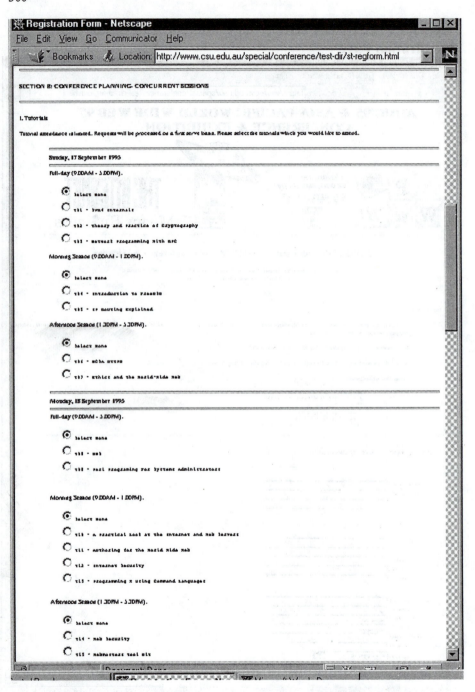

11.00AM -12.30PM

☐ 301 - Unix Developments

☐ 302- Internet For Business☐

☐ 303- Building the World Wide Information System 2☐

☐ 304- On-line Learning. Education on the Web 1☐

14.00AM -15.30PM

☐ 305- Graphics☐

☐ 306- Web For Business☐

☐ 307- The Publishing Revolution☐

☐ 308- On-line Learning. Education on the Web 2☐

THURSDAY 21 SEPTEMBER 1995

11.00AM -12.30PM

☐ 301- Client Serve

☐ 302- Internet Case Studies

☐ 303- The Web in The Region

☐ 304- The Web Society

14.00AM -15.30PM

☐ 305- Network Management

☐ 306- Publishing Revolution

☐ 307- Doing Business on the Web

☐ 308- Cyberlaw and Cyberethics. Legal and Ethical Issues on the Web

Section C: ACCOMMODATION- Please make reservations for me as follows:

Arrival date [＿＿＿＿]   Departure date [＿＿＿＿]

                        sgl/dbl

Novotel Sydney $155.00   ◉ select none ○ single ○ dbl/twin

Hotel Ibis Sydney $155.00   ◉ select none ○ single ○ dbl/twin

Parkroyal Darling Harbour $145.00   ◉ select none ○ single ○ dbl/twin

Furama Sydney $125.00   ◉ select none ○ single ○ dbl/twin

if dbl/twin, share with [＿＿＿＿]

TOTAL Section C(one night deposit required to guarantee accommodation) A$[＿＿]

Section D: SOCIAL PROGRAMME

*Included in full registration.

Date	Event	Cost (A$)	
Monday 18 September	Harbour Cruise	$45.00	no. persons [＿]
Tuesday 19 September	Cocktail Reception*	$45.00	no. persons [＿]
Wednesday 20 September	Conference Dinner*	$55.00	no. persons [＿]
		TOTAL Section D A$	[＿＿]

Appendix B: Asia-Pacific Web Conference Registration Page Source Codes (See http://www.csu.edu.au/special/conference/st-reform.html")

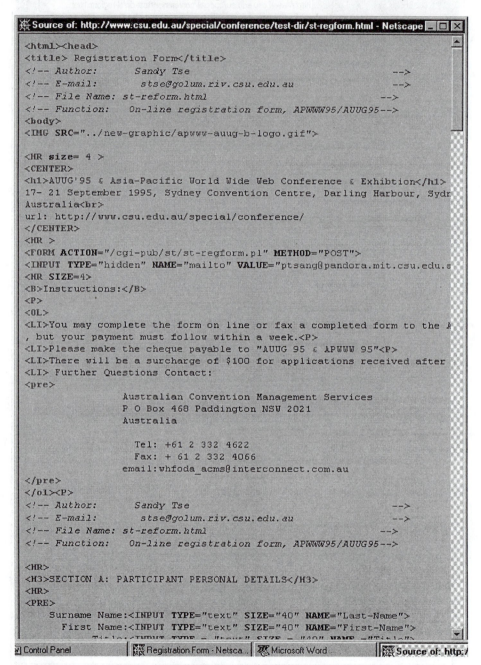

```
Source of: http://www.csu.edu.au/special/conference/test-dir/st-regform.html - Netscape

<html><head>
<title> Registration Form</title>
<!-- Author:        Sandy Tse                               -->
<!-- E-mail:        stse@golum.riv.csu.edu.au               -->
<!-- File Name: st-reform.html                              -->
<!-- Function:    On-line registration form, APWWW95/AUUG95-->
<body>
<IMG SRC="../new-graphic/apwww-auug-b-logo.gif">

<HR size= 4 >
<CENTER>
<h1>AUUG'95 & Asia-Pacific World Wide Web Conference & Exhibtion</h1>
17- 21 September 1995, Sydney Convention Centre, Darling Harbour, Sydr
Australia<br>
url: http://www.csu.edu.au/special/conference/
</CENTER>
<HR >
<FORM ACTION="/cgi-pub/st/st-regform.pl" METHOD="POST">
<INPUT TYPE="hidden" NAME="mailto" VALUE="ptsang@pandora.mit.csu.edu.e
<HR SIZE=4>
<B>Instructions:</B>
<P>
<OL>
<LI>You may complete the form on line or fax a completed form to the A
, but your payment must follow within a week.<P>
<LI>Please make the cheque payable to "AUUG 95 & APWWW 95"<P>
<LI>There will be a surcharge of $100 for applications received after
<LI> Further Questions Contact:
<pre>
                Australian Convention Management Services
                P O Box 468 Paddington NSW 2021
                Australia

                Tel: +61 2 332 4622
                Fax: + 61 2 332 4066
                email:whfoda_acms@interconnect.com.au
</pre>
</ol><P>
<!-- Author:        Sandy Tse                               -->
<!-- E-mail:        stse@golum.riv.csu.edu.au               -->
<!-- File Name: st-reform.html                              -->
<!-- Function:    On-line registration form, APWWW95/AUUG95-->

<HR>
<H3>SECTION A: PARTICIPANT PERSONAL DETAILS</H3>
<HR>
<PRE>
    Surname Name:<INPUT TYPE="text" SIZE="40" NAME="Last-Name">
      First Name:<INPUT TYPE="text" SIZE="40" NAME="First-Name">
```

Control Panel | Registration Form - Netsca... | Microsoft Word | Source of: http:/

```
Source of: http://www.csu.edu.au/special/conference/test-dir/st-regform.html - Netscape

<HR>
<H3>SECTION B: CONFERENCE PLANNING- CONCURRENT SESSIONS</H3>
<HR>
<H3>I. Tutorials</H3>
Tutorial attendance is limited. Requests will be processed on a first serve ba

<DL><DL>
<HR>
<B>Sunday, 17 September 1995</B><BR>
<HR>
Full-day (9.00AM - 5.00PM):
<PRE>
    <INPUT TYPE="radio" NAME="17Sept-Full-Day-Tutorial" VALUE="NO" CHECKED>Sele
    <INPUT TYPE="radio" NAME="17Sept-Full-Day-Tutorial" VALUE="T01 - SVR4 Inter
    <INPUT TYPE="radio" NAME="17Sept-Full-Day-Tutorial" VALUE="T02 - Theory and
    <INPUT TYPE="radio" NAME="17Sept-Full-Day-Tutorial" VALUE="T03 - Network Pr
</PRE>
<P>
Morning Session (9.00AM - 1.00PM):
<PRE>
    <INPUT TYPE="radio" NAME="17Sept-Morning-Tutorial" VALUE="NO" CHECKED>Select
    <INPUT TYPE="radio" NAME="17Sept-Morning-Tutorial" VALUE="T04 - Introductio
    <INPUT TYPE="radio" NAME="17Sept-Morning-Tutorial" VALUE="T05 - IP Routing
</PRE>
<P>
Afternoon Session  (1.30PM - 5.30PM):
<PRE>
    <INPUT TYPE="radio" NAME="17Sept-Afternoon-Tutorial" VALUE="NO" CHECKED>Sel
    <INPUT TYPE="radio" NAME="17Sept-Afternoon-Tutorial" VALUE="T06 - NCSA HTTP
    <INPUT TYPE="radio" NAME="17Sept-Afternoon-Tutorial" VALUE="T07 - Ethics an
</PRE>
<P>
<HR>
<B>Monday, 18 September 1995</B><BR>
<HR>
Full-day (9.00AM - 5.00PM):
<PRE>
    <INPUT TYPE="radio" NAME="18Sept-Full-Day-Tutorial" VALUE="NO" CHECKED>Sele
    <INPUT TYPE="radio" NAME="18Sept-Full-Day-Tutorial" VALUE="T08 - DNS">T08 -
    <INPUT TYPE="radio" NAME="18Sept-Full-Day-Tutorial" VALUE="T09 - Perl Progr
 </PRE>
<BR>
Morning Session (9.00AM - 1.00PM):
<PRE>
    <INPUT TYPE="radio" NAME="18Sept-Morning-Tutorial" VALUE="NO" CHECKED>Selec
    <INPUT TYPE="radio" NAME="18Sept-Morning-Tutorial" VALUE="T10 - A Practical
    <INPUT TYPE="radio" NAME="18Sept-Morning-Tutorial" VALUE="T11 - Authoring f
    <INPUT TYPE="radio" NAME="18Sept-Morning-Tutorial" VALUE="T12 - Internet Se
    <INPUT TYPE="radio" NAME="18Sept-Morning-Tutorial" VALUE="T13 - Programming
```